# Beyond the Bake Sale

## AMERICAN ASSOCIATION
## FOR STATE AND LOCAL HISTORY
## BOOK SERIES

## ABOUT THE SERIES

The American Association for State and Local History Book Series addresses issues critical to the field of state and local history through interpretive, intellectual, scholarly, and educational texts. To submit a proposal or manuscript to the series, please request proposal guidelines from AASLH headquarters: AASLH Editorial Board, 2021 21st Ave. South, Suite 320, Nashville, Tennessee 37212. Telephone: (615) 320-3203. Website: www.aaslh.org.

## ABOUT THE ORGANIZATION

The American Association for State and Local History (AASLH) is a national history membership association headquartered in Nashville, Tennessee, that provides leadership and support for its members who preserve and interpret state and local history in order to make the past more meaningful to all people. AASLH members are leaders in preserving, researching, and interpreting traces of the American past to connect the people, thoughts, and events of yesterday with the creative memories and abiding concerns of people, communities, and our nation today. In addition to sponsorship of this book series, AASLH publishes *History News* magazine, a newsletter, technical leaflets and reports, and other materials; confers prizes and awards in recognition of outstanding achievement in the field; supports a broad education program and other activities designed to help members work more effectively; and advocates on behalf of the discipline of history. To join AASLH, go to www.aaslh.org or contact Membership Services, AASLH, 2021 21st Ave. South, Suite 320, Nashville, TN 37212.

# Beyond the Bake Sale
## Fundraising for Local History Organizations

## Jamie Simek

ROWMAN & LITTLEFIELD
Lanham • Boulder • New York • London

Published by Rowman & Littlefield
An imprint of The Rowman & Littlefield Publishing Group, Inc.
4501 Forbes Boulevard, Suite 200, Lanham, Maryland 20706
www.rowman.com

86-90 Paul Street, London EC2A 4NE

British Library Cataloguing in Publication Information Available

**Library of Congress Cataloging-in-Publication Data**

Names: Simek, Jamie, author.
Title: Beyond the bake sale : fundraising for local history organizations / Jamie Simek.
Other titles: Fundraising for local history organizations
Description: Lanham : Rowman & Littlefield, [2021] | Series: American Association for State and Local History book series | Includes bibliographical references and index. | Summary: "Beyond the Bake Sale: Fundraising for Local History Organizations meets organizations where they are, cutting through all of the assumptions and mumbo-jumbo, taking professional fundraising strategies and scaling them to an accessible level"— Provided by publisher.
Identifiers: LCCN 2021042399 (print) | LCCN 2021042400 (ebook) | ISBN 9781538148778 (cloth) | ISBN 9781538148785 (paperback) | ISBN 9781538148792 (ebook)
Subjects: LCSH: United States—History—Societies, etc.—Finance. | United States—History, Local—Societies, etc.—Management. | Fund raising—United States.
Classification: LCC E172 .S56 2021  (print) | LCC E172  (ebook) | DDC 658.15/224—dc23
LC record available at https://lccn.loc.gov/2021042399
LC ebook record available at https://lccn.loc.gov/2021042400

For Dr. Robert E. May, my teacher, mentor, and friend.

Thank you for encouraging me to always be a student of history.

# Contents

# Preface

Several years ago, I had the opportunity to be part of a team charged with developing a state grant program for local history organizations. What made this program special was the educational component. We weren't simply giving away money; the fundraising education curriculum was a key component. We were tasked with teaching leaders at local history organizations and small museums to become more competent, confident, and comfortable with fundraising.

In the process, bake sales became an analogy for sporadic, reactive, one-off fundraising efforts common with many organizations. My quest became to help them move "beyond the bake sale" to develop knowledge and processes that would introduce more professional fundraising approaches into their daily operations. Based on countless hours of research, workshops, and discussions with heritage leaders and fundraising practitioners, *Beyond the Bake Sale: Fundraising for Local History Organizations* is the result of this work.

This book, and the curriculum on which it is based, was created on a premise that I wholeheartedly embrace: local history work is important and worthy of support. From local historical and preservation societies to small museums and historic sites, heritage organizations are critical to our cultural memory. The bulk of our collective history lives on Main Street in thousands of towns across the country. It's in wet basements and stuffy attics, in old post office buildings and former homes of well-known but long-gone townspeople. However, many of these leaders—paid and volunteer—didn't sign-on to be caretakers of this history because they wanted to launch fundraising campaigns or lead strategic planning sessions. They are there for the history—for the love of old things and old stories unique to their community. They come for the history but stay for the future because they understand their critical role in making sure these objects and stories are available for the next generation. However, as we know all too well, running local history organizations costs money, and chances are, at some point, that money will have to come from fundraising. Not bake sale fundraising, but genuine, relationship-building, asking-people-for-money fundraising.

If you're one of these leaders, perhaps you've felt that fundraising isn't your forte. Or you've come to realize, a bit more optimistically, that it's a skill you just haven't added to your wheelhouse yet. Maybe you've been looking for educational resources written with you in mind and have found that many fundraising books and even online articles are written for professional fundraisers. After one look at the theories, charts, jargon, and recommendations, it's no surprise that some small organization leaders feel disheartened or overwhelmed. Very few resources say "start here." Very few recognize and accept that some organizations have never done a strategic plan, or don't have a system in place to track their contacts, or maybe don't even work from an annual budget (yet). As a result, very few offer resources that meet these users where they are. *Beyond the Bake Sale* is designed to do just that. We're going to start with a big-picture view of nonprofits and fundraising in general. We then narrow our focus through the fundraising cycle to more specific topics like involving your board in fundraising, treating your members like donors, and offering "friend-raising" special events.

As you make your way through the book, you will find worksheets and blank templates to help you think through some activities or share them with your board, staff, or volunteers. Please keep in mind that these are tools, not tests, so use them in whatever way is helpful to you. You will also notice that many of the resources cited in this book are available online, usually for free. Most small organizations don't have the budget to stock their libraries full of museum and fundraising how-to books, and I want you to be able to refer back to these sources for further reading and reflection. When possible, I have tried to include statistics from studies pertinent to the small nonprofit fundraising discussion. Many of these studies are updated annually or at least every few years, so depending on when you're reading this book, you might want to look for more recent findings.

Above all, my goal for this book is to help you feel more comfortable and confident in your ability to professionalize your fundraising approach. I want you to proactively (rather than reactively) bring in enough money to help you fulfill your mission. To do this, I've broken the book down into twenty chapters over three sections: Organizing your Organization, Mastering the Fundraising Cycle, and Refining Your Approach.

## Organizing Your Organization

In chapter 1, Fundraising Perception and Reality, we will take an honest look at how we think and feel about fundraising and how these perceptions are often our first (and maybe most significant) hurdle to clear. We'll also look at a few income sources and consider how putting people and relationships at the center of our fundraising efforts can change our perception and reality.

Chapter 2, Nonprofit Basics, doesn't make assumptions about your nonprofit background or knowledge. It provides insight into some basics such as how nonprofits are created, what types of financial and accounting processes are important (such as budgets, financial statements, and 990 tax forms), and what core documents should be in place to govern your organization.

From there, we will start to narrow our focus a bit in chapter 3, A Fundraising Overview. We'll cover fundraising ethics and take a look at the process for registering your nonprofit in all the states you plan to solicit donations. The bulk of this chapter will break down essential fundraising policies for board involvement, donor relations, gift acceptance, and committee work.

The goal of chapter 4, Plans and Priorities, is to help you do some of the prep work to identify your most critical (and fundable) needs. We will reframe strategic planning to make it more accessible with a series of brainstorming activities that can help you analyze your current situation, identify your goals, and set priorities.

Chapter 5, Budgets, will walk you through an accessible budgeting process. After covering the basics, we'll look at budgeting to cover your full costs and implementing your procedures for creating, approving, and monitoring (and even sometimes revising) your organizational and special project budgets.

Chapter 6, Charitable Giving, rounds out the first section of the book. We'll look at donor motivation and talk about US giving trends. We'll also touch on identity-based philanthropy and different cultures of giving, which is an integral part of diversity, equity, accessibility, and inclusion (DEAI). From there, we'll consider all the different ways people give to charities and then prepare to launch into the fundraising cycle in section 2.

## Mastering the Fundraising Cycle

In section 2, each chapter will address one part of the fundraising cycle. In chapter 7, Identify, we'll start looking at our constituents—our current and potential audience, friends, supporters—and spend some time talking about how to track and manage constituent information. From there, we'll consider how to identify and qualify prospective donors.

Chapter 8, Cultivate, is all about building relationships. After identifying potential supporters, it will focus on donor-centered efforts to bring them closer to your organization and its mission. We'll finish up looking at strategic ways to interact and communicate with donors as segmented groups.

There's a lot more to fundraising than asking for money. But we do still need a chapter that specifically addresses some of the finer details. Chapter 9, Ask, will examine different solicitation methods from most to least personal. This chapter also includes an interesting activity that will help you think like a donor to refine your approach.

Chapter 10, Stewardship, is another relationship-building chapter covering the organization's responsibility to accept donations gracefully and gratefully. We'll break this down into accountability and gratitude and then talk about how you can tailor your approach and build stewardship into your institutional operations to ensure it remains a priority.

If you want your plans to become a reality, write them down. That's our approach for chapter 11, Annual Fundraising Plan. This chapter will help you craft your fundraising plan through a series of strategic questions and suggestions with guidance for creating a calendar and measuring your fundraising success.

If you want to raise money for your initiatives, you're going to need to make a good case: part information and part persuasion. Chapter 12, Case for Support, will walk you through developing your internal case resources to build an external case statement that details your compelling need and makes a persuasive request for support.

## Refining Your Approach

Once we have the basics down, section 3 will cover specific focus areas that can refine your fundraising approach. We'll start with the board of directors and their role in developing resources for the organization in chapter 13, Involving Your Board. We'll begin with legal duties and then examine how education and communication can contribute to a board's interest and effectiveness in fundraising.

In chapter 14, Members and Donors, we look at two foundational aspects of fundraising—annual giving and membership—that help you grow your base, recruit new supporters, build relationships, and create habits of giving to your organization. We also look at the similarities and differences between these two approaches.

Small organizations can raise large donations. In chapter 15, Major Gifts and Targeted Project Funding, we consider some of the most common questions when it comes to asking for money (such as "Who do I ask?" or "How do I know how much to ask for?"). We apply each step of the fundraising cycle to the major gift process, spending extra time on tactics for "the ask." This concludes with tips to help with fundraising for specific projects.

Chapter 16, Grant Funding, takes you through the grant process, from determining if you are "grant ready" and identifying potential funders to developing and submitting your proposal. We also cover a few best practices for end-of-cycle reports to help you prepare for your next successful grant award.

Special events are an important part of fundraising, as long as they support the organization's greater fundraising efforts. Chapter 17, Special Events, starts with choosing the right event for your organization's mission and capacity, and from there launches into the considerations for planning and executing successful events.

Volunteers power many local heritage organizations. They are, many times, essential to an organization's operations. In chapter 18, Volunteers, we look at the positive impact volunteers can have on fundraising and discuss how to recruit, manage, and recognize how they help make our fundraising more successful.

Evaluation doesn't have to be complicated. Chapter 19, Evaluation, takes a myth-buster approach, addressing some of the most common misconceptions about program evaluation. Through this, we also break down the evaluation process, providing tips to help you collect and measure the data you need.

Some aspects of fundraising are universally applicable, and others are specific to the field. In Chapter 20, Fundraising for Local History, you'll be the beneficiary of observations, tips, and lessons learned about fundraising for heritage organizations—from collections care and digitization to education, interpretation, human resources, and building projects.

Please, don't get me wrong. I love a good bake sale. Recipes I've never tried, treats I don't have time to make. What could be bad about a bake sale? Well, nothing. As long as you're not resting the hope and fate of your entire nonprofit organization on its proceeds. Or getting pulled away from your mission at the expense of your organization's core work and purpose. Or, maybe most tempting of all, doing bake sale after bake sale to avoid setting up a more formal fundraising process. Maybe for your organization, it's not a bake sale. Maybe it's some other (fill-in-the-blank) fundraiser that has you spinning your wheels, feeling like there has to be a better way. If you're tired of being disappointed by reactive, one-off fundraising pushes and feel like you could be more successful with a genuine, personal, professional, and structured approach, this book is for you.

# Acknowledgments

I owe an outstanding debt of appreciation to several friends, colleagues, and family members for the role they each played in supporting me throughout the writing of this book. First and foremost, I want to recognize and thank the local history and small museum leaders who have graciously shared their challenges and victories over the years. I extend my sincerest appreciation for their dedication to their organizations and their willingness to step out of their comfort zones to become better fundraisers. Their work is important and worthy of support.

I would also like to recognize all the other fundraising and nonprofit practitioners and teachers out there who share their experiences, ideas, lessons learned, and suggestions to make fundraising more accessible. I have referenced their work throughout this book.

Sometimes we're blessed with people in our lives who enthusiastically support our work and are even willing to help contribute to it. This is the case with my museum colleagues and friends who served as beta readers-extraordinaire:

- The crew from Local History Services at the Indiana Historical Society, including Tamara Hemmerlein and Bryce Gorman who had the tough job of being my first sets of eyes, and Jeannette Rooney who caught errors the rest of us missed. Thanks also to Karen DePauw for giving me guidance with my proposal.
- My friend, fellow fundraiser, and charter member of the Philanthropy Rocks! team, Jennifer Hiatt.
- Dr. Rebekah Beaulieu, who knows her stuff when it comes to finance fundamentals at museums. (Check out her book *Financial Fundamentals for Historic House Museums*.)
- And finally, Deanna Hindsley, one of the hardest-working volunteer museum leaders I know. Her feedback and affirmations were a constant source of encouragement to me.

I would also like to extend sincere thanks to the Indiana Historical Society (IHS) for giving me permission to use worksheets and activities created when I served as the fundraising educator there and to Lilly Endowment Inc. for funding IHS's Heritage Support Grants program that allowed me to create and share this content.

As a first-time author, I had a lot to learn about the publishing process. I am grateful to Charles Harmon, executive editor at Rowman & Littlefield, for his interest in my book and patient guidance throughout the writing and editing process. Sincere thanks also go to Erinn Slanina, editorial assistant at Rowman & Littlefield, for sharing her style and formatting expertise and always answering my (many, many) questions and to Meaghan

Menzel, associate production editor, for shepherding me and my book to the production finish line.

Finally, I want to recognize my family for their endless support when I decided to write a book in the middle of a global pandemic. To my husband, Mike, my biggest cheerleader throughout this marathon process: thanks for believing I could do it and for making space in our lives so it could happen. To Kate and Tyler for being active, involved teenagers, giving me undisturbed hours of writing time in parking lots while I waited for you to get done with practice. You're good kids and blessings to me every day. To my brother, Ryan, for his impeccable design skills. And to my parents, Mike and Diana, for being the ever-encouraging, ever-loving people I've always known you to be.

# ORGANIZING YOUR ORGANIZATION

# Fundraising Perception and Reality

What's the first thing that comes to mind when you hear the word "fundraising?" When I've asked this question of workshop attendees, the first thing I get is silence, followed by the sound of people exhaling through their noses, like a mix between a sigh and a chuckle. Then one brave person from the back will shout something out.

"Uncomfortable." Others will nod.

Another will say, "Challenging, confusing." More agreement from the crowd.

Sometimes someone even offers what others are thinking but are too afraid to say: "Begging."

And then it will happen. Someone else will chime in with what may be the bottom-line answer: "But it's necessary."

Let's frame this in an analogy that would fit those standardized test questions we all love to hate: fundraising is to nonprofits as food is to humans. In most cases (and I'm guessing in your case since you've picked up this book), fundraising is not an option; it's a necessity. The problem is many of us aren't comfortable in the fundraising kitchen. We're cooks with no training, no instructors, and no "thirty minutes or less," easy cookbook recipes. Combine that with some of our preconceived notions and the fact that the kitchen is hot, and we don't really want to be there. It's no wonder we can't wait to get out of that kitchen (or avoid going there altogether).

Sometimes we presume what fundraising looks like and how it's "supposed" to be carried out. We think it's supposed to be a perfect, prescribed process. It's neat and refined. There's a right way to do it. The pros make it look easy. Our college alumni associations, hospital networks, and prominent local nonprofits make it look effortless and so put together. How are we supposed to compete with that?

First and foremost, let's remember that those organizations are large, and their fundraising processes are well established. They have staff, money, and the benefit of years of experience. But behind closed doors, I can tell you that even their fundraising is not picture-perfect. You know why? Because fundraising is messy. It's trial and error. There are on-the-fly recipe revisions and last-minute ingredient substitutions. And even at those big "professional" places, sometimes fundraising efforts end up in the garbage.

What's our takeaway here? We don't have to cook up a perfect fundraising campaign on our first try. We can start small and simple, and then add to it as we get better, more comfortable with the process, and more confident in ourselves.

In meeting with local history organization leaders, a few themes come up time and again when talking about common fundraising perceptions that seem to get in the way of progress. The first is an idea I mentioned earlier, coined by the leader of a new start-up heritage organization as "Begging for Bucks." After hearing him explain his situation, I can understand why he was frustrated. He told me that in trying to secure funding to finance the launch of his new organization, he had a routine. He got up in the morning, put on his jacket, kissed his wife goodbye, and told her he was going out again to "beg for bucks." By this, he meant that he was going to make his way around the town square and down Main Street, trying to convince local business owners that they should donate to his cause. This became a dreaded practice for him. It was unpleasant, and it leeched away his joy and excitement for the start-up organization. It was a lot of time and effort, and it yielded mediocre results.

Another scenario we often encounter is what I call "Eventing Ourselves to Death." This has many different forms. For some groups, it's repeated, small fundraisers (e.g., bake sales, rummage sales, craft shows, direct sales parties, etc.) that take a lot of time and people to pull off. Most people only have so much bandwidth for things like these, whether they are organizing or attending. Another version happens when groups dedicate a considerable amount of resources (time, money, and people, specifically) to a gala event with high hopes of pulling in some major bucks, only to be disappointed after they pay the bills, do a little math, and realize how little they actually netted. By that time, staff and volunteers are burned out, sour about the low return on investment, and completely opposed to trying it again next year, which prevents it from ever growing into a successful signature event.

A third theme, one of the most common pitfalls for small nonprofits, is "Reactive Fundraising." This frequently looks like a series of one-off efforts or sporadic pushes, rather than a consistent, integrated process. The scariest part about this situation is that organizations often make these pushes in times of crisis. Too frequently, they are the result of building issues and deferred maintenance. The roof is leaking. The basement is flooding. The HVAC is failing. These make stressful, desperate times for organization leaders and serve as red flags for potential donors.

That's not to say there haven't been some genuinely valiant and impressive rallying efforts by communities committed to helping in times of trouble. But there is a better way that involves institution-wide planning, process development, and consistent efforts to build good relationships. These are the things on which successful (and yes, sometimes still messy) fundraising is made.

If any of these situations sound familiar, or if you could identify a few others yourself, it's time to start talking about how we can move from reactive to proactive fundraising.

## Sources of Revenue

Let's talk a bit about how organizations get their money. Although you might see it broken down under different category names, funding for nonprofits generally comes from one of the following:

- Individuals: These are your members and donors—the people who support your mission through their generosity. They may contribute through membership, donations to your annual fund appeals or special projects, or they could give larger donations (known as major gifts) or support your endowment or capital campaign. (More on all of this in future chapters.)
- Private foundations: Also nonprofit organizations, but not considered "public charities" because their funding typically comes from a single source (like an individual or family), instead of the general public. Private foundations usually conduct their tax-exempt work through grantmaking, although some have their own charitable activities.
- Corporations and businesses: In addition to corporate sponsorships, where there is an exchange of benefits between the company and the organization, corporate social responsibility programs also provide donations, usually in the form of grants, to charitable organizations.
- Special events: From a traditional fundraising gala to a community 5K race to a chili cook-off, these events are held for the express purpose of raising funds for a charitable purpose.
- Government sources (local, state, federal): While funding from state and federal government frequently comes in the form of grants, some nonprofit heritage organizations also receive support directly from government sources, particularly if they are closely tied to their municipality. Some receive a lump sum each year, while others have a portion of their expenses (such as rent, utilities, or IT services) covered. While this support can be helpful, especially for new organizations, it's not necessarily a stable source of funding. This is particularly true if the organization must make a new case or manipulate its budget for governing authorities each year. Organizations should work to diversify funding from other sources to wean themselves from annual government funding. Local, state, and federal grants for specific projects are exceptions (as long as they fit with the organization's strategic direction).
- Investment income: This is income from money in the bank in the form of interest, dividends, and capital gains.
- Earned income: Here, we're talking about money made from mission-related sales or services. Think admissions tickets, gift shop sales, add-on experiences, or even specialized training through workshops or webinars.

## REVENUE FROM DEACCESSION

Collections-holding institutions like museums are unique because they occasionally generate income from the disposal by sale of deaccessioned objects from the collection. Although this is technically a source of revenue, you should administer both the process and income according to museum best practices. For more information, seek guidance from the American Alliance of Museums, American Association for State and Local History, or from your state's Field Services office.

If you put each of these sources into a pie graph, it would look different for every organization. Some have the benefit of reliable attendance, so they count on ticket sales. Others were the beneficiaries of large bequests or have built an endowment that allows them to operate on the interest of their investments. (We'll talk about endowments later in the book.) Others have done amazing things with sizable federal government grants. But here's something that might surprise you. According to Giving USA's *Annual Report on Philanthropy*,[1] individual giving (as in giving by people from their own sources of wealth) makes up around 70 percent of all giving. If you combine that with donations from bequests (money given after death as the result of end-of-life planning), that number is closer to 80 percent. The takeaway here? Foundations and corporations are generous in their giving. However, the majority of philanthropic giving is overwhelmingly done by people.

## People Give to People

What if we could shift the way we think about fundraising a little? What if, instead of making it about money, we made it about people? If we put the people we serve and the people who support us front and center, does that refocus our efforts? Influence our comfort level? Does it give us more confidence in the fundraising work we are doing?

There's a popular fundraising adage: people give to people.

It might sound a little oversimplified, but it's true. People don't donate to organizations or causes; they give to those who are being served and those who are serving. And that's not unique to social service organizations alone. It also applies to heritage and cultural organizations, small museums, and local historical societies. You are absolutely serving people in your communities. That's why your organization exists.

Sometimes when we're doing history work, when we're up to our necks in artifacts and archival material, it's easy to focus on "the stuff" instead of the people. So, task number one in our fundraising process is to refocus on the human aspect: the people we serve, the people who make up our staff and volunteers, the people whose stories we preserve and share through our collecting initiatives, and on ourselves as people doing good work and building strong relationships. This is going to get us to the foundational philosophy that grounds this entire book and will move us forward on our fundraising journey together, because believe it or not, fundraising is not about money. It's about people.

> ### FUNDRAISING IS
>
> Fundraising is an intentional, people-focused process built on genuine, personalized relationships.

When the pressure is on, and things seem to be getting a little out of hand—when the kitchen gets hot—it's helpful to ground ourselves with this simple idea. The work you're doing is valuable and worthy of support. That support can be achieved through fundraising, as long as we engage people in deliberate, meaningful, thoughtful ways.

## The Fundraising Cycle

A search through some of the most well-known fundraising texts or online philanthropy resources will eventually lead you to something called the Fundraising Cycle. It's usually a circle graphic with arrows pointing in a clockwise direction. Every arrow points to a step in the fundraising process. There might be anywhere from three to fourteen arrows, depending on the source. For our purposes, we're going to talk about a four-step cycle: identify, cultivate, ask, and steward. Each step will have its own chapter in section 2, where we'll spend plenty of time defining them and examining what happens in each phase.

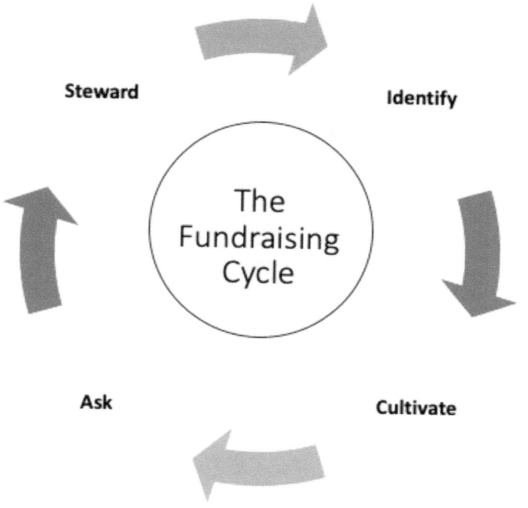

**Figure 1.1.** Fundraising Cycle

Let me tell you, though—the graphic in figure 1.1 is deceiving. It makes the process appear neat and orderly. The reality is that fundraising can be messy. One thing to keep in mind about the fundraising cycle is that each potential donor gets his or her own cycle. The organization doesn't move from step to step for its own sake. It proceeds from step to step with each prospect. Each of those people will be in a different part of the cycle at any given time. Some will take longer to get around the circle. Often, you will be working on small donations; other donations will be larger. And let's be honest—not every prospect will give a gift to the organization. It seems a bit like organized chaos, with all these individual fundraising cycles happening all at once. In truth, it looks a little more like figure 1.2.

**Figure 1.2.** Fundraising Cycle

You will sometimes see the fundraising cycle referred to as the "four Rs." The process is the same; it's just another way to name the activities. Instead of identify, cultivate, ask, and steward, it's research, romance, request, and recognize. I first saw the four Rs in an online resource by the Council for the Advancement and Support of Education. In its guide *Fundraising Fundamentals*, the council breaks down the fundraising cycle by how much time you might expect to spend with any one donor.[2] Are you ready for the good news here?

Cultivation (the "romance" part of the cycle) will probably take up about 60 percent of your time and effort.[3] Why is that good? Because that's the fun part! That's the getting-to-know-you, relationship-building part where you are helping prospective donors know and understand the work of the organization a little better. Do you know what else is encouraging? The ask—the request part—is estimated at only 5 percent.[4] That means that the part we worry most about, that makes us most uncomfortable, actually takes up a tiny percentage of our time and effort. Also, if you add the 10 percent of recognition time to the 60 percent of romance time, you can see that nearly three-quarters of your time is spent building relationships. Again, we can see that fundraising is about people rather than money.

The good news is that each time you move through the cycle with a prospective donor, you are learning more about each other. You are building a relationship. From how they like to communicate and what events they like to attend, to what your goals and priorities are for the future of the organization, there is a mutual exchange of information and, hopefully, a growing commitment to one another.

## TRANSACTIONAL VS. TRANSFORMATIONAL RELATIONSHIPS

As we get into the logistics of fundraising and start creating our "to-do" lists, we run the risk of losing our donor-centric focus. Like many personal and professional interactions, fundraising can be transactional. I ask you for money. You (hopefully) give me money. I ask the next person on my list for money. They (hopefully) give me money. And so on until I'm ready to start the process over again. In most transactional relationships, each party is looking out for themselves and their interests first, trying to get as much as they can while giving as little as possible. As a result, these relationship bonds are superficial and easy to break.

But fundraising doesn't have to be this way. You can be intentional about building transformational relationships instead. These types of interactions let the donor see how their support is positively affecting the work you do and the people you serve. They allow the donor to be part of the progress and take ownership of positive outcomes. It can be tempting to focus your attention on short-term measures, such as dollars raised, new donors acquired, and supporters retained. It's good to be aware of these things, but remember that it's much more difficult to quantify the value of relationships. Focus on genuine, interpersonal connections and be deliberate in including your supporters in your successes.

## It's a Process

Before we get into the fundraising cycle and start talking about tactics with donors, we need to do some strategy work. We have to make sure your organization is prepared to raise money. It's tempting to think, "We are always ready to raise money!" and sprint right out of the gate. Remember, though, that we're in this for the long haul. The goal is to integrate fundraising into your organizational operations—to make it an almost seamless part of your everyday processes. To do that, you'll need to establish some structured plans, including well-defined policies and procedures, and then figure out how they fit into your daily work.

Fundraising rarely happens by accident. Certainly, sometimes we get lucky, and things go better than expected, but that's usually because we've been intentional in our preparation. We've been proactive instead of reactive. Our goal in making these processes official is not only to create a fundraising recipe but also to develop institutional knowledge. When it becomes part of your organization's operations and is ingrained in the work you do, knowledge is passed from person to person over time. It becomes automatic and less likely to be lost during leadership turnover. Consistency and intentionality are keys to success.

If you want good results, you need to create the right environment. The next few chapters will help you prep your fundraising kitchen. We're going to use the rest of section 1 to talk about formalizing some of those processes. We'll start off with basic nonprofit responsibilities and fundraising ethics and then touch on some best practices when it comes to finances. Next, we'll consider how fundraising fits into the work you're already doing. Finally, we'll put some things in writing and formalize a few policies. Once we have a good foundation where philanthropy can thrive, we'll be ready to get cooking and share everything your organization has to offer to donors and the community!

## Notes

1. Indiana University Lilly Family School of Philanthropy, *Giving USA 2020: The Annual Report on Philanthropy for the Year 2019*, Giving USA Foundation, 2020, https://givingusa.org/.

2. "Donor Cultivation," Fundraising Fundamentals, Part 2, Section 7, Council for the Advancement and Support of Education, accessed July 1, 2020, https://www.case.org/7-donor-cultivation.

3. "Donor Cultivation," CASE.

4. "Donor Cultivation," CASE.

# Nonprofit Basics

Before we start working on a fundraising plan for your organization, let's go over a few of the basics. You may already be familiar with some or all of these concepts. However, many people come into nonprofit work (either as volunteers or staff members) from different backgrounds. Let's make sure we're all on the same page.

## Defining Characteristics

Have you ever heard the saying, "Nonprofit doesn't mean no profit?" Sometimes, people assume that nonprofits can't make money. Or they think public charities have to zero out their balance sheets at the end of the year. Money in, money out. This belief creates a misunderstanding of nonprofits right from the start. So, what makes a nonprofit? What are some defining characteristics?

First and foremost, nonprofits exist to further a social cause and provide a public benefit. To do this, they can and should make money. The difference between a nonprofit and a for-profit is that nonprofits do not distribute that money to shareholders or investors. Instead, income is reinvested into the organization's mission. It funds staffing and programming, provides for facility maintenance, and builds long-term security through operating reserves or endowments.

## State Oversight

Regulation and oversight of nonprofits occur at the state level. Nonprofit organizations can take advantage of a few benefits that are not available to for-profit corporations. In exchange for the beneficial community work done by nonprofits, federal and state governments have established certain tax incentives specifically for these groups.

When a group decides to form a nonprofit corporation, they submit articles of incorporation to the state department responsible for corporations. This is usually the secretary of state or attorney general's office. Nonprofits then establish bylaws and elect directors to lead the organization. These groups are expected to hold regular meetings of their directors (and possibly the entire membership, depending on the organization's bylaws). They must also keep good corporate records (including meeting minutes) and maintain a separate banking account specifically for the organization. There is also an expectation that leaders will follow an annual reporting system with the state oversight office, according to that office's rules.[1]

## STEPS TO START A NONPROFIT[1]

1. File Articles of Incorporation with your state's corporation's office (usually the secretary of state) using your business name.
2. Apply for a federal tax ID number, also called an employer identification number (EIN).
3. Submit your federal 501(c)(3) federal tax exemption application to the IRS. Apply for state tax exemption if needed in your state.
4. Draft organizational bylaws.
5. Hold a meeting of the board to adopt bylaws, elect officers, and make note of all filings in the official meeting minutes.
6. Initiate state licensing, registrations, and permits.

1. For more information see Bethany K. Laurence, "Form a Nonprofit in Eight Steps," Nolo, accessed October 2, 2020, https://www.nolo.com/legal-encyclopedia/form-nonprofit-eight-steps-29484.html; "Starting a Nonprofit Organization," USAGov, April 19, 2019, https://www.usa.gov/start-nonprofit; "How to Start a 501(c)(3) Nonprofit," Foundation Group, accessed October 2, 2020, https://www.501c3.org/how-to-start-a-501c3-nonprofit/.

## Tax Benefits

Once the state has granted nonprofit status, the group may qualify to apply for both state and federal tax benefits. At the federal level, organizations can apply for tax-exempt status from the IRS, meaning they don't pay income taxes. There are many different types of tax-exempt organizations defined by other sections of the US tax code. Section 501(c)(3) covers public charities and private foundations. In general, 501(c)(3) organizations exist for a public or community benefit and further a social cause. In addition to being exempt from federal (and possibly state and local) income taxes, donations made to these organizations are tax-deductible for contributors. We'll discuss this a little more in section 2.

## TAX EXEMPTION

Tax-exempt status should not be confused with sales tax exemption. Nonprofits may be able to forgo paying sales tax on purchases made for the organization by presenting a sales tax exemption certificate to merchants during transactions. This is different from your IRS determination letter, which is the original confirmation of tax-exempt status. (If you can't find the organization's original determination letter, you can apply for an affirmation letter from the IRS to serve the same purpose.) It's also worth noting that even with tax-exempt status, you must still collect and pay sales tax on items you sell (from your museum gift shop, for example).

# Finance and Accounting

There are books written solely about nonprofit finance and accounting. It would be impossible for us to cover everything in one section of one chapter. The suggestions below are a good jumping-off point:[2]

- Follow standard accounting procedures and IRS regulations. Many organizations follow Generally Accepted Accounting Principles (GAAP). Designate financial oversight responsibilities to the board-elected treasurer and general accounting to a bookkeeper. If you're unsure of your process or want to improve it, seek advice from a certified professional accountant (CPA).
- Create an annual budget for the organization (and consider individual project-specific budgets when needed). Update these budgets with actual numbers regularly to track financial activity.
- Take time to write out formal policies. Document rules for things like confidentiality, conflict of interest, and gift acceptance. (We'll talk more about this in future chapters.) These documents, along with your articles of incorporation and bylaws, will define how the organization operates. Put the policies and responsibilities in writing and get board approval when appropriate.
- Put important procedures in writing too. Consider everything from collections care to how to handle payments and donations. (More to come on this as well.) If you have a sound system in place, document it. This helps build a strong, consistent institutional memory.
- Maintain a system of checks and balances. Make sure there is more than one person with oversight of how money flows in and out of the organization's coffers. This includes involving multiple people in signing and depositing checks and requiring board approval for spending over a set threshold.
- Discuss financial statement formats with board members and determine how and when they want to see the organization's numbers. Create meaningful financial reports and make sure board members review and understand them.
- Determine whether your financial statements need an independent audit or whether a review or compilation is more appropriate (more on this below).
- Keep long-range financial plans in mind when setting your annual budget. Think beyond your current fiscal year and anticipate potential future expenses. This can influence short-term budget decisions as well as funding request strategies.
- Build operating reserve funds. Much like our personal emergency money, organizations should ideally have about six months of operating reserves as a "rainy day fund."
- Don't forget to track in-kind donations and volunteer time.

## Budgets

A budget is a plan. It's an outline that helps the organization estimate and control revenues and expenses for a given period (usually a fiscal year). By defining and following a budget strategy, the organization can work toward quantified goals. Financial statements, which we will discuss next, are reports. They provide records of money-related activities that help the organization's leaders better understand the current financial situation.

The extent to which organizations develop and use annual budgets varies as much as the organizations themselves. Some have a chief financial officer (and support staff) who work with the executive director and board finance committee to develop detailed budgets that line up with monthly income statements. At the other end of the spectrum, some use their check register and monthly bank statements to understand their financial situation but don't develop a formal annual budget. Most small nonprofits probably fall someplace in-between. For a heritage organization looking to offer programming (including caring for a collection), it's worth the effort of developing a basic budget, which is a key component for sustainability. We will talk more about budgets and how they relate to fundraising in the following chapters.

## Financial Statements

Financial statements help tell the organization's story in numbers rather than words. Leadership uses them internally to understand the organization's financial situation over a specific period, usually one year. For external audiences, financial statements help donors, funders, and others understand the organization's financial health.

Unfortunately, not every organization has a financial guru among its staff or volunteers. Sometimes even the treasurer lacks the knowledge and resources to create and maintain an ideal accounting system. Luckily, there are many online resources—including nonprofit accounting software—that can help make the process easier. Start with a consultation with a nonprofit tax accountant to help set up or refine your approach.

Generally, there are four types of financial statements that nonprofit organizations are encouraged to prepare and review:

1. Statement of Financial Position: This is akin to the balance sheet in the for-profit world. It tracks assets (what you have or what you are owed), liabilities (what you owe to others), and net assets (the organization's total worth). Net assets are broken down by "without donor restrictions" (unrestricted) and "with donor restrictions" (restricted). Remember, restrictions are defined by donors and funders, whereas unrestricted refers to funds the organization can direct as needed. Assets are listed in order of liquidity or those most easily converted to cash. Liabilities are ordered according to when they are due. Net assets represent the organization's net worth; basically, they equal assets (minus) liabilities. Put another way, your total liabilities and net assets should be equal to your total assets. (They balance each other out, thus the "balance sheet.") This provides a snapshot of the organization's current financial position. Figure 2.1 provides an example.
2. Statement of Activities: You might know this as an income statement, budget report, or profit and loss statement. This report shows the organization's income and expenses over a specified period. It explains changes in net assets and reflects much of the data in the annual operating budget. By comparing the current financial situation to last year's actuals, the current year's approved budget, and financial activity to date, leaders can recognize and address inconsistencies, if needed. Year-to-date data inform the report, but the goal is to track projected end-of-year results.[3]

## Heritage Historical Society
### Statement of Financial Position
### 12/31/19

**ASSETS**

|  |  | 2019 |
|---|---|---|
| Cash | $ | 58,000 |
| Accounts receivable | | 800 |
| Contributions receivable | | 5,500 |
| Investments | | 110,000 |
| Prepaid expenses and other assets | | 2,500 |
| Property and equipment, net | | 63,000 |
| Total assets | $ | 239,800 |

**LIABILITIES**

|  |  |  |  |  |
|---|---|---|---|---|
| Accounts payable | $ | 25,000 | | |
| Lease obligation | | 12,000 | | |
| Total liabilities | | | $ | 37,000 |

**NET ASSETS**

|  |  |  |  |
|---|---|---|---|
| Without donor restrictions | | 148,000 | |
| With donor restrictions | | 54,800 | |
| Total net assets | | | 202,800 |
| Total liabilities and net assets | | $ | 239,800 |

**Figure 2.1.** Financial Position

## Heritage Historical Society
### Statement of Activities
### Year Ended December 31, 2019

| | Without Donor Restrictions | With Donor Restrictions | Total |
|---|---|---|---|
| | $ | $ | $ |
| **Revenue and Other Support** | | | |
| Museum admissions | 15,000 | - | 15,000 |
| Memberships | 12,300 | - | 12,300 |
| Contributions and grants | 31,200 | 23,800 | 55,000 |
| In-kind contributions | 4,000 | 8,000 | 12,000 |
| Sponsorships | 11,000 | - | 11,000 |
| Program fees | 2,200 | | 1,200 |
| Fundraising events revenue | 7,000 | - | 7,000 |
| Merchandise | 8,200 | - | 8,200 |
| Facility rental | 12,000 | - | 12,000 |
| Investment income | 8,500 | - | 8,500 |
| Other revenue | 2,000 | - | 2,000 |
| | 113,400 | 31,800 | 145,200 |
| Net released from restrictions | 25,300 | 25,300 | - |
| Total revenue and other support | 138,700 | 5,000 | 143,700 |
| | | | |
| **Expenses** | | | |
| Program services | 103,100 | | 103,100 |
| Management and general | 22,640 | | 22,640 |
| Fundraising | 11,200 | | 11,200 |
| Total expenses | 136,940 | | 136,940 |
| | | | |
| Change in net assets | 1,760 | 5,000 | 6,760 |
| | | | |
| Net assets: Jan. 1, 2019 | 146,740 | 49,800 | 196,540 |
| | | | |
| Net assets: Dec. 31, 2019 | $ 148,000 | $ 54,800 | $ 202,800 |

**Figure 2.2.** Statement of Activities

3. Statement of Functional Expenses: Organizations that undergo independent audits must break their expenses down by function. Specifically, we break them down by program services, management and administration, and fundraising. They are then categorized in further detail within each of those areas. As you can see in figure 2.3, the functional expense category numbers mirror the expense totals on the statement of activities in figure 2.2. The statement of functional expenses is a useful tool in calculating exactly how much of an organization's costs directly benefit its mission.

4. Statement of Cash Flow: This report shows cash coming in and out of the organization during a specific time. It is usually categorized by cash flow from operations, investing, and financing. Not every state requires a statement of cash flow, so

**Heritage Historical Society**
**Statement of Functional Expenses**
**Year Ended December 31, 2019**

| | | Support Services | | |
|---|---|---|---|---|
| | Program Services | Management and General | Fundraising | Total |
| Salaries, wages and benefits | 65,000 | 16,000 | 7,000 | 88,000 |
| Advertising | 1,000 | 250 | 500 | 1,750 |
| Cost of goods sold | 4,000 | - | 500 | 4,500 |
| Insurance | 4,700 | 300 | - | 5,000 |
| Maintenance | 7,000 | 1,000 | - | 8,000 |
| Printing and postage | 2,700 | 600 | 1,500 | 4,800 |
| Supplies | 1,500 | 500 | 500 | 2,500 |
| Depreciation | 1,500 | 500 | - | 2,000 |
| Travel | 300 | 200 | 300 | 800 |
| Professional development | 200 | 200 | 200 | 600 |
| Professional fees | 250 | 90 | - | 340 |
| Licensing | 500 | 500 | 500 | 1,500 |
| Collections care | 1,500 | - | - | 1,500 |
| Collections acquisitions | 550 | - | - | 550 |
| Janatorial and utilities | 10,800 | 2,200 | - | 13,000 |
| Other | 1,600 | 300 | 200 | 2,100 |
| | $ 103,100 | $ 22,640 | $ 11,200 | $ 136,940 |

**Figure 2.3.** Functional Expenses

you will want to check your state guidelines. Cash flow statements help determine how long an organization can function with its current resources. We'll talk more about this in chapter 5.

While there are certainly wrong ways to prepare financial statements, there is also no one right way to do it. These reports are specific to your organization, so make them useful to your organization first and foremost. Understand what information your board needs and how they want to see it. Compile them in a way that is most helpful to your stakeholders, including your board of directors, leadership team, and potential donors and funders.

I'm the first to admit that I find financial statements a little confusing. I have trouble keeping track of which reports are which, and I don't always connect all the numbers. If you're feeling the same, don't despair. Talk to a CPA or another financial guru with experience in the nonprofit world and ask them to walk you through each report. You can also review the samples in this chapter. Finally, consider that some (or all) of your board might also benefit from more formal training on reading and examining nonprofit financial statements to be fully prepared for their money-related responsibilities to the organization.[4]

## Audits

Some nonprofits are required to have independent audits of their financial bookkeeping. There are different triggers for independent audits, including federal and state thresholds. For example, it is necessary for organizations that spend more than $750,000 in federal funding in a year. Requirements for audits also vary by state. The National Council of Nonprofits provides a good state-specific nonprofit audit guide on its website.[5]

In some cases, lenders may need a certain level of CPA assurance to secure financing or credit. Funders may request audited financial statements as part of their required documents for grant applications. Some may only ask for the Statement of Activities from your previous fiscal year. Still, others may require your most recently approved audit records, including the certification letter and all financial reports. The organization's annual budget often determines what is needed. Some funders make allowances for organizations that don't undergo a formal audit, but the requirements can vary, so it's good to be aware of the possibility.

Audits can be costly and time-consuming. Unless you require an audit due to the circumstances listed above, there may be more affordable ways to use an accountant's services. This is especially true for small nonprofits with fewer or less complicated financial transactions. Accountants generally offer a continuum of services from simply preparing your financial statements to conducting a formal audit. Other options include a compilation or a review.

## Financial Statement Services a CPA Might Perform

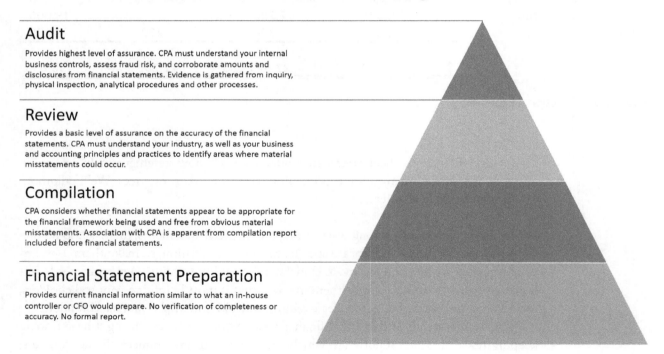

**Audit**

Provides highest level of assurance. CPA must understand your internal business controls, assess fraud risk, and corroborate amounts and disclosures from financial statements. Evidence is gathered from inquiry, physical inspection, analytical procedures and other processes.

**Review**

Provides a basic level of assurance on the accuracy of the financial statements. CPA must understand your industry, as well as your business and accounting principles and practices to identify areas where material misstatements could occur.

**Compilation**

CPA considers whether financial statements appear to be appropriate for the financial framework being used and free from obvious material misstatements. Association with CPA is apparent from compilation report included before financial statements.

**Financial Statement Preparation**

Provides current financial information similar to what an in-house controller or CFO would prepare. No verification of completeness or accuracy. No formal report.

**Figure 2.4.**   Financial Statement Services a CPA Might Perform

"Guide to Financial Statement Services: Compilation Review, and Audit," American Institute of Certified Professional Accountants, accessed October 3, 2020, https://www.aicpa.org/content/dam/aicpa/interestareas/privatecompaniespracticesection/qualityservicesdelivery/keepingup/downloadabledocuments/financial-statement-services-guide.pdf.

With a compilation, the CPA reads the financial statements, considers whether they are in an appropriate form, and issues a report to accompany the financial statements. They do not, however, verify the accuracy of the financial information. Organizations may also choose to engage in a review. This involves the accountant issuing a report detailing necessary material modifications for the reporting framework. Reviews offer a level of assurance from the accountant but do not include the opinion of financial accuracy provided by an audit.[6]

It's always a good idea to get counsel from a CPA or professional bookkeeper experienced in nonprofit work, especially if you are transitioning to Generally Accepted Accounting Principles or preparing for an audit. If you plan to enlist the help of an accountant, be sure to set aside time to help that person understand museum vocabulary and how it translates to your financial statements. There are some accounting standards, such as guidance on collections care and proceeds from deaccessioning activities, that are unique to museums.[7]

## CAPITALIZATION OF COLLECTIONS AS ASSETS

Typically, museums don't include the appraised value of their collections on their statements of financial activities (balance sheets), and they don't report collections as assets on their IRS 990 forms. According to the Financial Accounting Standards Board, museums don't need to recognize contributions of "art, historical treasures, and similar assets" if:[1]

1. they are held for public exhibition, education, or research for public service rather than financial gain;
2. they are protected, kept free of credit claims ("unencumbered"), cared for, and preserved; and,
3. they are subject to an organizational policy that requires any proceeds from items that are sold be used to acquire new collection items, for the direct care of existing collections, or both.

Organizations such as the American Alliance of Museum, the Association of Art Museum Directors, and the American Association for State and Local History all have policy statements against capitalizing collections, using them as collateral, or otherwise treating them as financial assets.[2]

---

1. "Accounting Standards Update 2019-03--Not-For-Profit Entities (Topic 958): Updating the Definition of Collections," Financial Accounting Standards Board, accessed October 30, 2021, https://www.fasb.org/cs/Satellite?c=Document_C&cid=1176172375318&pagename=FASB%2FDocument_C%2FDocumentPage.

2. See also, "Questions and Answers about Selling Objects from the Collection," American Alliance of Museums, accessed October 30, 2021, https://www.aam-us.org/programs/ethics-standards-and-professional-practices/questions-and-answers-about-selling-objects-from-the-collection/.

## Form 990s

Before we wrap up this bit about finance and accounting, let's mention the Form 990. This is the annual report that tax-exempt organizations must return to the IRS each year. Who files what version of Form 990 depends upon the organization's annual gross receipts and total assets. Organizations with lower gross income or those that are part of a larger parent organization will have to do very little (and nothing at all if you don't have a unique Employer Identification Number).[8]

**Table 2.1.** 990s

| FORM 990 ANNUAL RETURN TO IRS | SPECIFICATIONS |
| --- | --- |
| 990 N, Electric Notice (e-Postcard)—completed and filed electronically | Gross receipts less than or equal to $50,000 |
| 990 EZ ("Short Form") | Gross receipts less than $200,000 and total assets less than $500,000 |
| Standard Form 990 | Gross receipts greater than or equal to $200,000 or total assets greater than or equal to $500,000 |
| 990 PF | Private Foundations |

"Annual Filing and Forms," Internal Revenue Service, accessed July 22, 2020, https://www.irs.gov/charities-non-profits/annual-filing-and-forms.

It's important to note that 990s are made available for public inspection. Form 990s (or 990-PF in the case of private foundations) are accessible, free of charge, on websites such as Guidestar.org. All versions of 990s (including 990-N and 990-EZ) filed since 2018 are available on the IRS website, and Form 990, 990-EZ, and 990-PF data from electronically filed forms are available through Amazon Web Services.[9]

# Core Documents

When it comes to formally written and board-approved documents, some are required, and some are just really nice to have. While the process of putting them together on paper and making them official can be a little tedious, it will save you time, effort, and some grief on the other side.

Consider what you already have. If your group has nonprofit status, you probably already have your articles of incorporation. This is legal documentation detailing the structure and purpose of the organization. Your founders likely submitted them to your state's charity office as part of the incorporation process. If you don't have a copy on file, you can request a certified copy from the state office in charge of nonprofit registration.

Unless your group is newly created, you probably also have a set of bylaws, which lay out rules for structuring the organization and provide details about the roles and responsibilities of board members. You may find that your bylaws offer more specific organizational guidance than your articles of incorporation, especially if the articles followed a template or included boilerplate language.[10] In practice, bylaws should only address high-level policies because changes to them require approval by the board or membership (depending on how they're written). It is good to review the bylaws every few years and make sure that staff, board members, and key volunteers have access to them for reference. It is also important for the group to keep the minutes of all board and committee meetings.

So, what other formal documents should you put on your shortlist? The ones you will probably see most commonly referenced in the museum world are the American Alliance of Museum's (AAM) core documents based on the Core Standards for Museums. Core Standards cover the areas of public trust and accountability, mission and planning, leadership and organizational structure, collections stewardship, education and interpretation, financial stability, and facilities and risk management.[11] Verification of these documents is a required component of museum accreditation. However, even if your museum does not plan to become accredited, the core documents provide a helpful foundation for everyday operations.

Since each of these areas could merit a chapter of its own (if not an entire book), your best reference for more information, guidance, and examples of these documents will be the AAM and American Association for State and Local History websites.

Table 2.2.  AAM Core Documents

| ✓ | AMERICAN ALLIANCE OF MUSEUMS (AAM) CORE DOCUMENTS |
|---|---|
| | Mission Statement |
| | Institutional Code of Ethics |
| | Strategic Institutional Plan |
| | Disaster Preparedness and Emergency Response Plan |
| | Collections Management Policy |

"Core Standards," American Alliance of Museums, https://www.aam-us.org/programs/ethics-standards-and-professional-practices/core-standards-for-museums/.

How do you decide what other policies and procedures you should document and formalize? You probably already have a few others in mind just based on the daily operations of your organization. Writing and approving policies and procedures can be time-consuming and can feel a little overwhelming. Make a list and prioritize those that are most pressing. For our purposes, we will look at fundraising-specific policies and procedures in the following few chapters.

# Notes

1. See "State Government," National Association of State Charity Officials, https://www.nasconet.org/resources/state-government/.

2. Adapted from Sandy Rees, "12 Best Practices in Accounting for Small Nonprofits and Startups," Get Fully Funded, August 27, 2019, https://getfullyfunded.com/best-practices-in-accounting-for-small-nonprofits-and-startups/.

3. Elizabeth Hamilton Foley, "Reporting and Operations: Statement of Financial Activities," Nonprofit Accounting Basics, 2008, https://www.nonprofitaccountingbasics.org/reporting-operations/statement-financial-activities.

4. See "Financial Literacy for Nonprofit Boards," The National Council of Nonprofits, https://www.councilofnonprofits.org/tools-resources/financial-literacy-nonprofit-boards and "Welcome to Your Key Financial Statements: A Primer for Board Members," BoardSource, https://boardsource.org/product/financial-statements-primer/.

5. See "State Law Nonprofit Audit Requirements," The National Council of Nonprofits, https://www.councilofnonprofits.org/nonprofit-audit-guide/state-law-audit -requirements.

6. "Guide to Financial Statement Services: Compilation, Review and Audit," Association of International Certified professional Accountants, 2015. Available for download at "Comparative Overview: What Is the Difference Between a Financial Statement Preparation, Compilation, Review and an Audit?" https://www.aicpa.org/interestareas/ privatecompaniespracticesection/qualityservicesdelivery/keepingup/what-is-the -difference-between-compilation-review-audit.html.

7. "Updating the Definition of Collections," Financial Accounting Standards Board, March 2019, https://www.fasb.org/cs/ContentServer?c=FASBContent _C&cid=1176172408217&d=&pagename=FASB%2FFASBContent_C%2FCompleted ProjectPage.

8. Rebekah Beaulieu, Director, Florence Griswold Museum, comments in manuscript review, October 15, 2020. For more information about financial best practices for small museums, see Dr. Beaulieu's book, *Financial Fundamentals for Historic House Museums* (Lanham, MD: Rowman & Littlefield, 2017).

9. "Charities and Nonprofits," Internal Revenue Service, February 3, 2020, https:// www.irs.gov/charities-and-nonprofits.

10. Tamara Hemmerlein, Director, Local History Services, Indiana Historical Society, comments in manuscript review, November 6, 2020.

11. See "Core Standards," American Alliance of Museums, https://www.aam-us.org/ programs/ethics-standards-and-professional-practices/core-standards-for-museums/.

# Fundraising Overview

A lot of resources out there are intended for professional fundraisers. They're written for people with formal training in fully staffed offices. In many cases, their only job is to raise money. Sometimes it's a challenge to translate fundraising information into useful to-do items for our small heritage organizations. We're going to spend the rest of this book trying to do precisely that. But first, let's take a look at some "big-picture" fundraising concepts. They apply no matter the size or makeup of the organization.

## Fundraising Ethics

Just like museum work, fundraising has its own ethics and professional standards. One of the most important is respect for the donor's rights and intentions. As fundraisers, we represent not only our organizations, but public charities as a whole. Our actions directly influence donors' confidence in philanthropy. The Donor Bill of Rights of the Association of Fundraising Professionals outlines several basic donor rights and expectations.[1]

If we follow the Donor Bill of Rights, we will serve both our donors and our organization. Use these standards and rights in your fundraising practice. Weave them into your policies and procedures. Share them with stakeholders in your organization. We can help everyone be accountable for ethical fundraising.[2]

## DONOR BILL OF RIGHTS[1]

1. To be informed of the organization's mission, of the way the organization intends to use donated resources, and of its capacity to use donations effectively for their intended purposes.
2. To be informed of the identity of those serving on the organization's governing board and to expect the board to exercise prudent judgment in its stewardship responsibilities.
3. To have access to the organization's most recent financial statements.
4. To be assured their gifts will be used for the purposes for which they were given.
5. To receive appropriate acknowledgment and recognition.
6. To be assured that information about their donation is handled with respect and with confidentiality to the extent provided by law.
7. To expect that all relationships with individuals representing organizations of interest to the donor will be professional in nature.
8. To be informed whether those seeking donations are volunteers, employees of the organization, or hired solicitors.
9. To have the opportunity for their names to be deleted from mailing lists that an organization may intend to share.
10. To feel free to ask questions when making a donation and to receive prompt, truthful, and forthright answers.

---

1. "The Donor Bill of Rights," The Association of Fundraising Professionals," accessed July 5, 2020, https://afpglobal.org/donor-bill-rights. Used with permission.

## Fundraising Registration

In many states, nonprofit organizations are required to register with the state charity official in order to ask for charitable donations. (This is separate from registration and approval for your nonprofit 501(c)3 status.) Fundraising registration allows you to legally ask for philanthropic donations in your state. You may need to register (and possibly pay a fee) in other states as well. Regulations, requirements, and registration processes are different in every state. These regulations are in place to protect donors—to keep unscrupulous organizations from misrepresentation and fraud. However, they can be burdensome for small nonprofits.

So how do you know if you need to register in a particular state? As of this writing, thirty-nine states and the District of Columbia require registration when an organization asks its residents for donations.[3] This applies to face-to-face asks and appeals, whether mailed, emailed, sent through text, or possibly even through online donation buttons. Unfortunately, the process varies from state to state; each has its own form and filing requirements. This can be cumbersome to manage—especially for organizations strapped for time, money, and people resources. In addition, many states will require renewal each year.

The good news is that some states do have a minimum donation threshold. If you raise less than that amount (which, of course, varies by state), you may not have to register. You may, however, have to apply for an exemption.[4] Some states also have specific disclosure statements. You may need to include these with appeals and gift acknowledgment statements or reference them on your website.

The work of a paid professional fundraising counsel (consultant) also requires registration in some states. (A fundraising counsel is a professional fundraiser who is paid to plan, manage, advise, counsel, consult, or prepare materials to solicit donations for charitable purposes—including grant writers.) Although this registration is the responsibility of the individual consultant, it is a good idea to verify that person's registration before hiring them. Permanent staff do not need to register separately; they are under the umbrella of the organization. Also, volunteers who are not being paid for their services do not need to register.

Some larger national nonprofits choose to register in every state to be sure they can legally solicit donations without restrictions or threat of fines. Often, they have the resources to hire a compliance company, attorney, or a certified public accountant to assist with filing. Others designate a staff person to handle the process. Unfortunately, this isn't a realistic solution for most small heritage organizations.

There is a push at the national level to have a single multistate portal for registration, but this work is ongoing.[5] If you feel overwhelmed by this information and process, or just have specific questions that need to be answered, seek guidance from your organization's tax attorney or accountant. The National Council of Nonprofits and the legal information website Nolo also provide helpful information and resources.[6]

## Fundraising Policies

Creating policies is an important step in professionalizing your fundraising. A little bit of structure now can save you from a lot of headaches in the future. Your policies don't have to be overcomplicated. We have a lot of practical information to come, including spotlights on each step in the fundraising cycle and even some museum-specific fundraising tips. But first, we need to cover a few basic policies that will help you and your board lay a solid foundation.

BoardSource has identified four policy focus areas in *The Nonprofit Policy Sampler*: fundraising, donor relations, gift acceptance, and sponsorship.[7] Let's expand on these and consider how they apply to our heritage organizations.

## Board Member Roles and Expectations

We're going to cover how to involve your board in fundraising in depth in chapter 13. For now, we'll focus on how to include the board in your fundraising policy. It's important to note that the board has financial responsibility for the organization. This can be seen through their different roles—from approving the annual budget to reviewing the financial statements we talked about in the last chapter. But one of their most important responsibilities is making sure the organization has resources to achieve its mission. This happens, in part, by their involvement in fundraising. When it comes to your written fundraising policy, you might want to consider addressing the following areas:

*Role of the board in fundraising:* It might be a good idea to start this section by reaffirming the board's important role in fundraising. This includes establishing that financial contributions and assistance with the solicitation of gifts are expected of each board member.[8]

*Expectations for giving:* Board members should be expected to include the organization among their top giving priorities. Each should make at least an annual financial contribution to the organization. I realize that for some organizations, this can be a contentious issue. I have spoken to leaders who insist they could never require board donations. This is usually followed by the justification that "they give so much of their time." This is undeniable. Many organizations have a small cadre of volunteers who go above and beyond, giving unselfishly of their valuable time. But hear me out on this one and consider why 100 percent board participation in donations is so meaningful:

- Financial support signals an investment in the organization's mission and work. If members of the board won't donate to its cause, it's more difficult to make the case that donors outside the organization should support its work.
- Board members may be involved in asking for cash or in-kind donations. They will be much more comfortable asking for support from others if they can say that they have already made a financial commitment. And because they have invested in the organization, they have ownership over the success not only of the programs but the fundraising efforts.
- You don't have to set a minimum threshold. As a matter of fact, I'd recommend against it. The policy can simply state that board members are expected to give according to their means and comfort level.
- These expectations should be communicated to potential board members as part of the recruitment process. If someone is not comfortable with giving, they have the opportunity to decline a board position.
- Funders expect to see 100 percent board giving. Foundations and donors want to see that those closest to the organization are committed to the cause and believe in the organization's work. Less than 100 percent board giving may be a red flag for some.

This is in no way meant to devalue someone's contribution of time. Because board members also serve as voluntary staff at so many small heritage organizations, the time they spend at work for the organization is invaluable. The museum or historical society couldn't survive without them. If fundraising is not yet part of the organization's culture, it may take a while to get everyone on board and comfortable with annual financial gifts. In the end, it will depend on the individual organization and its leaders. If it's not something that can be implemented immediately, at least consider whether it could be a future goal.

*Expectations for participation in solicitation:* Not every board member is cut out to make face-to-face asks for money, and that is okay. However, they should each expect to participate in the fundraising process. Examples include providing a prospective donor list, hosting small gatherings, attending organization-sponsored fundraising events, signing appeal letters, sending personalized notes of thanks, attending donor visits, or even, in some cases, making asks themselves.

Again, the fundraising policy needs to set expectation for participation. Each person can choose how they will take part according to their interests and comfort level. It might be helpful for the fundraising policy (or an accompanying document) to give board members an overview of annual fundraising appeals and events. It could be billed as a sort of "choose your own fundraising adventure." This will help them understand and commit to fundraising activities that are within their interest and skill level.

## Donor Relations

The organization's relationship with its donors is of paramount importance; it's the backbone of the entire fundraising effort. In light of this, spell out how the organization will handle a few specific issues related to these supporters, especially when it comes to respecting donors' wishes. This is an area where everyone needs to be on the same page. The fundraising policy can help accomplish this. Fundraising is built on a high degree of trust; it's essential for good donor relations. You can refer back to the Donor Bill of Rights as you craft this section of your policy.

*Donor intent: restricted verus unrestricted gifts:* You won't get too far into a conversation about fundraising before you run across the words "restricted" and "unrestricted." This means that donors may choose whether their gifts should go to a particular area. Perhaps the gift is designated for collections care or a specific educational program. This gift is considered to be restricted (or "with donor restrictions" to use the wording from Form 990). A donation given without specifications is unrestricted (or "without donor restrictions"). It can be used where it's needed most, including general operating funds. There is a legal and moral obligation to use this money according to the donor's specifications. But it might be a good idea to reaffirm this in the policy to make sure everyone understands.

*Confidentiality:* The organization will have information on potential donors, donor gift records, and other personal data related to people's finances. For this reason, organization representatives must maintain strict confidentiality. The fundraising policy should include a statement about this and should also explicitly say that donor information should be used solely for the organization's resource development efforts. (We will talk more about the organization's responsibility for safeguarding donors' personal information in section 2.)

*Recognition and donor anonymity:* Recognize donor contributions properly. Do this in a timely, consistent manner, including public recognition when appropriate. However, respect and adhere to donor requests for anonymity. According to Philanthropy Roundtable, "Donor privacy allows charitable givers to follow their religious teachings, insulate themselves from retribution, avoid unwanted solicitations, and duck unwelcome publicity. It also upholds and protects important First Amendment rights of free speech and association."[9] Your fundraising policy should address your commitment to donor anonymity. Failure to uphold this important aspect of fundraising can infringe on your donors' rights and result in serious damage to valuable relationships.

## Gift Acceptance

If you've ever referred back to your collections management policy to refuse an object that doesn't fit your mission or collections scope, you can probably imagine having the same "power of the policy" when it comes to monetary donations. Not every gift is right for every organization. This holds true when it comes to money too. Establish a baseline for what you will and will not accept. The bottom line is that your fundraising policy should give the board power to refuse a gift. A few common reasons for doing so might include a misalignment with funding objectives, suspect sources, or complicated gift provisions (stipulations).

*Funding objectives:* You don't have to accept every gift offered, so it's a good idea to specify that donations must match the organization's priorities and strategies. You also don't want to accept gifts that may create an undue burden on the organization. Be careful not to create extra work for the organization or risk "mission creep" by chasing funding for programs that are outside of the organization's goals. For example, it can be tempting to create a special program to fit a grant funder's requirements or consider taking a donor up on their offer to fund a pet project. However, if that program isn't advancing your current goals or isn't in line with the strategies you've established, your time and effort might be better directed toward funding opportunities that will help you meet your objectives.

*Suspect sources:* You want to receive gifts that enhance your mission and help build your programs. Ideally, you also want your donors to share your values and goals. Nonprofits may need to take a pause before accepting donations from controversial figures who would damage the organization's reputation. Sometimes, ethical issues about how a potential donor gained their wealth may need extra consideration. Above all, you want to avoid the appearance that the organization is "selling out" or undermining its mission for cash. An organization may never face this situation, but it's better to address it proactively ahead of time so that the board can refer to policies that will provide sound guidance if they need to refuse a gift.

*Gift provisions:* When you're dealing with cash, checks, and credit card payments, accounting for gifts is relatively straightforward. However, when you get into other kinds of donations—such as land, vehicles, stocks, or valuable objects that won't be accessioned into the collection—things can get more complicated. Certain types of gifts come with different tax responsibilities, which may require the assistance of an attorney, nonprofit accountant, or other tax professional to help sort out.[10] For example, you may want to define a policy regarding the valuing and sale of securities when received. Donated property may need its own process. Gifts from an estate may require guidance from legal counsel.

Sometimes, an organization may feel that there are just too many "strings attached" to a donation. Donor-imposed restrictions on how the money is spent should be considered when determining whether to accept a gift. As with more complex donations, the organization should assess its capacity to administer the donation and decide whether it's worth the extra care and attention that would be required.

With the help of a trusted professional, you can craft policies that will help the board consistently navigate more complex donations. It's prudent for the organization to understand its capacity for accepting and processing gifts and to reflect that in the fundraising policy.

## Sponsorship

The board may want to address corporate sponsorships in its fundraising policy. This should clarify who is responsible for initiating, negotiating, and approving sponsorships. It may also set sponsorship levels and what type of recognition will be provided at each level. Policymakers may also want to define the types of companies the organization seeks for partnerships.[11] For instance, a local historical society might prioritize sponsorships from community-based businesses.

It will probably come as no surprise that the IRS regulates charitable sponsorships and classifies them separately from taxable business activities. For this reason, make sure corporate sponsorship agreements fall within IRS regulations to avoid paying taxes on the income. Generally, this involves offering recognition of the corporation without providing a substantial, tangible benefit to them. It's worth noting that from the corporation's perspective, sponsorships are generally classified as business expenses, rather than charitable contributions.[12]

Each corporate agreement should be separate, with specific stipulations, depending on what is negotiated between the nonprofit and the business. Groups may want to consider drafting a Memorandum of Understanding if the corporation does not provide one. Depending on the resources available to you, it might not be a bad idea to have your legal counsel review these agreements or at least provide feedback on a template.

As you begin crafting your policies, look for examples from other nonprofits—especially museums—to help you get started. There are many sample policies available online and in print. You can also use the Fundraising Policies Worksheet. These questions will help you set up a framework for your policy document. Remember, your policies can be updated and refined as your fundraising efforts grow, so address your current needs and refine the process as you go.

## Fundraising Procedures

You will want to get a few of your fundraising procedures in writing. Even if one person always handles the process and doesn't need written instructions, documentation allows someone else to step in and replicate it if needed. You may want to formalize your procedure for processing donations, including how to update records and when to make deposits, what types of acknowledgments should be sent for different donation levels, and how to handle credit card and other personal information. We will talk about this more in section 2 when we discuss stewardship.

FUNDRAISING POLICIES WORKSHEET

## Board Member Roles and Expectations

*Board Member Involvement*
How do you want your board to be involved in fundraising?

*Financial Contributions*
Do you expect each board member to make a financial contribution to the organization?

How will this be communicated to current board members?

How will it be communicated to prospective board members? How will it be included in the board member recruitment process?

*Role in Fundraising*
What role will board members play in the fundraising process?

Do you provide an overview of fundraising tasks to help board members understand how they might contribute to the effort?

What are some of those tasks?

## Donor Relations

*Gift Designations (Restricted vs. Unrestricted)*
Include a statement confirming the organization's commitment to recognizing, tracking, using, and reporting gifts according to their designations as restricted or unrestricted. (Refer to the Donor Bill of Rights if needed.)

Does everyone on the board and staff understand the difference between restricted and unrestricted gifts?

How is this communicated?

What procedures are in place to assure gift restrictions are honored?

*Confidentiality*

Include a statement affirming the organization's commitment to confidentiality when dealing with personal and otherwise sensitive information. This should apply to prospect research, contribution records, and other personal information privy to agents of the organization.

Include a statement affirming that donor information will be used solely for the organization's resource development efforts.

*Recognition*

How will donors be recognized for their contributions?

How will the organization adhere to donor requests for anonymity?

## Gift Acceptance

*Funding Objectives*

Include a statement to specify that donations must match the organization's priorities and strategies. Emphasize who in your organization has the power to refuse a gift and why.

*Gift Provisions*

With help from a trusted tax professional, determine how the organization will handle more complex donations such as land, vehicles, stocks, or other valuable objects that won't be accessioned into the collection.

## Sponsorship

Will the organization pursue sponsorships? If so, clarify who is responsible for initiating, negotiating, and approving sponsorships.

Are there specific sponsorship levels? If so, what type(s) of recognition will be provided at each level?

Will the organization seek or prioritize sponsorships for certain types of companies or businesses?

Will the organization require a memorandum of understanding (MOU) or other official document for sponsorships?

## Other

Are there other fundraising issues that should be addressed in your fundraising policy document?

# Development Committee

The development committee can be a valuable resource to expand the organization's fundraising network. So, what is the development committee's role? It will vary depending on the structure of the organization, as well as its fundraising history and goals. Traditionally, the development committee is made up of individuals who are well-connected and can grow the organization's network by building and strengthening relationships in support of the organization. They work closely with fundraising staff to inform and reinforce the fundraising plan and to encourage other board members to do their part.

For volunteer-led organizations or those with minimal staff, the development committee may take a more hands-on role, helping to build, plan, and execute fundraising strategies. Recommendations and timelines may originate with the development committee, which then takes ideas to the larger board for approval when needed.

It's important to note that this committee is not solely responsible for raising the money; they are in charge of looking at how the board can support and influence the organization's fundraising. They can also support other board members by helping them embrace their roles in the process. The development committee's work is not prescribed. It's beneficial to formalize their objectives, but these may change depending on the needs of the organization.

Another benefit of the development committee is that (assuming it's allowed by your bylaws) you can invite nonboard members to participate. This is a great way to involve new people in the life of the organization and to possibly benefit from their expertise in areas not covered by the board. It can also be a recruitment and screening tool for potential board members.

A word of caution: Don't be tempted to just pass development committee responsibilities on to your finance committee. While it might seem logical to lump all the "money people" together on one committee to handle both areas, they serve two very different functions. The finance committee is responsible for oversight and recommendations to maintain the organization's overall financial health. The development committee provides leadership for fundraising goals and strategies. These two committees should work closely together, and some members may serve on both committees, but their responsibilities aren't interchangeable.

The development committee should draw on the influence of multiple perspectives. It's important to have members who are good with figures and understand the organization's finances. You'll also want to include those who are good at making connections and building relationships. Also, consider whether you could recruit someone familiar with the logistics of fundraising appeals and event planning. What about volunteers who are good at internet research or someone who might be willing to look into technology upgrades that could make fundraising easier? Your fundraising efforts will benefit from a development committee with diverse skills, perspectives, and connections.

Now that we've covered some basic fundraising policies, let's talk strategy. In the next chapter, we're going to go through some brainstorming activities that can help you identify and prioritize your most pressing needs. With these in hand to inform a realistic budget and your "wish list" for special projects, you will be ready to develop a fundraising plan that can meet the needs of both your organization and your donors.

# Notes

1. "The Donor Bill of Rights," Association of Fundraising Professionals, https://afpglobal.org/donor-bill-rights. Reprinted with permission. July 5, 2020.

2. See also "Code of Ethical Standards," Association of Fundraising Professionals, https://afpglobal.org/ethicsmain/code-ethical-standards.

3. Venable LLP, "Does My Nonprofit Really Have to Register Before Asking for Money? What You Need to Know about Fundraising Regulations," National Council of Nonprofits, October 25, 2019, https://www.councilofnonprofits.org/thought-leadership/does-my-nonprofit-really-have-register-asking-money-what-you-need-know-about.

4. For resources to determine where and how to register with individual states, see "State Government," National Association of State Charity Officials, https://www.nasconet.org/resources/state-government/. Also find the most recent Annual Survey on State Laws Regulating Charitable Solicitation under "Special Reports and Spotlights," Giving USA, https://store.givingusa.org/collections/special-reports-spotlights (available for purchase).

5. See "Multistate Registration and Filing Portal," MRFP, Inc., http://mrfpinc.org/about.html.

6. See "Charitable Solicitation Registration," National Council of Nonprofits, https://www.councilofnonprofits.org/tools-resources/charitable-solicitation-registration. Also see Stephen Fishman, "Fundraising Registration: An Overview," Nolo, https://www.nolo.com/legal-encyclopedia/fundraising-registration-does-nonprofit-need-33598.html.

7. This section was adapted, in part, from "e-Policy Sampler—Fundraising," *The Nonprofit Policy Sampler* (BoardSource, 2013). See this source for additional explanations, tips, and sample policies.

8. James M. Hushagen and Emily Happy, "Establishing a Fundraising Policy for Your Nonprofit Board," AFP Connect, February 27, 2019, https://community.afpglobal.org/afpwasouthsoundchapter/blogs/portal-wa2-admin/2019/02/26/fundraising-policy-for-your-board.

9. Sean Parnell, "Protecting Donor Privacy: Philanthropic Freedom, Anonymity, and the First Amendment," Philanthropic Roundtable, accessed December 2, 2020, https://www.philanthropyroundtable.org/docs/default-source/default-document-library/protecting-philanthropic-privacy_white_paper.pdf, p. 1.

10. "e-Policy Sampler—Fundraising," 11.

11. "e-Policy Sampler—Fundraising," 21.

12. "e-Policy Sampler—Fundraising," 22.

# 4

# Plans and Priorities

If you want to raise money, you have to know what to ask for. That takes some prep work. You have to identify your needs and understand how they are interconnected. It's easy to understand why groups are frustrated and overwhelmed by fundraising when they haven't had a chance to map out what they want to accomplish, share their ideas with other leaders, and prioritize the projects that will get them where they want to be. In short, they need a plan—a recipe for fundraising success, if you will. In this chapter, we will go over a few brainstorming and planning activities that can help you get organized. After all, you have to know what you want to make before you can get cooking!

## From Aspiration to Operation

What do you aspire to do? Do you daydream about building an educational resource space? Making your way to the end of a collections backlog? Hiring an executive director or someone to manage your programs? Stashing away six to twelve months of operating reserve funds? We all have goals for our organizations. The challenge comes in making the aspirational operational. In order to get from point A (where you are now) to point B (where you want to be in the future), you need to know your goals and have strategies in place to meet them. When you see your priorities written down and can estimate their cost, you can begin focusing your fundraising efforts. You know how much you need to raise and can identify possible sources. Most importantly, you can put together a proactive plan.

We're going to look at this from a few different perspectives. We'll talk a (very) little bit about the formal strategic planning process. Then we'll consider some alternative ways to get good ideas on paper if an intensive strategic planning initiative isn't in the cards right now. You don't have to focus on everything all at once. Still, the daily business of running your museum or historical society will be much easier and more productive if you can put a few goals and action items on paper and work from an informed, realistic budget.

# A Little Bit About Strategic Planning

Strategic planning is often the go-to recommendation when it comes to setting goals and identifying strategies to move the organization forward. It involves big-picture planning and calls on participants to think beyond daily business to reaffirm the organization's purpose and strategic direction. The formal process can take several weeks (or months) and usually produces a comprehensive written plan.

Those in favor of strategic planning appreciate the structure it offers by aligning stakeholders' visions for the organization into goals and strategies, determining how to allocate resources, and setting a timeline for implementation. Opponents say that the process is too drawn out or that the plan itself is not useful because it is too rigid. Another common critique is that the strategic planning binder sits unopened on the bookshelf, lost to the demands of day-to-day business. Personally, I think it's all of the above.

It's important to remember that strategic planning is not one-size-fits-all. A formal, intensive strategic planning process might be exactly what your organization needs. Or the thought of doing that might make you laugh (or cry) out loud because it just isn't feasible right now. It's fine to be in either of those places or anywhere in between.

We aren't going to get into the details of strategic planning here. There are countless resources available, including websites, articles, books, consultants—even entire college courses—that can help guide you through the process. The American Alliance of Museums offers institutional planning resources as part of their Core Documents program,[1] and your local field services office may also be able to help.[2] Your local community foundation, state charity office, or SCORE chapter may provide training, planning templates, or mentors.[3] Business schools at local universities and colleges sometimes offer the expertise of their faculty, and some even seek community partnerships to provide real-world projects for students. You will also find plenty of resources online or through your local library.

---

### AAM STRATEGIC PLANNING

The American Alliance of Museum's reference guide, *Developing a Strategic Institutional Plan* provides a good overview of the strategic planning process for museums.[1] It includes:

1. setting goals and establishing strategies;
2. developing and allocating human, financial, and physical resources to advance mission and sustain viability;
3. gathering feedback to guide actions (including input from stakeholders and data from benchmarking);
4. establishing measures to assess achievements;
5. prioritizing action steps;
6. establishing timelines; and
7. assigning responsibilities for implementing the plan.

---

1. American Alliance of Museums, Developing a Strategic Institutional Plan, 2018, https://www.aam-us.org/wp-content/uploads/2017/12/Developing-a-Strategic-Institutional-Plan-2018.pdf.

# Planning Strategically

Does an organization have to go through an extensive, formal strategic planning process to be successful? It depends on what you're trying to achieve. Strategic planning is undoubtedly a valuable activity, and in some cases, such as for museum accreditation or a significant grant proposal, you may be required to submit your written plan. However, for a variety of reasons, strategic planning isn't always doable for everyone all the time. So, what if we try to reframe the process and make it more accessible for these cases? Instead of a strategic plan, what if we just "plan strategically?" What would this look like? To me, it means beginning with the end in mind to create a work plan that will help us identify where we should focus our valuable resources (specifically time, money, and people) so we can get a few wins. It still involves doing some work—brainstorming, thoughtful conversations, putting things down on paper—but with less structure and pressure.

Your organization might want to put strategic planning on your to-do list for the future; it's a great goal. But that doesn't mean you have to remain in limbo between now and then. You can still engage in discussions and planning activities that will help you move forward strategically, making good use of your current resources and identifying new sources of support. My goal for the rest of this chapter is to offer a few quick brainstorming exercises you can use with your planning team to get everyone on the same page.

## PLANNING TO-DO LIST

1. Consider the organization's internal and external environment.
2. Agree on big-picture goals.
3. Identify and prioritize projects that support and advance those goals.
4. Consider how to reflect these priorities in the budget.

## SWOT Analysis

SWOT stands for strengths, weaknesses, opportunities, and threats. SWOT analyses frequently show up in the strategic planning process because they're an excellent way to get a collective assessment of the organization's current situation. I like it for the following reasons:

- It's a good starting point. Even though it's often a kick-off activity for formal strategic planning, it can also be used for "in the moment" assessment and planning.
- It involves making lists, which I think is a great way to spend a few minutes when you're trying to get organized.
- It can be done fairly quickly during part of a meeting.
- The acronym is easy to remember.

You can work through a SWOT analysis on your own, but you'll likely benefit from the perspectives of a diverse group of stakeholders. During your designated time for brainstorming, you can have everyone work on one part at a time, or you can divide into four teams and assign sections. If you are planning virtually, you can create a document for each section using a cloud-based program and ask team members to make updates that can be tracked in real time.

Your goal for this activity is simply to identify these factors so you can consider them when developing strategies and action plans. Think of strengths and weaknesses as internal (under the influence of the organization) and opportunities and threats as external (happening in the environment outside the organization). It's a good way to start formulating the needs list that will inform your fundraising plan.

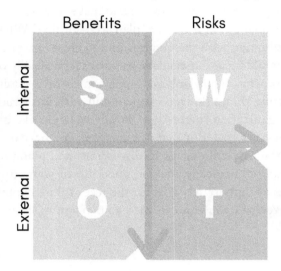

**Benefits**

**Risks**

**STRENGTHS**

What does your organization have going for it right now? What does it do well? What does it do for your community that no one else can?

**WEAKNESSES**

What areas are lacking right now? What needs improvement? Are resources adequate? What do others do better than you?

**OPPORTUNITIES**

How could you better serve your audiences? What's on the horizon? Could you take advantage of new or current external circumstances?

**THREATS**

What obstacles are you facing? Are you tracking any worrisome trends? What are factors outside of your control?

**Figure 4.1.** SWOT Overview

*Strengths:* What does your organization have going for it right now? What does it do particularly well? What does it do for your community that no one else can? This could relate to the scope of your unique collection, the location of your museum, or your staff expertise, for example. The sky is the limit as long as it's a strength you can tap into and build upon.

*Weaknesses:* What areas are lacking right now? What needs improvement? Although you should certainly capture the "fixable" things, it's also fine (and beneficial) to acknowledge and consider the weaknesses you can't change right now. Maybe you're lacking board diversity or some of your exhibitions are starting to get a little rundown and out-of-date.

*Opportunities:* What could you be doing to better serve your audiences? What's on the horizon? Consider whether you could take advantage of external circumstances. There may be partnerships to explore or community efforts to join. You may have an upcoming event to commemorate or choose to pursue new collections objects. Ask yourself what could work in your favor going forward.

*Threats:* While internal weaknesses can undoubtedly serve as threats to the organizations, in this case, we're taking stock of risks outside our control. Examples could be competing attractions, declining interest from younger demographics, changes in local, state, and national laws, or economic downturns.

You may find that it's sometimes difficult to classify strengths versus opportunities and weaknesses versus threats. Remember, this is a brainstorming and organizing exercise. Perfect classification is less important than capturing all considerations.

Make the SWOT analysis fit your needs. You can S today, W tomorrow, and OT next week, or you can tackle them all during one work session. It's a great way to brainstorm with some unstructured structure. From a logistical standpoint, make sure each team has a notetaker and designate one person to compile notes and identify themes, as these can be focus areas for goal setting (and creating your needs list for fundraising).

Once you've made your lists, try to identify how your quadrants relate to each other. Can you use a strength or opportunity to mitigate a weakness or threat?[4] You might want to ask the members of your SWOT team to prioritize which of these areas need attention first and why. Identifying these connections is an important part of the process; otherwise, you're just making lists.

## Decide What You Want to Accomplish

Before you can plan and prioritize where to focus your energy, decision makers need to agree on the organization's goals. Begin with the end in mind. In this case, you're going to need (1) big-picture goals and (2) objectives, which break those goals down into smaller, actionable achievements. It's a good idea to spend a little bit of time talking about these goals to make sure everyone is on the same page. If you've done the SWOT analysis, you may also have identified a few focus areas.

You can begin by asking, "What is the work of my organization?" What action verbs guide how you spend your time? In the museum world, we tend to use some of the same words to describe our work. Do any of the following sound familiar?

- Collect
- Educate
- Share
- Inspire
- Preserve
- Interpret
- Exhibit

These are essential words and actions for us. And they likely also translate well as "big-picture goals" because they represent our daily accomplishments. They are directly tied to our missions, and as a result, they probably won't change much from year to year. We will have achievements within each of these goal areas, but we probably won't ever check them off as "complete" because they are ongoing.

Feel free to use the words above to get started on your own list of big-picture goals, or come up with a few of your own. Don't forget to solicit input from your stakeholders, including your board, staff, members, visitors, and community partners. Since we are trying to come up with a manageable, actionable plan, it's probably a good idea to narrow your focus to three to five big-picture goals. (You may want to use the results of your SWOT analysis to help you decide where to focus.) As you define your goals, make note of any strategies or projects that could help support each individual goal. It could be something you're already doing, or it could be a new idea.

## Prioritizing Projects: Mind-Mapping

It's not unusual for organizations to have competing priorities and projects that are running simultaneously. You probably also have board members, volunteers, and other invested supporters and partners who are always coming up with new ideas and opportunities. Maybe you're trying to decide how to allocate your valuable resources to respond to the most pressing issues (both opportunities and threats).

A mind-mapping activity can identify how specific projects are connected to one or more of your goals and how they might also be interconnected to each other. This can be helpful for those of us who are visual learners or who don't necessarily like to brainstorm by making lists. It can also be a good group activity to help everyone get their thoughts on paper for further discussion and sharing.

I like to do this with an extra-large piece of paper and a few different colored markers. Start with the mission at the center to focus on the purpose of your work. Next, list your top goals for the year around the mission. This needs to be a manageable list of goals—ideally, three to five—that are realistic and strategic. But they are also big-picture goals. Examples might include:

- Increase educational outreach and community learning.
- Improve collections care to provide better public access.
- Provide meaningful, professional development opportunities to staff and volunteers.

**Figure 4.2.** Mind Mapping

From here, consider what types of programs, projects, or other initiatives would bring you closer to each goal. List them around the goal and connect them with a line. As you think of each activity, consider whether it might support more than one goal at a time. For instance, sending your collections care staff to a workshop about developing an emergency management plan might serve to improve collections care and provide meaningful professional development. If that's the case, make sure to connect that activity to both goals.

**Figure 4.3.** Mind Mapping

When you're finished, your paper will probably look a bit of a mess. That's okay because you can then transfer those thoughts into a written format that will help you rank your highest priority projects. While some areas are more pressing than others, you can also consider whether a project that helps meet more than one goal should move up the priority list. There are a few other considerations when prioritizing projects:

- Urgent versus important: It's easy to be consumed by the daily "fires" that pop up. They detract from our ability to do the things we've identified as strategically important. That said, we also have to leave room and flexibility in our planning to respond to urgent situations as they arise. Leave yourself (and your budget) a little wiggle room to come up with contingency plans.

- Strategy and capacity: Part of your strategy should stem from a realistic under-standing of your organizational (and even personal) capacity. In this case, you have to weigh the outcomes. If a project consumes too many resources—especially at the expense of other important initiatives—it may be less of a priority.
- Effort and time: Along the same lines, you have to consider your return on invest-ment in terms of the time and effort required to make something happen. If a project or event is going to suck the life out of your staff and volunteers or take up more time than it's worth, it may deserve a lower place on the priority list.
- Resources needed: Consider the ratio of resources required to resources available or accessible. A high-cost or complicated project may need to be broken down into smaller, more achievable steps or phases.
- Springboard effect: Some initiatives better prepare your organization for the next big thing. If you are considering a project that will set the groundwork for a more significant and impactful effort, strategy might dictate you focus on that sooner rather than later.

Creating a list of priority projects and a plan for implementing them is an essential step in preparing your organization—and your budget—for the year ahead. We're going to talk about annual budgets (and how they inform your fundraising plan) in the next chapter. Before we do that, I have one more activity that can help you prioritize expenses. If you already have an annual budget (either from your current fiscal year or in draft form for the year ahead), you can use it in this activity. If you don't have a budget, that's okay. This activity will still work for you (and hopefully make creating a budget that much easier).

## Needs Continuum

When weighing priorities, it's our responsibility to sort the wants from the needs. A needs continuum can help us establish these priorities. If you do have your annual budget, keep it in your top drawer and we'll come back to it.

1. Set a timer for five minutes. Without looking at your budget, make a list of all your organization's needs. These could be needs for the next year, for three years, or even for ten-plus years. This is a brainstorming activity, so don't censor yourself. If you think of it, write it down. You can go back and move things around to organize your list better later. For now, your goal is to capture your ideas.
2. Once you have your list, categorize it by:
   - short term (this year)
   - midterm (two to five years)
   - long term (five-plus years)
3. If you have your budget, pull it out and see how things line up. Determine how many of these needs are reflected in your budget. If you have mid- to long-term goals, is there any evidence of them on your annual budget? If not, should there be? For example, if one of your goals is to create an operating reserve (a "rainy day" fund), is that reflected on your budget? There will also probably be some needs addressed through line items on your budget that didn't make it to your list. Go ahead and add them and any others you happen to think of as you're going through this process.

4. For the next step, assign each need a place in line. You can use a chart similar to Table 4.1. Specifically, determine where each need fits in these four categories:
   • Must Happen
   • Should Happen
   • Nice to Happen
   • Shouldn't Happen

**Table 4.1.** Needs Continuum

| MUST HAPPEN | SHOULD HAPPEN | NICE TO HAPPEN | SHOULDN'T HAPPEN |
|---|---|---|---|
|  |  |  |  |

Are you wondering about that "shouldn't happen" category? Although there may not be many on your list, you might identify one or two on the budget. If you can do this activity with your board members, staff, volunteers, or a mix of all three, there's a decent chance that someone will have strong feelings about a "need" that others classify as a "shouldn't happen." These can often be identified as pet projects. If these low-priority activities don't advance the organization's mission and suck up resources that could be redirected, they need to be addressed.

5. Next, go back through your needs list one more time and note any that would require additional fundraising. If possible, assign a rough estimate. When I say additional fundraising, I mean needs that aren't covered from general operating funds. Hopefully, your reoccurring annual expenses—frequently classified as your "must-haves," such as mortgages, lease payments, salaries, insurance, supplies, etc.—are covered with general operating funds. But if something on your priority list isn't accounted for on your budget, or if you know there's a fundraising gap to fill, go ahead and note that now.

6. Finally, give your list some thought. Let it simmer for a day or two and come back to it. Your next task is to put these priorities in order. You may find that the top and bottom of the list are easy, but the middle is a little messier. The order of "should happens" and "nice to happens" will likely be influenced by the availability of resources and whether additional fundraising would be required. A "should happen" with a hefty ticket price and a long, intensive timeline may fall below a "nice to happen" that requires fewer resources. Of course, the urgency and importance of a "must happen" will probably take precedence over both.

7. Bonus: Go back to those "should happens" and "nice to happens" and see if you can break them into smaller pieces. Can you separate them into a series of steps or phases that are more manageable or affordable? Reorder your list if needed.

In the next chapter, we are going to talk about how your priorities—from "must-haves" to "nice-to-haves"—will inform the budget. This will have you well on your way to developing a fundraising plan that can support what you want to accomplish.

# Notes

1. "Strategic Institutional Plan," Ethics, Standards and Professional Practices, American Alliance of Museums, accessed July 28, 2020, https://www.aam-us.org/programs/ethics-standards-and-professional-practices/strategic-institutional-plan/.

2. Find your local or regional field services office through "Field Services Alliance," Affinity Communities, American Association for State and Local History, accessed May 10, 2021, https://aaslh.org/communities/field-services-alliance/.

3. SCORE is a resource partner of the U.S. Small Business Administration that offers free business mentors and education. See https://www.score.org/ for more information.

4. Tamara Hemmerlein, Director, Local History Services, Indiana Historical Society, comments in manuscript review, November 6, 2020.

# Budgets

Creating an annual budget could be the single most important planning exercise a non-profit undertakes. It provides an opportunity to consider the past, present, and future and reflect on the organization's priorities. The budgeting process helps you identify what's important and realistic to achieve over the next twelve months and serves as a guide for distributing precious resources. It is also a working document that needs to be responsive to changes during the fiscal year due to uncertain (or even emergency) situations. Your budget is a critical ingredient for fundraising success. With budget in hand, we have a much better idea what we want to make of our organization and can start putting together a plan for how to make it happen.

## Budgeting for Your Priorities

The budget goes hand-in-hand with your financial documents, but it's more than just a reporting tool. It's a vital part of the planning process, and it deserves a little more space. Now, if you already feel like you have a solid budgeting process, this chapter may not be for you. But a little review never hurts, and if nothing else, you might be able to dog-ear a few pages for your next treasurer. If you have been doing an annual budget for years and the process is working well for you, I wish we were in a workshop setting so I could ask you to stand up and testify: "Budgeting is a very good thing!" (to paraphrase Martha Stewart).

If budgeting is new to you or your organization, or if you feel like your budget needs a proverbial kick in the pants, welcome to the budget chapter. We are going to talk our way through the process, and hopefully, I can provide some helpful tips. Luckily, there are many budget resources available for nonprofits of all sizes, and I will share some of those throughout this chapter and in the notes section.

You were able to identify some of your priorities in the last chapter and maybe even compare them to your current budget, if you have one. The needs continuum activity demonstrated how easy it is to see a budget without really looking at it. When we take some time to examine our numbers and verify that our priorities—our "must happens"—are represented, we start to see strategy at work. This is especially true when we think about our goals not just for next year but for the next several years. If we want to accomplish these goals, we have to allocate resources to them. And if we're going to allocate resources, we have to secure them first. Budgeting is all about that balance between revenue and expenses, and fundraising plays a major role.

# The Budget Process

Reading and analyzing the financial statements we covered in chapter 3 does not come easily for everyone (me included). Personally, I appreciate the big financial picture painted in financial statements, but prefer the line item details a budget provides. It is a numerical plan, quantifying our priorities and serving as a practical guide for decision-making. Once established and refined, your budgeting process can be a springboard for strategic operations and fundraising.

## Start Early

Begin working on next year's budget three to six months before the end of the current fiscal year. You want to give yourself time not only to compile your numbers (which can take some legwork) but to plan for a review/revision phase before final board approval. Remember to document your work, including where you got your numbers and how they were calculated. It's really difficult to go back and try to figure that out later; retroactive math is no fun.

## Assemble Your Team

Generally, staff prepare the budget, and the board approves it. Depending on the size and functional areas in your organization, individual department heads may put their budgets together and forward them to the executive director or financial officer. In other cases, the executive director may be responsible for compiling the entire budget for all program areas. For all-volunteer groups, the task of creating the budget may go to the treasurer, volunteer staff who serve as administrators, or even to a small team of leaders.

## Gather Your Reference Materials

A budget is a plan—an estimate—but it should be built using the most accurate data you can find. That means using current and previous years' numbers to better inform your process. According to the Nonprofit Finance Fund, that information can come from several sources, including:[1]

- the current year's budget, ideally including year-to-date actuals or six-month results, and a forecast for how the year will look at the end;
- past financial performance in the form of the last fiscal year's budget compared to actual revenue and expenses;
- other relevant institutional historical data, such as past project budgets or ongoing projects that will need to be incorporated;
- cost estimates for any major purchases or new contracted services; and
- funder information, which can include anything you might know about your larger funders' intentions for next year.

**Worksheet 5.1.** Sample Budget Worksheet

| REVENUE | FY 2021 ACTUAL | FY 2022 BUDGET | ACTUAL TO DATE | DIFFERENCE | NOTES |
|---|---|---|---|---|---|
| Admission | | | | | |
| *(Identify separate admission categories)* | | | | | |
| Contributions | | | | | |
| *Restricted* | | | | | |
| *Unrestricted* | | | | | |
| Facility Rental Fees | | | | | |
| Fundraising Events | | | | | |
| Grants | | | | | |
| *(Identify separate grants)* | | | | | |
| Interest | | | | | |
| Dividends | | | | | |
| Investment Income | | | | | |
| Member Dues | | | | | |
| Program Fees | | | | | |
| *(Identify separate programs)* | | | | | |
| Retail Sales | | | | | |
| Tours | | | | | |
| Miscellaneous | | | | | |
| REVENUE TOTAL | | | | | |
| **EXPENSES** | | | | | |
| Cost of Goods Sold | | | | | |
| Bank Fees | | | | | |
| Insurance | | | | | |
| *(Identify separate insurance coverage)* | | | | | |
| Collections | | | | | |
| *Acquisitions* | | | | | |
| *Archival Supplies* | | | | | |
| *Conservation* | | | | | |
| Exhibits | | | | | |
| *(Identify by exhibit or by cost category)* | | | | | |
| Marketing | | | | | |
| *(Identify different types of marketing)* | | | | | |
| Occupancy Expenses | | | | | |
| *Mortgage or Lease* | | | | | |

| | | | | | |
|---|---|---|---|---|---|
| Alarm System | | | | | |
| Building Maintenance | | | | | |
| Building Repairs | | | | | |
| Equipment Repairs | | | | | |
| Groundskeeping | | | | | |
| Housekeeping | | | | | |
| Gas | | | | | |
| Electricity | | | | | |
| Internet | | | | | |
| Telephone | | | | | |
| Water | | | | | |
| Utilities | | | | | |
| Office Expenses | | | | | |
| Equipment Purchase | | | | | |
| Equipment Repair | | | | | |
| Office Supplies | | | | | |
| Printing | | | | | |
| Postage | | | | | |
| Personnel | | | | | |
| Salaries | | | | | |
| Payroll Taxes | | | | | |
| Contract Labor | | | | | |
| Professional Development | | | | | |
| Professional Fees and Subscriptions | | | | | |
| Accounting | | | | | |
| CRM Database | | | | | |
| Website Design and Maintenance | | | | | |
| Web Designer | | | | | |
| Program Expenses | | | | | |
| (Identify separate programs) | | | | | |
| Fundraising Expenses | | | | | |
| Other Expenses | | | | | |
| Dues Paid | | | | | |
| Sales Tax | | | | | |
| EXPENSES TOTAL | | | | | |
| | | | | | |
| SURPLUS/DEFICIT | | | | | |

Tamara Hemmerlein, "Sample Small Museum Budget," in the author's possession, 2020. Adapted with permission.

As you review your previous and current years' budgets, keep your eyes open for outliers or other variances that could influence next year's budget numbers. This might include revenue in the form of a significant grant or the sale of noncollections assets or expenses such as capital repairs to the building or the salary of a departing staff member who will not be replaced.

If this is your organization's first budget, you can begin with the priorities you identified from our previous activities and start estimating expenses from there. I've included a sample budget template (see worksheet 5.1) that might provide some categories you hadn't considered. Go ahead and gather whatever financial information you do have, such as bank statements, check registers, and treasurer's reports to understand how cash flowed in and out of your organization in the past few years. If you have at least three years of records, this will help you recognize trends.

If board members are new to nonprofits, or to museums specifically, they may identify unfamiliar budget lines that are specific to the work we do. Examples might include collections care materials or exhibit loan transfer fees. It's always a good idea to educate new board members (and even remind the long-timers) about why these line items exist and are important to the work of the organization.[2]

## Start Plugging in Numbers

You are probably going to want to use a spreadsheet program such as Excel to format your budget. This gives you flexibility with your columns and rows, and it enables quick calculation, making it a better option than Word tables. Your main budget should be on one tab in the spreadsheet. You may find that you want to use other tabs for notes or separate project budgets, but for now, just start with one.

As you set up your spreadsheet, you may wonder what row and column headers you should include. There's no one set formula; you should have the information that will be most helpful to your staff and board. Since you're (hopefully) starting this process well before the end of your fiscal year, you won't have all of your actual numbers for the current year. So, you have a few options here. You can include the actuals from your last completed year, the forecast for the current year, or both. For example, if you are in FY2022 and you're planning for 2023, your last completed fiscal year would be 2021. Your budget column headers might look something like those found in table 5.1.

**Table 5.1.** Sample Budget Column Headers

| REVENUE | FY2021 ACTUALS | FY2022 FORECAST | FY2023 BUDGET | NOTES |
|---------|----------------|-----------------|---------------|-------|
|         |                |                 |               |       |
|         |                |                 |               |       |
|         |                |                 |               |       |
| EXPENSES | FY2021 ACTUALS | FY2022 FORECAST | FY2023 BUDGET | NOTES |
|          |                |                 |               |       |
|          |                |                 |               |       |
|          |                |                 |               |       |

As you start working on your numbers, be sure to make good use of the notes section, or possibly even create a separate document, if needed. You're going to be making a lot of assumptions to do your calculations, so you'll want to make sure you know how you got your numbers. Document this information in your notes so you can explain it to others if they have questions. The notes will also help you remain consistent in your calculations from year to year. Don't forget to list exactly what's included in any "miscellaneous" categories and to refer to any special project budgets that might exist outside of the main budget.

## Revenue

Revenue usually comes first on budgets, so it can go at the top. Consider where your money might come from next year, including charitable, earned, and institutional income (such as investments and endowment distribution). Common sources of contributions might include membership, annual fund, major gifts, grants, special projects, and events income; earned income includes anything for which goods or services are received in exchange for money, such as museums or grounds admission, gift shop sales, or program registrations. If you receive regular funding in the form of grants or other support from your town, county, or another funder, it might be a good idea to check in with them to confirm your expected amount for next year.

### IN-KIND DONATIONS

Don't forget to include in-kind donations, including things like products, services, space, and even volunteer time. If you add these to your revenue, make sure to also add them to your expenses so they cancel each other out. IndependentSector .org releases updated data on the hourly value of a volunteer,[1] so check that out at before assigning your volunteers' annual worth in your budget. (It will make you appreciate them even more!)

1. "Value of Volunteer Time," Independent Sector, July 2020, https://independentsector .org/value-of-volunteer-time-2020.

When it comes to estimating your charitable income, it's part art, part science, and a decent amount of guessing. But these are educated guesses, so consider your past performance in this area. You want your numbers to be realistic. If you've never done an annual appeal (separate from a membership appeal), you may want to be conservative in your estimate until you know how your supporters will respond. Similarly, if $1,000 is the largest gift you've ever received, you probably don't want to set your annual major gifts goal for $10,000 right off the bat (unless you have an excellent prospect waiting in the wings). Other potential areas for fundraising income include grants, special events, and planned giving. (More on all of these topics to come.)

You're going to have some back and forth as you move through the budget, and that is okay. By the time you fill in your expenses and get your surplus or deficit total at the end, you may very well find that you need to come back to your fundraising income and readjust. It's a process trying to balance revenue and expenses. Just remember to be realistic and practical. You may have to cut costs or seek a new revenue stream rather than padding your fundraising income projects with unrealistic numbers.

## Expenses

In a typical "sources and uses" budget, expenses follow sources. Your fixed expenses—those that don't change much from year to year—may be the easiest to estimate. These are more than likely your "must happen" expenses. Examples would be staff salaries and benefits, lease or mortgage payments, insurance, and loan repayments. Others might include technology needs, such as your website and any databases you use, as well as expected utilities and facilities costs. Double-check your records on these, and you should be able to come up with a pretty reliable estimate.

Your variable, or flexible, expenses are a little more fluid. They can change depending on the situation, and there may be some level of discretion when it comes to spending in this area. For example, expenses associated with programming, collections care supplies, exhibits, printing and mailing, travel, and professional development are less set in stone. They can vary according to schedule, and some might fit into the "nice to happen" category, subjecting them to possible cuts if your expenses outpace your revenue.

## Covering "Full Costs"

Alice Antonelli of the Nonprofit Finance Fund recommends doing something she calls covering "full costs" or "below-the-line budgeting."[3] This refers to any activity that does not fall within the general operating budget, giving nonprofit leaders a chance to address short- and long-term nonoperational needs. Capital expenditures and technology are two common examples. These strategies help organizations create reserve funding (a "rainy day" fund) and plan ahead to repair, replace, or purchase new fixed assets. They also help link operational planning with annual financial reporting.[4]

Anyone in charge of a nonprofit organization during the 2020 COVID-19 pandemic can attest to the value of having operating reserves (whether you had them or not). They are the result of careful planning and controlled spending through the budget process. It is commonly recommended that organizations have three to six months of operating reserves (and, at the very least, enough to make one month's payroll).[5]

Consider deferred maintenance as another example. If you are responsible for your building or property, you probably know what I'm talking about (even more so if you're in an historic building). We all have looming projects—pending roof replacements, air handlers that should have been replaced years ago, windows and lights that need UV treatments. The list goes on. How are you actively planning to pay for these inevitabilities? Are they showing up on your budget right now? If not, below-the-line budgeting may help you put them in place. This is the best way to elevate them as a proactive priority (and a much better option than the reactive, one-off, frantic fundraising we talked about in chapter 1).

To add a nonoperating section to your budget, create a separate space below your surplus/deficit line, and add additional rows for revenue and expenditures. Examples of nonoperating revenue might include outliers like one-time bequests or large project or capital grants that are not reoccurring. Under expenses, Antonelli[6] recommends including categories such as:

- Debt payback
- Repair or replacement of fixed assets
- New fixed asset purchases
- Operating reserves

The surplus or deficit from this section is then combined with the operating surplus/deficit from the operating section to give you a total for the bottom line.

## Line Items

How many line items are too many? How do you know when you need more? Again, there's no specific number. Your goal is to provide enough lines that someone reviewing it can have a comprehensive understanding. But you also want to set your budget up so that they can make good decisions quickly, without getting "into the weeds" with too much detail.

You will find some standard accounting categories you can include to make classifying expenses and revenue simpler. This is known as natural classification in accounting. In some cases, you will have to adjust according to your organization's unique needs. Refer to the budget I included to help you decide which categories make sense for you. Also, consider whether you might want to create a more detailed budget for staff and committee members responsible for implementation while providing the board a less complicated version for review and approval.

In trying to decide whether to break a particular category down into subcategories, consider whether that line item includes 10–15 percent of your total budget. If the answer is yes, you might want to break it down into subcategories.[7] You want your categories and subcategories to be useful to decision makers and those responsible for daily budget management. If they accurately encompass your income and expenses and can be used consistently by everyone over subsequent years, your end-of-year, budget-to-actuals reports can serve as useful planning tools.[8]

As you work through your budget lines, consider whether you want to add any "cushion" to help manage expenses that are higher than originally anticipated. Incorporating contingency funds into your budget (10% or more) gives you some wiggle room you may appreciate at the end of the year.[9] And if you end up under budget, remember that it's okay to end the year with a profit. It's far better to be in the black because you used contingency planning than to end up in the red because you underestimated expenses.

## Special Projects

You may find that you need to create budgets for special projects such as programming and events. This will be especially true in instances of grant-funded work. Grant guidelines will likely require a separate project budget, and income from the funder for that project would be considered restricted (as would any matching gifts included in the agreement). Special events such as fundraising galas or awards ceremonies may also require a separate budget. Not only is this helpful when trying to determine the return on investment based on net proceeds, but a budget makes planning for subsequent years much easier and more effective.

You can keep special project budgets on additional tabs in your spreadsheet workbook, or they can be separate files. These budgets should be easily accessible to staff (paid or volunteer) responsible for carrying out the work. You can include the net revenue and expenses from these projects on your main budget along with additional notes to make it clear what's being included; just make sure the numbers are reflected in both sections to balance each other out.

## Review, Approve, Monitor

Once you have your draft budget compiled, you can send it out for review. If you have a finance committee, this process may start with them before moving on to the full board. Be sure to include any notes about your assumptions or calculations. Carve out time for questions, discussion, and revisions in your timeline before scheduling a vote to approve the budget.

As you move into your next fiscal year with your approved budget, be sure to refer back to it frequently to monitor your progress. Depending on the needs of your staff, finance committee, and board, you may want to create monthly or quarterly reports to help you take note of and monitor any variances in your budget. This report might include year-to-date actuals, as well as forecasted numbers for the rest of the fiscal year. Budgets can also be a good tool for evaluation and in preparing for future projects, so updating the actual expenses and revenue is a valuable exercise.

## Cash Flow

In addition to tracking your budget-to-actuals each month, you will also want to look at your cash flow. You need to get a sense of how and when money comes in and out of your accounts.[10] Timing is essential here. Even if your budget numbers are accurate, you could still find that you don't have enough money in the bank to pay your bills at the end of the month, depending on your influxes of cash.

For instance, let's say your museum is regularly closed for a few months over the winter (so no admissions income). Your most profitable group tours don't happen until late summer. In this case, you may need to come up with a plan to address possible

### SAMPLE CASH FLOW TEMPLATE

Fiscal Year Begins (Month):
Actuals Through:
Beginning Cash Balance:

| | Prior Year Carryover | Current Yr Budget | Q1 | Q2 | Q3 | Q$ | TOTAL | Year-to-Date | Remaining to Budget | Projected Difference |
|---|---|---|---|---|---|---|---|---|---|---|
| CASH RECEIPTS | | | | | | | | | | |
| | | | | | | | | | | |
| | | | | | | | | | | |
| | | | | | | | | | | |
| TOTAL CASH RECEIPTS | | | | | | | | | | |
| CASH DISBURSEMENTS | | | | | | | | | | |
| | | | | | | | | | | |
| | | | | | | | | | | |
| TOTAL CASH DISBURSEMENTS | | | | | | | | | | |
| EXCESS (SHORTFALL) | | | | | | | | | | |
| CAPITAL AND FINANCING | | | | | | | | | | |
| Cash Receipts | | | | | | | | | | |
| Cash Disbursements | | | | | | | | | | |
| NET CASH EXCESS (SHORTFALL) | | | | | | | | | | |
| ROLLING CASH BALANCE | | | | | | | | | | |

**Figure 5.1.**   Cash Flow Template

shortfalls during the spring and early summer months. Would it make sense to do your annual appeal in the spring to generate more cash on hand? Can you possibly adjust your insurance payment schedule, so it doesn't hit during those lean months? A cash flow projection, broken down by month or at least by quarter, can help you and the board make better, more strategic decisions that can keep you from having cash-poor months. You then have a strategic approach that can influence the timing of your revenue and expenses.

You can refer to Figure 5.1 as a basic quarterly cash flow template, although you may find monthly tracking better fits your needs. There are many cash flow examples on the internet and your accounting software may also provide a suitable report.

## Revisions

Generally speaking, once the board has approved your budget, it is your official numbers plan for the year. When your actual numbers vary from what you budgeted (and they will), you will track and monitor them, keeping your eyes open for any concerning trends. On occasion, you may find that you need to reallocate resources from one line to another, but you should rarely need to revise your approved budget completely. This should be reserved for situations where unforeseen circumstances outside of the organization's control lead to significant gaps in projected income or expenses. One example might include forced extended closure (such as during a pandemic or as the result of building damage from a fire or storm), leading to a significant loss of revenue. Unexpected capital repairs such as roof failure, water damage, or asbestos remediation could cause expenses to far exceed projections. In these cases, the budget team should try to implement some scenario planning and reforecast the budget using any new information they have gathered since the budget was created. Although it may be abbreviated somewhat, the revised budget should still go through the same review and approval process as the original.

Your budget is an essential piece in your overall fundraising puzzle. Your written fundraising plan is another. These two go hand-in-hand and inform each other. You will probably want to work on them together, and there will be some back and forth as you make decisions about how to balance your budget and implement a realistic fundraising strategy. We are going to work on a written fundraising plan, but first, we need to talk about charitable giving in general and circle back around to cover the fundraising cycle. We'll revisit the fundraising plan at the end of section 2.

## Notes

1. Alice Antonelli, "Nonprofit Budgeting Basics," *Making Your Budget the Backbone of Your Nonprofit—Part 1* (blog), Nonprofit Financial Fund, November 14, 2017, https://nff.org/blog/nonprofit-budgeting-basics.

2. Tamara Hemmerlein, Director, Local History Services, Indiana Historical Society, comments in manuscript review, November 6, 2020.

3. Alice Antonelli, "Below-the-Line-Budgeting," *Making Your Budget the Backbone of Your Nonprofit—Part 4* (blog), Nonprofit Financial Fund, December 5, 2017, https://nff.org/blog/below-line-budgeting.

4. Rebekah Beaulieu, Director, Florence Griswold Museum, comments in manuscript review, October 15, 2020. For more information about financial best practices for small museums, see Dr. Beaulieu's book, *Financial Fundamentals for Historic House Museums* (Lanham, MD: Rowman & Littlefield, 2017).

5. "How Much Should My Nonprofit Have in Its Operating Reserve?" Candid, accessed August 14, 2020, https://learning.candid.org/resources/knowledge-base/operating-reserves.

6. Antonelli, "Below-the-Line-Budgeting," Part 4.

7. Sandy Rees, "The Small Nonprofit's Guide to Budgeting," (blog), *Get Fully Funded*, January 15, 2019, https://getfullyfunded.com/the-small-nonprofits-guide-to-budgeting/.

8. Stacy L. Klingler and Laura B. Roberts, "Building Better Budgets," *AASLH Technical Leaflet #268*, Autumn 2014.

9. Rebekah Beaulieu, October 15, 2020.

10. Stacy L. Klingler and Laura B. Roberts, "Improving Financial Management," *AASLH Technical Leaflet #269*, Winter 2015.

# Charitable Giving

So far, we've talked about why fundraising is vital to our mission-focused successes, even if we perceive it to be complicated or uncomfortable. We've looked at some basic information about nonprofits—especially financial information that can impact or be impacted by our fundraising efforts. We made our way through some of the policies and procedures that we need to draft to formalize our fundraising intentions. Finally, we've brainstormed, made plans, set priorities, and slugged our way through the budgeting process. It seems like we should be about ready to get down to the business of raising some money, right? We are—almost. Before we jump into the fundraising cycle, let's talk a little about donors, including why and how they give.

## Donor Motivation

Donor motivation is a fundraising topic that is well-studied and discussed. From academics to practitioners to consultants, everyone is trying to figure out why people give, where they give, and how to influence that behavior (or at least understand it). This information is constantly evolving because of more research and because donors themselves change individually and as groups.

## Why People Give

While charitable causes and organizations certainly influence donors' lives, we can't dismiss the fact that the philanthropic choices they make result from their individual experiences. Donor motivation, and therefore choice, varies from person to person. From when and how they donate to the causes they support, each person participates in philanthropy on their terms. But why do people give to charities in general? Below are several different reasons:

*Belief in the organization's mission or having a personal passion for the cause*[1]
We all have natural affinities to certain causes, and as a result, organizations that address these causes tend to attract our attention. Sometimes in history work we compete with health and human services (or other charities) for valuable fundraising dollars. Don't lose

sight that there are donors out there who are motivated by the work you do. They embrace your mission because they see the value in preserving, interpreting, and sharing history.

*The belief that a gift can make a difference or that the organization depends on them*
Donors want to make a difference. They want to be a catalyst for change, and they want to feel needed. For this reason, it's essential to value the contributions of donors at every level and to communicate that all forms of support are impactful. To create even more meaningful experiences for your donors, provide them access to information that demonstrates the impact of their contributions, individually and collectively.

*A personal connection to the cause*
As we've already discussed, charitable giving is a profoundly personal experience. This is particularly true for donors who know someone affected by the work of the organization. While we might look to health and human service organizations again as examples, history organizations play an important role in many people's everyday lives. From telling stories of our ancestors to providing educational resources to our teachers to engaging visitors looking for new experiences, the history work we do is important and worthy of support. (We'll discuss how to identify these connections in the next chapter.)

*Habit*
Sometimes, giving just becomes a habit. As long as the organization meets their expectations, some donors will support the same causes or organizations year after year. These long-term, dedicated supporters make up a significant segment of our donor base.

*Engagement beyond donation*
"Doing" drives loyalty. According to the Donor Loyalty Study, people are 74 percent more likely to donate after attending an event and 73 percent more likely to give after volunteering.[2] These numbers illustrate the importance of making fundraising an organization-wide commitment. The work done by event and volunteer managers clearly contributes to the overall development objectives of the organization.

*Personal satisfaction and fulfillment*
People give to charitable causes because it makes them feel good. We will talk more about stewardship in chapter 10, but this speaks to why demonstrating an appropriate level of gratitude is essential in good donor relations.

*Personal financial situation*
The choices people make about their giving are, of course, influenced by their personal capacity. According to a U.S. Trust study, high-wealth donors are almost twice as likely to support charitable causes than the general US population.[3] Blackbaud's study found that donors are more likely to make regular contributions as their financial situations improve.[4] Providing good stewardship and plenty of opportunities for engagement is essential for donors at all levels.

## Where People Give

That same U.S. Trust survey also examined how people determine which nonprofits to support. Interestingly, the top three reasons identified in the study were profoundly personal to the donor.[5] First and foremost, 74 percent of donors in this study looked for causes and organizations aligned with their values. Looking at it another way, we can reasonably conclude that these supporters might deliberately exclude a charity whose mission deviated from their principles.

Similarly, 57 percent of donors reported they directed funding to organizations that addressed issues of interest. The takeaway for organizations here is twofold. First, we should look to identify and engage those who are interested in our work. We want to find people who love history and museums. But should we be surprised that this number isn't higher, and if so, what does that tell us? Perhaps we can conclude that there is an opportunity here to make a connection with the other 43 percent of those prospective donors who might be receptive to learning more about our work, whether they are self-described "history people" or not.

As we might expect, 54 percent of donors said they gave to organizations where they had firsthand experience. Not only should we ask for support from those we currently serve, but we should look to engage new audiences and provide unique experiences. It also can't be overstated how meaningful personal connections are for us as cultural organizations.

The fourth and fifth factors that donors identified in deciding where to direct their funds are more in the organization's control: the organization's reputation (50%) and the perceived need of the organization (49%). Although these are factors a nonprofit can influence from within, you may need to turn to your external community to get a good read on them. Community town hall conversations or focus groups can help you understand how your organization is perceived, as well as whether or not the objectives you're trying to achieve (your needs) are clear.

## Identity-Based Philanthropy

An emerging topic in fundraising is identity-based philanthropy and the idea of different cultures of giving. Within this is the acknowledgment and acceptance that people have diverse giving preferences based not only on their experiences but also on their personal identities. These can vary not only from culture to culture but also from person to person within those cultures.

Consider the diverse community your organization serves, including your staff and volunteers, donors, and supporters. Cultural factors such as race, nationality and ethnicity, language, religion and spirituality, age and generation, gender identity, sexual orientation, socioeconomics and education, family customs, and accessibility can all play roles in how individuals experience and participate in philanthropic giving.[6] As you determine how best to meet these different groups' needs through your programming, also reflect on whether your fundraising approaches are inclusive.

A colleague and I once visited with a small heritage group in a rural Indiana town. After meeting with their board of directors, we outlined our action items, including following up with them via email. In response to this, one man at the table—an Amish gentleman—asked if we could please send a paper copy to him in the mail. He provided his address and promised to write back immediately with his response. Cultural factors—such as using certain tools we take for granted—influence communication, participation, and even giving.

There is no one-size-fits-all approach to diversity, equity, accessibility, and inclusion (DEAI). You must tailor your strategies for including cultural competence in your fundraising to meet your unique population's needs. Further, they will change and mature as you continue to learn more about different cultures and your individual donors. These changes can be intimidating, and it can be tempting to stick to business as usual. However, according to Dr. Lilya Wagner, a thought-leader and researcher in this area, "To ignore or remain unaware of the rich and varied giving traditions of the many population groups in North America is not only unwise but leaves our fundraising practice incomplete and unbalanced."[7]

How do you begin to introduce cultural competency into your fundraising?

1. Consider your own assumptions and biases. Examine your current practices and determine whether they pose a disadvantage to any particular group connected to your organization. For example, are you holding events that overlap with religious observances that might prevent some from attending?
2. Reflect on who is missing from your visitors, staff, and board. Does the work you do reflect the identity of your current and potential audiences, and therefore, motivate them to consider it worthy of philanthropic support? Do they see themselves in your exhibits, programming, and fundraising appeals? How would the work of your organization benefit from additional representation from different cultures?
3. Commit to asking questions and learning as much as you can about different cultures in your community. Intentionally invite prospective visitors, volunteers, and donors from underrepresented groups to be part of the conversation. Approach this with sincerity, humility, and grace for everyone involved; it's an ongoing effort in improvement, not a quick fix.
4. Identify and implement changes that will have both immediate and long-term impacts on your programming and fundraising. Keep lines of communication open and receive feedback with an open mind. You want all donors to understand that they are seen, heard, included, and respected. Learning about and responding to identity philanthropy, much like fundraising itself, is an ongoing process.

## How Do People Give?

As mentioned in the first chapter of this book, philanthropic giving comes from three sources: individuals, foundations, and corporations. From there, we can break it down a few other ways. In this case, we will look at methods for giving, types of gifts, and different gift purposes. As we get into the fundraising cycle in the next section, especially chapter 11, where we'll work through your fundraising plan, it's helpful to understand some of these classifications. Not only does it improve our fundraising vocabulary, but it helps us understand the strategy and logistics of setting up a solid annual development plan.

## Methods for Giving

We're going to talk about giving channels in chapter 9, but first, let's take a big picture look at different methods of giving from the donor's perspective. Generally, donations are either given outright, on a reoccurring basis, through pledges, or via planned giving.

*One-time gifts*

These are singular gifts that come in all at once via cash, check, or credit card. They could be annual fund, occasional, or sometimes even major gifts, although they are more common for smaller amounts.

*Reoccurring gifts*

Reoccurring gifts are also sometimes known as monthly gifts because that is when they are usually processed. Generally, the donor authorizes the organization to process their donation at the same time each month (or possibly each quarter). This is a win-win situation for both the donor and the organization. The donor can spread their generosity over a more extended period and does not have to go through the hassle of remembering to send a check each month. The organization can secure a reliable payment, which makes planning and budgeting more straightforward.

*Pledges*

More significant donations often come in the form of pledges paid over several years (usually one to five), depending on the gift's size. The donor signs a pledge form that indicates how much he or she will donate over a specific, mutually agreed upon time. It is then up to the donor to ensure those payments are received (hopefully on time). Pledges make it a little easier for organizations to plan their annual budgets, but you must approach pledges knowing that a donor could default on their promise to pay. If the donor can arrange automatic payments through their bank, this reduces the chance of default and ensures a more consistent cash flow for the organization.

*Planned giving*

Planned giving refers to nonliquid gifts such as securities, assets, and insurance policies.[8] It is also frequently part of end-of-life estate planning, which provides specific financial incentives to donors who include charities in their wills. Donors may direct these funds toward endowments or capital projects or even general operating funds. Planned giving is an important fundraising vehicle, but it can be more complicated than other giving types. For this reason, it is crucial to work with a trusted financial advisor who can provide professional advice when structuring planned gifts.

## Types of Gifts

There are several different ways to classify what type of gifts your organization receives. There's no one-size-fits-all approach to fundraising, and your strategies will develop and change over time. Many local history organizations start with memberships and progress into requests for annual giving. It's not uncommon to receive occasional gifts for other reasons. As organizations mature in their fundraising, some may also begin to pursue major gifts, which are generally larger and usually directed toward a specific need. We will also touch on capital campaign gifts; you may have heard of these before without being completely clear about what they mean.

We will go into greater detail about these types of gifts in section 3 when we discuss diversifying your giving. For now, an overview of each will be helpful when we make our way through the fundraising cycle and development plan chapters.

*Memberships*

Memberships are often the first step toward financial support for an organization. Generally, the member receives certain benefits in exchange for their dues. As we will discuss in chapter 14, there are good reasons to treat your members as donors and show them the same love and care. However, when it comes to tax purposes, memberships are not entirely tax-deductible. This means that your members will be able to deduct only the part of their payment that extends beyond the value of the benefits and services they receive for their membership. It also means that you will need to provide market value for those benefits and services. Can you consider memberships as donations? Should you? The answers are maybe and possibly. We will cover this situation, called quid pro quo, in more detail in chapter 14.

*Annual Fund*

The annual fund is another name for the fundraising you do to cover your yearly operating and programming expenses. But don't let the name fool you—annual does not necessarily mean "once a year." Many organizations have ongoing annual fund solicitations. Generally, these donations are small enough that they come from your donor's current income. In other words, they aren't digging into their assets, such as stocks or real estate, to donate.

Annual giving is a foundational part of fundraising. It is usually unrestricted, meaning the organization has the freedom to direct it to the greatest need. Not only does it generate critical income for your general operating fund, but it also helps build a more substantial fundraising base so you can identify prospects for larger gifts.

*In-kind Gifts*

In-kind gifts are contributions of goods or services rather than cash. Common examples of goods might include auction items, computer equipment, or office furniture. Services might include meeting space, printing and mailing, or "pro bono" expertise from professionals such as lawyers, carpenters, or graphic designers. Corporations, businesses, and individuals are all promising participants in this type of giving. The organization should provide written acknowledgment of in-kind donations that includes a note stating it is the donor's responsibility to determine a valuation of the goods or services and income tax deductibility. (As always, consult your tax professional if you have questions about acknowledging in-kind donations.)

*Major Gifts*

How big does a donation have to be before it's considered a major gift? The truth is, it depends on the organization's giving history and where they are directing the money. What you regard as "major" for your organization may not be for another. A smaller organization might consider $500 a major gift, whereas for a larger institution, maybe it's $5,000. Major gifts tend to be directed to special programs and projects or possibly to an endowment, although they can sometimes be marked unrestricted. Depending on the donor, the funds may come from a combination of income and assets. If you're trying to determine your major gift level, look at your gift history over the past several years to get a feel for your average donation size. This may help you determine a range. In all honesty, though, if it "feels" major for your organization, it probably is.

*Occasional/Even Gifts*

Although it's less about the amount and more about the situation, let's mention that sometimes (maybe even frequently, depending on the organization), we may receive occasional contributions. These funds may come in due to a specific appeal, event, or situation and are not necessarily the result of a targeted mailing to your usual annual fund supporters. In some cases, such as for gifts given in memoriam, the donors may be new to your organization. These gifts may be restricted or unrestricted according to the donor or the specific appeal.

*Capital Campaign*

It's easy to confuse capital campaigns with capital expenses or projects. A capital campaign is a formal, phased, organization-wide fundraising initiative that usually lasts for several years. Generally, gifts go to special projects, buildings, equipment, or endowments tied together as part of the overall campaign goals. (Capital expenses, on the other hand, are everyday expenditures that go toward buying, maintaining, or improving the organization's fixed assets such as buildings, property, or equipment.)

## CAPITAL CAMPAIGNS

While leading a grants workshop, I had a conversation with an organization leader that I think bears repeating. This particular organization was trying to raise funds to renovate a building—a capital project. While talking about grant guidelines, they mentioned that they were having trouble finding grants they qualified for because so many of the grants wouldn't fund capital campaigns. Because they were confusing capital projects with capital campaigns, this dedicated leader was self-selecting out of grant opportunities. Don't confuse capital expenses with formal capital campaigns. If you're trying to get funding for a building or equipment, look specifically for mention of these in the sections about priorities and exclusions.

## Gift Purposes

From the organization's perspective, different funds serve different purposes and will affect who you solicit (ask) and what type of appeal they receive. Donors want to know what an organization will do with their funds, so it's helpful to communicate with well-designed requests that allow for transparency. As we discussed in chapter 3 about fundraising ethics, organizations are legally and morally required to record, report, and manage funds according to their intended purposes as defined by the donor. It's crucial to introduce careful accounting procedures that will allow you to track whether gifts are restricted or unrestricted.

Unrestricted donations are those without any strings attached. You can use unrestricted dollars for the organization's general operating fund to cover overhead expenses like salaries, mortgages, and insurance. Or the organization can use them for specific programs or other areas of need. When you see a solicitation form that allows the organization to "direct these funds to the areas of greatest need," that means the funds are unrestricted. Although special project funding is important to the organization's fundraising goals, many will argue that unrestricted funds are the most critical because they allow the organization a greater degree of flexibility and strengthen its ability to respond to change.

Gifts can be restricted by purpose, by time, or both. In the case of purpose restrictions, the donor says that the money should be used to perform specific activities. For example, a donor might direct their gift toward collections care. Time-restricted donations, such as a three-year foundation grant, are on a timeline. Organizations should be deliberate in how they communicate requests to their prospective donors. If you request donations for a specific project—a roof repair or preservation project, for example—you are, in effect, restricting money to that project alone.

Some restricted funds go to specific programs or projects, such as grant funds for a particular exhibit or donations for a family day program. Others cover the organization's physical capital, like building additional storage space. Still other gifts are restricted to generate money through an endowment.[9]

## ENDOWMENTS

Endowments are assets that are set aside in a separate fund to be invested over time, allowing the original assets (the principal or corpus) to grow by continuing to add to the fund and reinvesting interest. Endowments are generally designed to keep the corpus intact, but organizations will usually take an annual draw from the endowment's interest rate to provide budgeted annual income for programs or operations.[1] This distribution rate is usually around 3 to 5 percent. The remaining interest is reinvested back into the corpus of the endowment.

If an organization has an endowment or is working with a donor to set one up, guiding documents will be needed to establish the endowment and its terms. Guidelines should address issues such as the endowment distribution, investment policies, and withdrawing money from the corpus. Seek expert legal and financial advice when necessary.

---

1. "Endowments," National Council of Nonprofits, accessed September 27, 2020, https://www.councilofnonprofits.org/tools-resources/endowments.

Although "without donor restrictions" and "with donor restrictions" are accounting standards, their application goes beyond the annual financial statements. It is essential to know which funds are restricted to which program or operating areas and diligently track their use.

## Fundraising Pyramids

With each donor, your goal is to move them through a progression of three steps:

1. Attract
2. Renew
3. Upgrade

You must first attract a donor's support; they must be motivated to sustain your cause. Next, your goal is to get them to renew their funding to you. This is easy enough to say, but you might be surprised to learn that the donor retention rate averages around 46 percent.[10] In other words, fewer than half of donors who give to a charity one year also include the same charity in their contributions the following year. As a general rule, it costs an organization less to retain an existing donor than it does to attract a new one. From there, your next goal is to upgrade the donor to higher levels of support each subsequent year.

You will often see this represented through a triangle diagram called a fundraising or donor pyramid. At the bottom of the pyramid is the sea of possible donors, frequently called your "total constituency."[11] (More on constituency to come in the next chapter.) From there, you have your first-time donors (or members if we're talking about a membership program). The next level belongs to renewed donors who give consistently. As we move up the pyramid, we split into those who have upgraded their donation amount each year and sustaining donors who have committed to increasing their donation frequency (either annual, quarterly, or monthly).[12] From there, we move up to major gift donors. Finally, at the top of the pyramid, we have planned gift donors who have chosen to include the organization in their legacy giving.

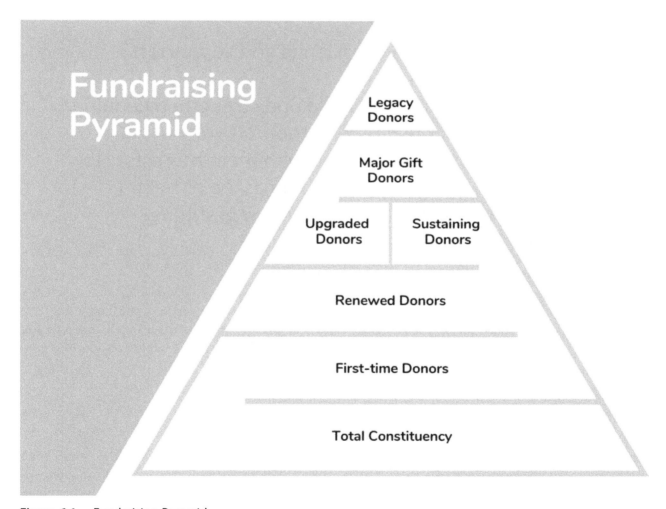

**Figure 6.1.** Fundraising Pyramid

The donor pyramid is helpful when evaluating an individual donor's relationship with the organization and when considering how to dedicate resources to your overall fundraising efforts.

## The Fundraising Cycle

We've covered a lot of material in this first section. Now that we've spent some time understanding nonprofits in general and fundraising specifically, let's move into some practical application. Back in chapter 1, we spent a little bit of time talking about the fundraising cycle phases. As I mentioned there, we are going to focus on a four-part cycle:

1. Identify
2. Cultivate
3. Ask
4. Steward

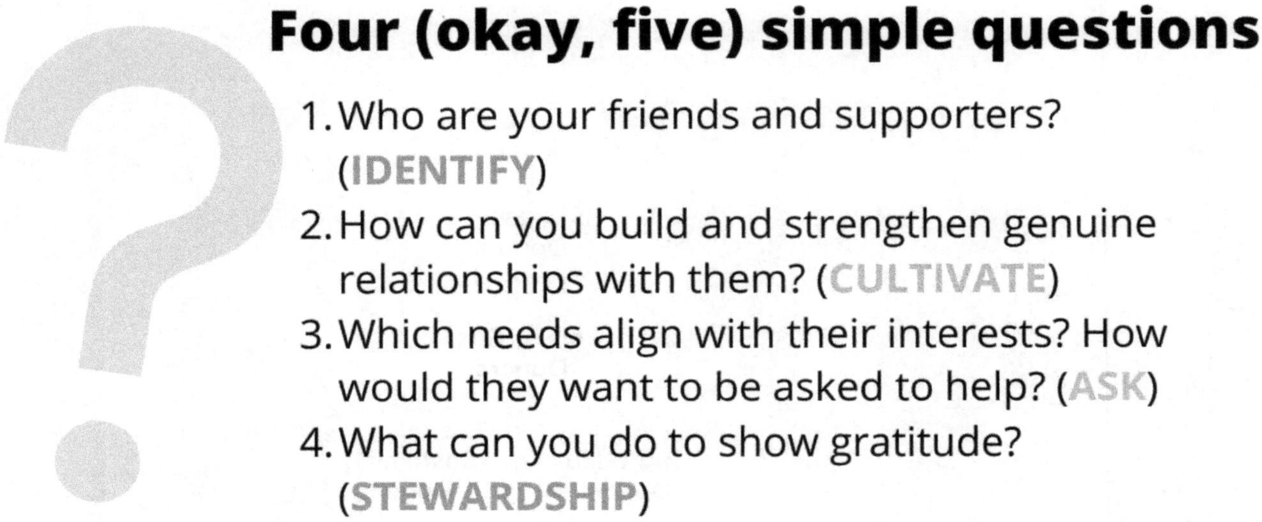

# Four (okay, five) simple questions

1. Who are your friends and supporters? (IDENTIFY)
2. How can you build and strengthen genuine relationships with them? (CULTIVATE)
3. Which needs align with their interests? How would they want to be asked to help? (ASK)
4. What can you do to show gratitude? (STEWARDSHIP)

**Figure 6.2.** Four Questions

How are these four little words going to help you professionalize your fundraising? We will spend the next few chapters looking at each of these phases separately and in greater detail. By the time we're done, we will answer four (okay, five) simple questions that provide the foundation for fundraising.

## Notes

1. Rich Dietz and Brandy Keller, "Donor Loyalty Study: A Deep Dive into Donor Behaviors and Attitudes," Abila, April 2016, http://www.thenonprofittimes.com/wp-content/uploads/2016/04/Donor-Loyalty-Study.pdf. "Donor Perspectives: An Investigation into What Drives Your Donors to Give," Blackbaud, November 2012, https://www.blackbaud.com/files/resources/downloads/10.12_DonorProfile_whitepaper_FINAL2.pdf. "The 2018 U.S. Trust Study of High Net-Worth Philanthropy," Bank of America

Private Bank and the Indiana University Lilly Family School of Philanthropy, accessed September 29, 2020, https://scholarworks.iupui.edu/bitstream/handle/1805/17666/high-net-worth2018-summary.pdf.

2. Rich Dietz and Brandy Keller, 9.

3. "The 2018 U.S. Trust Study of High Net-Worth Philanthropy," 2.

4. "Donor Perspectives," 3.

5. "The 2018 U.S. Trust Study of High Net-Worth Philanthropy," 3.

6. Patrick Kennedy, "Intercultural Competence for Nonprofit Fundraising," *CCS Fundraising* (blog), February 13, 2020, https://ccsfundraising.com/intercultural-competence-for-nonprofit-fundraising.

7. Lilya Wagner, "Culture, Code Switching and Fundraising—Including Immigrants in Our Circles of Giving," *Lilly Family School of Philanthropy* (blog), October 29, 2018, https://blog.philanthropy.iupui.edu/2018/10/29/culture-code-switching-and-fundraising-including-immigrants-in-our-circles-of-giving.

8. Bryce Gorman, Fundraising Educator, Local History Services, Indiana Historical Society, comments in manuscript review, November 6, 2020.

9. Michael Worth, *Fundraising Principles and Practice* (Los Angeles: Sage Publications, 2015), 88.

10. Bill Levis, Ben Miller, and Cathlene Williams, *2019 Fundraising Effectiveness Survey Report*, The Growth in Giving Initiative, March 5, 2019, https://afpglobal.org/sites/default/files/attachments/generic/FEP2019AnnualSurveyReport.pdf, 19.

11. Worth, 99; Timothy Seiler, "The Total Development Plan," in *Achieving Excellence in Fundraising*, ed. Eugene Tempel, Timothy Seiler, and Eva Aldrich (San Francisco: Jossey-Bass, 2011), 45.

12. Kurt Worrell, "8 Key Aspects for a Successful Monthly Sustainer Donor Program," *sgENGAGE* (blog), May 6, 2020, https://npengage.com/nonprofit-fundraising/healthcare-sustaining-donors-programs-tips/.

# MASTERING THE FUNDRAISING CYCLE

# Identify

In museums, we talk a lot about audiences. We want to know more about our current audiences to learn how we can better serve them. In addition, we also want to identify potential audiences and figure out how to reach them. In fundraising, we use the word "constituents." Your constituents are anyone and everyone who has been or potentially could be involved with your organization. Whether we call them audiences, constituents, members, donors, supporters, collaborators, partners, guests, or visitors—they all deserve our consideration because they represent actual and potential relationships waiting to be developed and nurtured.

## CONSTITUENCY DEFINITION

Constituency: "All people who have in some fashion been involved with the institution seeking support: consists of members, contributors, participants (past or present), clients and relatives of clients."[1]

1. Eugene R. Temple, Timothy L. Seiler, and Eva E. Aldrich, *Achieving Excellence in Fundraising* (San Francisco: Jossey-Bass), 467.

## Constituent Relationships

It's important to be deliberate in identifying your constituents and understanding their relationship with the organization. This helps us decide where and how to focus our efforts. One way to do this is with a constituency model. Philanthropy teacher Henry Rosso's model, which he called "concentric circles," looks a bit like the cross-section of a tree or a pebble dropped into a pond.

This model allows you and other stakeholders to consider how committed your constituents are to your organization. Those nearest the center are closest to your cause, with each ring outward representing a degree of separation, until you reach the general public at the outermost level. *Achieving Excellence in Fundraising* compares this to the flow and

# Hank Rosso's Concentric Circles Constituency Model

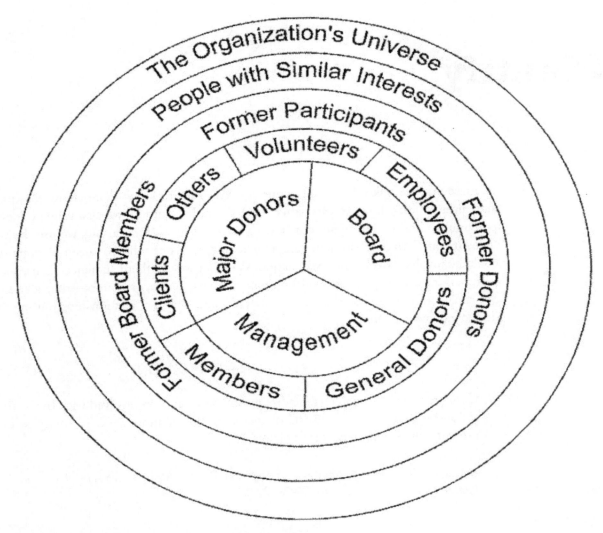

**Figure 7.1.** Constituency Model. The Fund Raising School, 2021

dissipation of energy. "The closer to the center of the action, the greater the energy, the stronger the bond."[1]

Those who gravitate to the center might include your board members, staff leaders (volunteer or paid), and possibly even some major donors. Moving outward, your second ring might include donors, members, regular visitors, and community partners. The next ring might list occasional visitors, newsletter subscribers, and social media followers. From there, you could consider people who used to be involved, such as former board members and lapsed donors. As you continue to move outward, you lose some of the momentum—the energy—that creates a connection to your cause.

In considering the constituency model, it's important to remember two things:

1. It's not static. People will move in and out of the rings as their involvement with the organization changes. A visitor could become a member, then a volunteer, and finally, a board member, moving progressively closer to the center of the circle. Likewise, board members, staff, and volunteers may leave their positions and migrate toward the outer rings.
2. Your goal is to move people toward the center by building and strengthening relationships. Every time you gain a new member, donor, or even a program participant, you strengthen the bond between that person and the organization. You're trying to create more energy, but keep in mind you will never get everyone to the center. Each ring and each person are important on their own.

## Blank Constituency Model

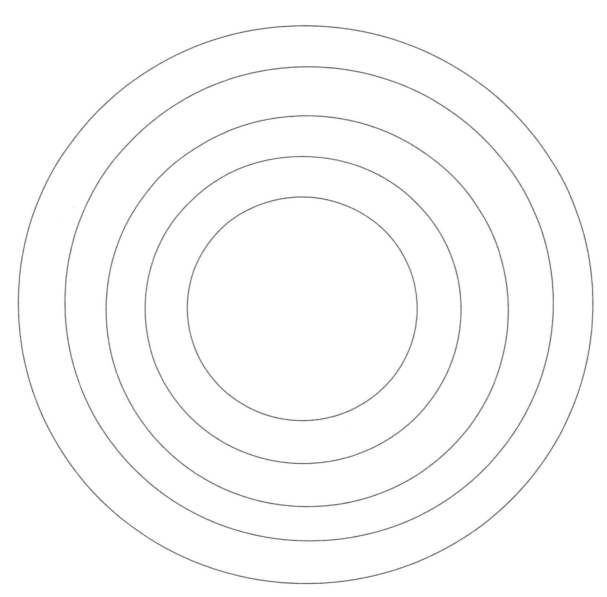

**Figure 7.2.** Blank Constituency Model. The Fund Raising School, 2021

# Constituent Management

One of the most important steps organizations can take to improve fundraising is to make sure they are keeping track of their friends. Without easy access to contact information and other details about donors, members, and potential supporters, your fundraising efforts will never get off the ground. Having a good system in place for managing your constituents is probably the single most important step you can take to improve your outcomes.

But what does this look like? The first thing to keep in mind is that your contact database is dynamic; it's always moving and changing. While a snapshot of your supporters at any given time can be helpful, you ideally want the information you have about them to increase, changing each time you learn more about them.

Let me give you an example. I once worked with an organization that kept its historical society membership list on an Excel spreadsheet. Every time someone new joined, they would add that person to their "mailing list," which they used to run mailing labels for their quarterly newsletter. However, their critical error came when it was time to note who didn't renew. Instead of moving those people to a different list or somehow marking them inactive, they just deleted the person (and their contact info). By doing this, they erased any record of that lapsed member's relationship with the organization; they effectively deleted an entire ring from the constituency model (and all of their contact info along with it) and significantly decreased their chances of reengaging with those supporters.

Keep, at the minimum, basic information about your current, past, and potential supporters. As is often the case, you can break this information down into "need to have" and "nice to have." So, what information do you need to track?

- Contact information (name, address, email, phone number)
- Giving information (membership history, gift history)

So, in addition to basic contact information, you'll want a record of each person's membership and donor history. Ideally, it's nice to know when each membership was activated, renewed, or lapsed. It's also helpful to have at least this level of information about monetary donations as well. By tracking how much someone gave, when they gave, and whether it was restricted to a specific area or in response to a particular appeal, you have greater insight into each person's relationship with the organization. This information is critical for researching and qualifying donors, which we'll talk about in just a bit.

Depending on the capabilities of your database, you may want to give some thought to how you handle married couples. Oftentimes, spouses are listed together and do not have their own entries. In the case of death or divorce, the organization can lose track of valuable constituent information. If your database has a relationship function, you may be able to link individuals together. If you decide to create individual entries and link them with a shared ID, pay attention to your queries. This can sometimes lead to double counting.

The more information you can track and retain about each of your constituents, the more effective you can be in building relationships. In terms of "nice to have" information, consider how you might track the following:

- Employment information
- Family information (spouse, children, parents, siblings, etc.)
- Volunteer activity
- Event attendance

- Object donation history (if you're a collections-based organization)
- Solicitation history (when they were asked to give or join and how they responded)
- Past contact details
- Notes

How you go about keeping this information is called constituent relationship management (or CRM for short). A CRM database is your best tool for this process.

## CRM Options

Imagine trying to mail holiday cards without your address book or sending a message to a friend without a phone number, email, or social media connection. If you want to be in contact with the people in your life, you have to keep track of them. The same is true when it comes to maintaining communication with your organization's friends and supporters. If you want to mail a letter or send an email, you need to have that contact information readily available. Establishing a good method for tracking your contacts is an essential step toward fundraising success.

When it comes to tracking your constituents, your options may fall into "good, better, best" categories, depending on your knowledge, resources, and budget. Many smaller organizations start out maintaining their records using Excel because it's accessible. As a widely available computer spreadsheet program, its primary functions are pretty straightforward. However, a spreadsheet program like Excel is designed for number crunching; it is a self-contained dataset. Spreadsheets are great for financial analysis but work less well when it comes to filtering and grouping information. Imagine creating columns for every category we discussed above and then adding new ones for each new year of membership or event attended. It wouldn't take long for your spreadsheet to become unwieldy, making it difficult to see patterns and opening your reporting up to errors.

The most effective constituent relationship management comes from a database. Complex collections of data are organized in relational tables. The tables are linked together in different ways and can support queries. In other words, you can sort information based on different relationships and generate reports. For example, if you were tracking both membership and event attendance in your database, you could then run a report to see which of your members attended your last gala event. You could take that a step further and find out which members have participated in the previous five galas or whether any lapsed members attended. Databases make this type of information more accessible and, therefore, more powerful, because you can use it to target your strategies and messaging.

Databases usually require a more significant investment. They are more complicated and robust, and generally require that you purchase a product and maintenance service from an outside vendor. When you're already strapped for cash, it can be difficult to justify a new investment. However, if at all possible, try to work database maintenance into your annual budget. (Perhaps a sponsor or multiyear grant can help you bridge the gap.) In addition to traditional commercial, nonprofit CRM systems, there are a few other options to consider:

- Open-source databases, such as CiviCRM, means the program's code is available to download, change, reuse, and share for free. Because they don't belong to a proprietary company, some require a bit more technical savviness. Open-source databases could potentially even disappear without much notice, so it's important to research your options to find one that's been around for a while. You should also consider options for backing up your data.

- Discounted or even free technology services may be available from businesses such as Salesforce.org, which offers CRM subscriptions at no cost through a program called The Power of Us. Some CRMs offer nonprofit discounts or even free versions of their product with data caps.
- Museums may find that they already have a suitable solution in place through PastPerfect, which is a desktop or cloud-based collections management software program that also offers contact management features. While PastPerfect is not a CRM specifically designed for nonprofit fundraising, it does have some features that make sense for museums, including the ability to cross-reference your object and monetary donors.

Because CRM databases are traditionally built for for-profit sales teams, it's important to look for a solution that is designed specifically for nonprofits. If you decide to start shopping for a CRM, gather as much information as you can up front. There are numerous online reviews and recommendations to help you become familiar with your options, but you may find that conversations with other nonprofit leaders will yield the best results. Reach out to other local history organizations or small nonprofits in your area and ask them how they manage their constituent information. Find out what they do and don't like about their system and software, and ask them what they wish they'd known going in. It may also be helpful to schedule demonstrations with a few companies when you've narrowed your choice down. Also, consider that many CRM providers offer free trial periods.

As you evaluate your options, keep in mind not only how you bring money in now, but how you'd like to grow that effort. If online giving isn't something you offer right

## CRM TIPS

- Research options and ask questions. Find out how long a new system would take to get up and running and how you would migrate your current data. Ask which merchants you can use (especially if you will be taking online donations or selling items online). Discuss how staff will be trained and how you access support if you have trouble.
- Budget for your CRM system. Consider not only the base price but also add-ons such as training, maintenance, updates, expansions, and processing fees.
- Create and document a process for data entry (and then use it consistently).
- Commit to making contact updates. Designate who will be responsible for ensuring the database reflects the most current information.
- Keep "everyone" in one place. Don't maintain separate contact lists.
- Make the system accessible to key personnel. Consider a cloud-based service or ensure the program is available in a common space to everyone who needs it.
- Consider integration with other systems as needed. You may want to expand and add-on new capabilities in the future. Make sure these platforms all "talk" to each other.
- Consider how you want to see your data onscreen and in print. Try to find the right balance between ease-of-use and functionality.

now, but it's a strategy you plan to implement in the future, make sure your CRM is designed to handle that. You will find that most software companies offer a range of products. They should be able to tell you whether the CRM you're considering can be integrated with current or future products and services. Examples might include online giving (including membership), as well as your store, ticketing, event registration, and marketing platforms.

Once you're working from a CRM platform that meets your needs, invest in training for users to get the most out of the features. It's vital to commit to updating records promptly. From there, you can create and document the procedure, making it available to everyone who has responsibly for making updates. In doing this, consider the different ways you receive contact info updates—from checks to emails to returned mail. You may find that you even need to create a guide (and possibly category definitions) to ensure that each record is updated in a consistent manner and format, with all relevant fields completed.

Make sure that there is only one "master list." Remind others not to keep separate contact lists; it's too easy to make changes in one place and not the other. Finally, make sure that the database is accessible to everyone who needs to use it. Depending on the software you choose, you may be able to network several computers, or it might be entirely accessible via the cloud. Some organizations may decide to put it on one computer in a museum office. This can be a good solution, as long as everyone making updates and running reports has a key to get in. It's also a good idea to keep a data backup offsite, if it can be done securely. Your CRM database is a valuable fundraising tool; you'll want to maximize its functions for cultivating current and prospective donors.

## Prospective Donors

You will find prospective donors in every ring of the constituency model. There are a lot of different factors that influence whether a person is a good prospect for any specific ask. We will take a look at some of these in a bit when we talk about "qualifying" donors.

Generally speaking, you have one of three goals when it comes to working with donors and members, depending on their current relationships with your organization:

1. Attract: Your first goal is to attract their support. In some cases, this will happen without much work; some people will just naturally gravitate toward your cause. At other times, you'll have to try a little harder to build that relationship.
2. Renew: Once someone has committed to supporting your organization, your next goal is motivating them to renew that commitment. This is called donor retention, and it's an essential aspect of successful fundraising. Why? Because it costs the organization less to keep a donor than it does to recruit one. Consider this: most major gifts are made after five years of giving (and eighteen to twenty-four personalized "touches" or interactions between the organization and the donor).[2] In addition, someone who gives at least three times is more likely to continue supporting your cause. Even smaller gifts given year after year from retained donors can add up significantly over a lifetime.
3. Upgrade: Among your committed donors, you will want to try and move them up to a greater level of giving, in terms of amount, frequency of giving, or both.

## Prospect Research

Prospect research is one of those areas where the heavyweight programs speak a whole different language. The major university or hospital system down the road has entire departments dedicated to prospect research, not to mention subscription access to expensive databases that will pull information on a plethora of wealth indicators. But that doesn't mean a small organization can't make prospect research work to its advantage. You can become a better-informed fundraiser. It just takes a little know-how, some curiosity, and a willingness to learn about people inside and outside your database.

Build a "suspect" list. Your prospective donors are out there. Some are already in your database, and some are outside just waiting for you to add them. The first thing to remember is that your current and past members and donors are your best prospects for future gifts. When it comes to building a network outside your current database, you are looking to make contacts, network, and begin building relationships. But how can you proactively go about identifying potential donors and adding them to your maybe list? In other words, how do you develop a list of people you suspect might be interested in the work your organization is doing? Here are a few ideas:

- Ask for recommendations from your board, staff, friends, donors, and volunteers.
- Consider object donors or those who have contributed items to your collecting initiatives.
- Collect names and contact information from visitors and event attendees when possible and ask for permission to add them to your mailing list.
- Provide options to sign up for e-newsletters and other communication on your website.
- Use social media to identify, inform, and engage your followers.
- Get involved and network locally. Get to know the people at your community foundation, chamber of commerce, and tourism bureau, as well as other local service organizations.
- Leverage partnerships with organizations with missions that complement yours.
- Form relationships with corporate and business partners.

Your prospective donor/volunteer/partner/collaborator list will take some time to grow. Still, each new connection provides an additional opportunity to invite that person to learn more about the good work you're doing. Be patient and persistent. The more you know about your prospective donors, the better you will get at targeting specific messaging and building profiles for major gifts.

## Qualifying Donors

Identifying potential donors is an ongoing process, but at some point we have to decide where and how to focus our energy. Not everyone on our list is a good fit for every priority. Some join once, and others renew faithfully every year. Some will contribute to an annual appeal; others will give monthly. Some will donate major gifts, and others will not give at all. Our challenge as fundraisers is to try and figure out who among our list of prospective donors might be a good fit for specific asks. Sure, we could just start throwing pasta on the wall and see what sticks, but gathering data to look for key indicators and trends will probably yield better results.

## Linkage, Interest, and Ability

Your goal with prospect research is to identify your most likely donors and begin trying to match their interests to your giving opportunities. *Achieving Excellence in Fundraising* identifies three factors that come together to influence a person's giving to a particular organization: linkage, interest, and ability, or LIA for short.[3]

1. Linkage: This is how closely affiliated a person is (or is not) with an organization, often based on a person-to-person connection with someone close to the institution. Linkage is developed through networking and intentional relationship building.
2. Interest: This gauges how closely the organization's mission aligns with the prospective donor's priorities. It's important to note that for someone to be interested in the work of the organization, they have to know about it first. Also keep in mind that a potential donor's interests might be specific to a particular area, such as education, exhibits, or collections. Communication is critical to increasing awareness and interest.
3. Ability: Each person or family has a different level of resources available to them. As fundraisers, we must gauge financial capacity and match it to an appropriate gift request. Research and peer evaluation can help in this area. For example, ask your board or even loyal major donors to review your prospect list to help you determine appropriate gift ranges.

Taken together, these three factors influence the best possible communication with potential donors. They can help us decide where to focus our efforts (and resources) in cultivation, which we will talk about in the next chapter. Organizations sometimes pursue a handful of wealthy donors (or foundations) without considering that there is no established linkage to or interest in their work. Because of this fixation, we might overlook a potential volunteer with less ability to give but with a strong linkage to and interest in the organization. Consider all these factors at work. While your immediate goal might be to raise money, your ultimate goal is to build overall support for and investment in the organization.

## Philanthropic Indicators and Wealth Markers

Determining the degree to which a prospective donor has linkage, interest, or ability requires some investigation. Sometimes there is a certain "ick factor" that accompanies prospect research because people feel like they are snooping or somehow invading others' privacy. It can feel a little awkward. My advice is to stay within your comfort level, but remember two things: First, your research will likely be confined to publicly available information or to something you learn about someone from personal interactions (either by you or others in your organization). Second, people who make charitable contributions give because they want to. Gathering information to make better-informed asks does not mean you're manipulating someone into giving to your nonprofit. It means you're investing time and resources to provide matches between potential donors and the people you serve.

According to DonorSearch, which is a company that uses philanthropy and wealth analytics to identify prospective donors, there are a few key indicators that can help you focus your efforts to qualify donors.[4] While the research does take some time, these resources are available without costly prospect research subscriptions or consultants. DonorSearch refers to these as philanthropic indicators and wealth markers.

Philanthropic indicators are as follows:

- Previous donations to your nonprofit: As we've already discussed, past support for your cause is a strong indicator of potential willingness to donate again. If you're collecting the right type of information, you can start your prospect research right in your database.
- Donations to other nonprofits: Gifts to other nonprofits, particularly if they are in the same sector, indicate a person's charitable habits, as well as their giving priorities. Don't be shy about studying other nonprofits' annual reports, donor walls, and sponsor lists.
- Nonprofit involvement: People who volunteer or work for nonprofits understand the challenges associated with fundraising and appreciate the importance of philanthropy.
- Personal hobbies and interests: Not every project is a good fit for every donor. That's why understanding prospective donors' priorities and commitments can help match them to opportunities.
- Employer philanthropy: Employers are often looking for philanthropic opportunities, whether it be through matching gift programs, social responsibility divisions, employee-directed giving and volunteerism, or donations of goods or services.

Wealth Markers are:

- Real estate ownership: Real estate can be a wealth marker, but it also serves as an indicator of philanthropic giving. According to DonorSearch, someone who owns $2 million-plus in real estate is seventeen times more likely to give than the average prospect.[5] From conducting online real estate searches to visiting the county tax assessor's website, you can learn a lot about your prospect by where and how they live. Just realize that your conclusions will probably (at least initially) be based on generalizations. While the average American spends more than 35 percent of their income on housing, some people live well above or below their means.[6]
- SEC transactions: The U.S. Securities and Exchange Commission (SEC) reports on all stock holdings at publicly traded companies on the website SEC.gov. While this information doesn't provide a complete picture of someone's wealth, you can consider it with other indicators.
- Business affiliations: Information on a donor's career, professional achievements, and business affiliations can provide information not just about the person's financial situation, but also about their interests and connections.
- Political giving: Giving to political campaigns is regulated by the Federal Election Commission. As a result, information about donations (and donors) to federal campaigns is publicly available on the website FEC.gov. A large contribution to a political campaign may indicate giving capacity, but it also demonstrates that the donor is willing to take action to support something they believe in.[7]
- Family wealth: Philanthropic giving tends to run in families and wealth is often transferred from one generation to the next. Sometimes it can be helpful to research the giving priorities of parents or children of potential or current donors.

These are a few ideas to get you started. This information can be helpful when considering capacity and whether support for a particular program or project might be a reasonable ask for a specific donor. You won't make all your decisions based on formal research. A lot of your best indicators come from getting to know your current and prospective donors on a more personal level and helping them learn more about your organization. That's called cultivation, and we're going to cover it in the next chapter.

## Notes

1. Timothy L. Seiler, "Developing a Constituency for Fundraising," in *Achieving Excellence in Fundraising*, ed. Eugene Tempel, Timothy Seiler, and Eva Aldrich (San Francisco: Jossey-Bass, 2011), 19.

2. Jay Love, "3 Reasons Why Donor Retention Trumps New Donor Acquisition," (blog) *Bloomerang*, November 28, 2017, https://bloomerang.co/blog/3-reasons-why-donor-retention-trumps-new-donor-acquisition.

3. Timothy L. Seiler, "Plan to Succeed," *Achieving Excellence in Fundraising*, ed. Eugene Tempel, Timothy Seiler, and Eva Aldrich (San Francisco: Jossey-Bass, 2011), 15.

4. "Prospect Research: The Ultimate Guide [Updated]," DonorSearch, accessed August 12, 2020, https://www.donorsearch.net/prospect-research-ultimate-guide/.

5. "5 Ways to Determine If a Prospect Has Significant Real Estate Holdings," DonorSearch, accessed 12, 2020, https://www.donorsearch.net/prospect-research-real-estate-holdings/. See this website for more detailed information about how to conduct real estate holding research.

6. "Consumer Expenditures Mid-year Update—July 2019 through June 2020," U.S. Bureau of Labor Statistics, accessed November 3, 2021, https://www.bls.gov/news.release/cesmy.nr0.htm.

7. "8 Types of Essential Prospect Data," DonorSearch, accessed August 12, 2020, https://www.donorsearch.net/prospect-profile-data-types/#estate.

# Cultivate

Most of us who do local history work didn't expect to ask people for money. However, there is a surprising transfer of skills between doing public history work and fundraising. Much like public history, fundraising is all about building relationships, sharing stories, and concentrating on the audiences we're trying to serve. In other words: cultivation.

## Cultivation: Not Just for Crops

You might associate the word "cultivation" with agriculture. It provides a good analogy. When we refer to farmers cultivating their crops, we are talking about how they care for their plants. It involves preparing the soil, and once seeds are planted, the farmer works to promote growth. But not every plant receives the same treatment. What works for corn may not be right for soybeans or wheat. Farmers have to consider what they know about the land and the seeds. They have to envision what tactics will produce strong, healthy fields with good yields. Perhaps most importantly, they have to rely on instinct and what they've learned over their careers. And of course, there's always a little bit of luck mixed in; rain when you need it, sun in-between. So it goes with fundraising, but instead of plants, we're taking care of people.

### HISTORIAN-TURNED FUNDRAISER

In a recent blog post on the American History Association's website, a historian-turned fundraiser detailed how her training in public history prepared her for a career in fund development. She explained, "In public history, I learned to write well, tell stories, read an audience, be empathetic, collaborate, and see myself as part of a larger historical narrative. All of these skills help me raise money and improve peoples' lives, and it is an incredible privilege to be able to use my history degrees in this way."[1]

1. Katherine Garland, "A Career in Development," *American Historical Association* (blog), November 28, 2018, https://www.historians.org/publications-and-directories/perspectives-on-history/december -2018/a-career-in-development-how-a-public-historian-became-a-fundraiser.

As we mentioned in chapter 1, cultivation—the time and effort spent growing healthy relationships—is where we will spend most of our fundraising time. The goal is to weave fundraising so seamlessly into the history work we're doing that it becomes second nature. You may be pleasantly surprised how well your skills in public history line up with the development of your abilities as a fundraiser.

Fundraising in general—and cultivation in particular—draws on skills we use every day to interpret history with thoughtfully curated exhibitions and programs. It's very much in line with our roles as community partners. More than likely, you are already doing a fair bit of cultivation. We just need to be a little more deliberate in those efforts to match potential donors with funding opportunities that are in line with their passions. Sounds easy enough, right? Let's get a bit more specific.

## What Is Cultivation?

A friend of mine, an executive director at a county museum, has a weekly ritual. Every Friday, he goes to the bakery across the street and buys two dozen donuts: one dozen for his kids and the other dozen for his community partners. Sometimes he delivers them to colleagues at another nonprofit; other times, they go to a local business where one of his board members works. He always attaches his business card and a note of appreciation. During delivery, he'll stop to chat, ask people how they're doing, and tell them about an upcoming event at the museum he thinks they might enjoy. He doesn't do these things because he expects a check in return; he does them to make connections and strengthen relationships.

### WHAT IS CULTIVATION?

Thoughtful, intentional relationship building and a genuine desire to know the donor better through a series of donor-centered touchpoints that build mutual understanding, loyalty, and commitment.

Cultivation shouldn't be confused with promotion. Cultivation—to build mutual understanding, loyalty, and commitment—is based on a series of donor-centered touchpoints. It's built on conversations, the back-and-forth exchange of information. As the fundraiser, you should come away from these conversations knowing as much about your prospective donors as they do about the organization.

## Donor-Centric Goals of Cultivation

We spend a lot of time talking about our goals as an organization, which of course is necessary if we're going to put plans in place to help us meet those goals. However, it's vital to focus on the perspective of the donor. When we are donor-centric, we focus on the donor's wants, needs, and expectations to help guide our cultivation activities. Let's consider what a donor might want out of the relationship with our organization.

1. Understand the organization's work.

Ideally, your donors appreciate the purpose of your mission and how you go about achieving it. They understand why your history-focused mission is relevant and have a feel for some of the moving parts. From exhibitions to tours and from collections care to educational programming, you can help them learn how each contributes to the organization's overall success.

Takeaway: help donors see multiple aspects of your work and how they all fit together.

Ideas:

- Compile a reference list of all your programs, services, and initiatives for your spokespeople (especially your board). Make sure they understand how these different parts fit together to achieve your mission, and help them be prepared to talk about the work of the organization out in the community.
- Plan a behind-the-scenes collection tour and discuss how you care for the objects in your collection. Think about including a demonstration of how you house and store objects.
- Highlight an object's "road to accession" in a newsletter article. Start when it arrives on your doorstep, and finish with it securely stored, awaiting exhibit (and don't forget to talk about what it costs the organization to care for it in perpetuity).
- Highlight (with permission) one of your program participants or partners and discuss how the organization's work affects them.


2. View the work as successful, meaningful, and well-planned.

The donor wants to have confidence that the organization's operations and programming are well-planned and well-executed. You want them to tell others that you do good work. That's not to say that everything you do has to be perfect all the time. It is to say that you should celebrate and promote your successes while also collecting feedback about how you can continuously improve.

Takeaway: donors want to feel like they are part of something successful.

Ideas:

- Ask visitors and participants to provide feedback about their experiences with you. Use that information to improve your work.
- Use your communication channels wisely to celebrate your successes. (If you're not sure which digital platforms to use for which messages, recruit the help of someone who uses them frequently. This can be an excellent way to engage younger volunteers.) Don't forget to promote your fundraising successes as well. If you secure a new sponsorship or receive a grant award, share these achievements with your followers.


3. Perceive that money is spent wisely.

Your supporters will vary on their opinions of how you should direct their money. Some will tell you to use it where you need it most, and others will tell you exactly where they want it to go. Understand from the beginning that this is as much about them as it is about you. But transparency is still important. Help prospective and current donors understand just how far their money could go.

Takeaway: show your donors the good work you're doing using the resources they provide.

Ideas:

- Provide supporters with regular updates about your progress, particularly if they donated to a specific project. Before and after photos are particularly useful for conveying the message of progress, making donors feel confident in their investment in you. It's also a good idea to be transparent with your project costs and budgets.
- Educate your stakeholders (including your board) and supporters about museum methods and best practices to help them understand why some of your funds need to be directed to things like collections care. You can have similar conversations about why your facilities and administrative costs (often called your F&A or overhead) are critical to the work you do.

4. Feel appreciated

Donors and fundraising experts alike will often cite failure to offer a proper thank-you for a gift as a primary reason why organizations don't receive subsequent gifts. We will talk more about this in the chapter on stewardship, but it's worth frequent mention. Showing appropriate and timely appreciation contributes significantly to building relationships.

Takeaway: make donors (and visitors, participants, partners, and generally everyone) feel valued and appreciated.

Ideas:

- Print and send photos from your big annual event or favorite program.
- Host a special recognition for your volunteers.
- Spotlight longtime members in your newsletter.
- Send personalized thank-you letters (or even handwritten notes). Enlist board members to make thank-you calls. The purpose of these calls is purely for appreciation with no requests for donations or membership.
- Recognize donors, members, partners, and volunteers on social media.

5. Believe their gift makes a difference.

Donors (and volunteers) give because they believe their resources can help you reach people in need of your services. They want to know that their generosity moves the needle. Focus on the donor and the people who benefit from the work you do (outward-focused), rather than the organization (inward-focused). Provide specific examples of their donation's impact.

Takeaway: track, measure, and communicate results that speak to your donors' desires to do good.

Ideas:

- Use "you" frequently in your communications while avoiding overusing "we" or "the museum," for example.
- If someone gave last year, take the opportunity to tell them what was accomplished for the people you serve. For example, "Because of your generosity last year, fifty students in after-school care participated in our know your local history virtual game show. Now, these kids and their families not only know more about our community, but they know that the museum is the place to go for more fun and facts. You made this possible!"

6. Feel individually noticed and cared about.

Sometimes it's easy to talk about "our visitors" or "our members" as one big, homogenous group. Of course, we know that's not the case. Each one comes to us with their own experiences and expectations. An important part of our challenge is to see and treat each one as an individual, whether they are a one-time visitor or a longtime supporter.

Takeaway: donors (and visitors) want you to see them and not their pocketbooks.

Ideas:

- Streamline your processes, from your website and social media comments to your welcome desk and main phone line. Train staff and volunteers on how to answer or refer questions and provide top-notch customer service.
- Make your communication to prospective donors as personalized as possible. A good CRM database and careful upkeep of individual records will make this process much easier and more effective. And if you're not currently using mail merge for your letters, now is the time to learn.

## Building Relationships: The Four I's

I created this model to think through how we can proactively engage potential and current supporters. Like most models, it doesn't have to flow in only one direction, and a donor could come in at any level. I call them the Four I's.

Inform: Do they have enough information about us?

- Organizational values and guiding principles: Donors are becoming more aware of and interested in organizational values. They look to support charities that align with and further their personal ideals. Define your organization's beliefs and priorities, and share them with current and potential supporters.
- Connection to the mission: We want to ensure supporters understand our mission—not using fancy terms and lofty goals, but how it looks when we practically apply it to the work we do. This includes how our priority projects and initiatives connect to the mission.
- Multiple engagement channels: We want to have many touchpoints with the donor, spread appropriately over a comfortable amount of time. We need to consider how and where prospective donors (including future visitors) learn about us. This often begins before they even step foot in our museum or historic site. Think about the organization's website and reviews on social media and travel sites.
- Brand management: This goes beyond our logo and the colors we use on our sign. Our brand is what comes to people's minds when they think about our organization. Do they think, "My kids had a great time there, and the staff was kind and helpful," or do they think, "I felt like I was in an antique shop, and it smelled funny in there?" Our constituents' experiences with us physically and digitally inform their impression of the work we do.
- Coordinated messaging: Information about our organization should be consistent and complementary. Our goal is to have it all fit together like a puzzle. When we get good at this, we don't just post the same information across all communication

channels. We introduce a strategy to engage our followers, conveying our message in different ways using different platforms. (Need more help here? See if you can find a pro bono marketing guru to offer some assistance, or reach out to a local university marketing professor; there might be opportunities to engage students with your project.)

- Case resources: We're going to talk about making a good case for support in chapter 12. Case resources, or case expressions, are the materials we create to help inform and persuade, from our website to our social media to our brochures and appeal letters.

Invite: Have we invited them to participate in ways that would be meaningful to them?

- Seeing is believing: As you develop relationships with people who have the potential to be your biggest supporters (and not just "big" in terms of dollar amounts, but also enthusiasm), make sure you include them in programming that will be of most interest to them. Sometimes this may mean inviting them to participate, and sometimes it will mean asking them to observe. Other times, especially for those who aren't likely to physically visit a site, this can mean engaging with them virtually through live webinars or content posted on social media.
- Provide "insider" opportunities: Extend invitations to special events, behind-the-scenes tours, or training workshops designed specifically for those closest to your organization. This could mean members-only day trips or exhibit openings. It could be special tours through your collections area or other parts of your museum not on the standard route.
- Make personal connections a priority: Invite your supporters to connect with you on a personal level. Schedule face-to-face visits. Take the time to send handwritten notes. Bring them donuts. Get to know them as people. Move from transactional to transformational relationships.

## FOUNDATIONS AND CORPORATIONS

Relationship-building applies not just to individual donors but to the people running foundations and corporations as well. Don't miss out on opportunities to draw them closer to your organization using the same strategies you would for individuals. They are also gathering information and trying to make decisions about how to do the most good with their resources. The more they know about you and the work you're doing, the more they can understand your needs and provide support.

Involve: How can we take them beyond participation to true involvement?

- Involve prospects in the life of your organization: Make them feel like part of the team. Print personalized membership cards if your budget allows, or create digital cards for a more cost-effective option. Invite them to participate in focus groups or serve on an appropriate subcommittee. Explore potential partnerships with their businesses.

- Provide volunteer opportunities: In one study, 73 percent of participants indicated they were more likely or much more likely to donate to an organization after volunteering. Helping to do the work can drive loyalty.[1]
- Introduce them to those you serve, directly and indirectly: Create a gathering place for members at your local festival. Invite individual prospects to observe a group tour or field trip. Share results from your latest program or event satisfaction survey. Teach them more about how the museum works.
- Help them understand your needs and opportunities: Don't be afraid to share your list of priorities—and even your big dreams—with your constituents. I have a colleague who frequently invites major donors to attend professional development training workshops with him to see firsthand how the organization is working to improve, using museum best practices.

Inquire: What could we learn about ourselves from them?

- Value their perspective: Ask questions that will help you get to know them and better understand their relationship with your organization. What's their passion? What motivates them? How could these things intersect with what you're trying to achieve? This information will also help you shape your eventual solicitation.
- Ask their opinion: There is a saying in fundraising: "If you want advice, ask for money. If you want money, ask for advice." Current and prospective donors can offer valuable insight, and they will be flattered that you asked. Get their opinions over coffee. Conversation grows relationships.

The Four I's address our ongoing efforts to engage donors. But let's not forget that our response to their incoming engagement—whether following up on phone calls and email, answering questions on social media, or spending time with them one-on-one—is also essential. Building relationships is back and forth, give and take. You're likely doing a lot of this work already. How can you be more deliberate? Use the donor engagement worksheet to think through your cultivation activities and capture new ideas.

## Donor Segmentation

Are you trying to be more deliberate with your communication to make it more targeted and personalized? One way to do that is with donor segmentation. It allows you to separate your constituents into different groups to zero in on what you ask for and even how you ask for it. This can significantly improve your ask strategies and results.

Remember how we talked about the importance of a good CRM database in the last chapter? To segment your donors, you need to have this system in place. You need to collect enough information about your constituents that you have good categories for segmentation, and you need to have it in a database that allows you to sort by one or more of these categories.

For instance, let's say you are preparing to send an annual appeal. You could use one letter for your entire contact list. That would certainly be more effective than not mailing to them at all. However, what if you could craft different messages for different people based on their giving history?

## CULTIVATION: GROWING RELATIONSHIPS

1. Who are your current donors?

2. Who are your prospective donors (people who might give but haven't yet)?

3. Where did these groups come from? How did you identify them?

4. How do you communicate and engage with these groups? Do you communicate with them differently than the general public?

5. Do you deliberately cultivate these relationships? If so, how?

6. What types of cultivation (relationship-building) efforts have worked for your organization? How do you know?

7. What new ideas do you have?

8. How could you segment your donors to better tailor your message to them? What would you say?

- Maybe your letter to those who give every year would focus on their loyalty to your organization and the significant impact they've had.
- Perhaps you might then send a message to lapsed donors saying that you miss them.
- Your letter to those who have never donated might serve as more of an introduction to your work.

Having a user-friendly CRM can help you segment your donors by running lists with different criteria. You might generate a mailing for volunteers, event attendees, or volunteers who are event attendees. You can mail to loyal donors who give every year, those who give to collections care projects, or loyal donors who support collections care. You could even segment your donors by how and when they give. This might prompt you to mail a letter with a reply envelope to donors who pay by check while targeting an email with a link to your donation page to those who tend to give online. The possibilities are endless—as long as you have a good CRM. (How easily donors can be segmented into different groups is an important question for potential CRM vendors. If you think your current system can handle this, but you're not sure how to use that function, seek training or find someone who can help you.)

While we're talking about our database again, let's also mention data tracking and evaluation as an option. Sometimes we hear the word "evaluation" or "data collection" and think we don't have the time or expertise for that. However, with a good CRM and a process for updating records, you can begin collecting some useful data with minimal effort. For instance, a good database will allow you to record and track trends and success rates. Through reports or a dashboard view, it can give you a better understanding of your overall fundraising, as well as individual campaigns and appeals.

In some ways, I think small organizations have an advantage (or at least a potential advantage) when it comes to donor cultivation. Unlike large national institutions, we're more likely to know our supporters personally because our work is often done closer to home. That doesn't mean we can't or shouldn't try to broaden our base and take our mission out to the constituency model's outer rings. We should because if we only look in our own backyard, we can quickly exhaust our options among our friends and neighbors (who are also the friends and neighbors of every other nonprofit in town trying to raise funds).

By focusing on people instead of money, deliberately building more genuine relationships, and finding some joy and fun in the cultivation process, "the ask" becomes a little less forced and a lot more natural.

## Note

1. Rich Dietz and Brandy Keller, "Donor Loyalty Study: A Deep Dive into Donor Behaviors and Attitudes," Abila, 2016, http://www.thenonprofittimes.com/wp-content/uploads/2016/04/Donor-Loyalty-Study.pdf.

# Ask

We're nine chapters into this book about fundraising. It's probably about time to talk about asking people for money. I say this in jest—sort of. There's a lot of work that comes at the front end of fundraising before we're ready to ask for money. At some point that ask is going to need to happen. Our goal is the "right" ask: asking the right person for the right amount for the right need at the right time via the right method. No problem, right?

## How to Ask? It Depends

There are many different ways to ask for money. Solicitations are influenced by the situation, the individual donors, their capacity to give, and the comfort level of the people doing the asking. If the thought of sitting across the table from someone, looking them in the eye, and asking for a four, five, or six-figure amount makes you blanch, don't worry. You don't have to start there. The situation will dictate when that's the appropriate course.

Gift solicitation can be divided into three categories: personal, impersonal, and cold call. As you might expect, more personal requests tend to have higher success rates. However, they also usually take the most time, a valuable and limited resource for most of us. There are many factors to consider with each method, from the degree of personalization to the number of prospective donors reached. This is where strategy and evaluation meet trial and error (and a little bit of luck).

## Personal

These asks are based on a personal one-to-one connection. Examples include face-to-face asks, personalized letters or emails, phone calls, and peer-to-peer fundraising.

### Face-to-face asks

These asks usually take the form of a prearranged meeting following a period of cultivation and planning. You can do them one-on-one or with a team of two people (usually a peer of the donor and a staff member from the organization, although in smaller organizations these can be one and the same). Formal asks are usually reserved for larger gifts, although they can also come from more informal, organic conversations with prospective donors. In the case of a formal ask, remember that these conversations should never surprise the donor. They are the result of information exchanged between the prospective donor and the fundraiser. They should be the natural continuation of a conversation already in progress.

- Pro: By far the most personal and effective way to ask for money. The donor can ask questions and get clarification. The fundraiser can better respond to verbal and nonverbal cues to help direct the conversation.
- Con: People can be uncomfortable or reluctant to make the ask. Prospect research and cultivation leading up to the meeting usually takes time and diligent attention. Face-to-face asks are more time-consuming as they require more planning, scheduling, and follow-up, in addition to the solicitation meeting.

## Personal phone calls

This is a call from someone the prospective donor knows from the organization, whether a staff member or peer serving in a volunteer role (as opposed to the "phone-a-thon" model we'll cover in a bit). These aren't cold calls; in this case, we're referring to substantive, personal conversations between people who likely know each other and have developed a rapport. Phone calls can be effectively combined with personal letters or emails, either before or after the call. Follow-up is important in these situations because it's often that second contact that spurs the gift.

- Pros: Phone calls allow for personal interaction and exchange of information but can feel less intimidating than a face-to-face meeting. Although you lose the advantage of reading body language, the fundraiser can still pick up verbal cues and get a feel for the conversation's overall tone. Calls are a good option when in-person meetings aren't feasible and can be easier to set up than a face-to-face appointment. Phone calls are also a good way to collect feedback from multiple donors.
- Cons: Some donors do not like to be contacted by phone (although this irritation should be diminished somewhat by receiving a call from someone they know and, ideally, like). Not every pledge made over the phone will be converted to a donation because not every donor will follow through.

## TIPS FOR PERSONAL ASKS

- Set an appointment and tell them why you're coming. Remember, you don't want the prospective donor to be surprised by your ask; it should be built on good cultivation. When you ask for a meeting with them, give them time and notice to prepare. You could say something along the lines of, "I'd like to talk about your involvement in the build-out of our new education space."
- Practice. Think through how you want to start the conversation. Make note of anything you want to be sure to say. What words do you want to use when you ask for their contribution? Practice saying a few different versions out loud to yourself (maybe even in front of a mirror).
- Meet in person when possible. Both you and the donor will benefit from the back and forth that comes with a personal meeting. It helps you read and respond to facial expressions and body language.
- Ask for a specific amount. This might be the hardest part. The amount you suggest should be based on your needs and your understanding of their capacity and interest in the project. Spend some time thinking about how you want to handle this and progress with what makes the most sense and is within (or maybe just a little beyond) your comfort level. You'll refine your process each time you make an ask.
- Don't speak first after the ask. Silence is a tool many fundraisers swear by. It can be tempting to make the ask and then keep talking to appease your own discomfort or fill what feels like an awkward silence. Try to resist; once you've made your ask, give the donor a chance to process the request and wait for them to respond before you say anything.
- Offer monthly giving or multiyear pledges. If the project allows, and you think it would be a good fit for the donor, you might suggest that their donation be paid through monthly or yearly pledges (depending on the situation and the amount). If this is a tactic you want to pursue, have the pledge form with you just in case.
- Don't burn bridges if you get a "no." Despite your best research and cultivation efforts, a prospective donor may say no, and that's okay. Note whether they are saying "no" or "not right now." An answer of no suggests you may need to revisit your strategy; not right now indicates this is just another step in the cultivation process. Ask for permission to follow up and to keep them in the loop. Continued conversation may help you understand why they said no. Maybe the project didn't fit their interests, the amount was too high, or the timing just wasn't right. Let them know you value their involvement with your organization and would like to keep them connected.

## Personalized letters

This is a step above simply running a batch of bulk mailing letters. In this case, personalized messages are crafted for each prospective donor, usually from a peer (such as a board member or other fundraising volunteer) or organization representative who knows the prospect well. A personal phone call can follow the letter (or the order can be reversed). Personalized letters can take the place of in-person meetings when they are not feasible, but they are still the result of ongoing conversations between the prospective donor and the fundraiser. They will usually include a specific amount requested for a specific need.

- Pros: Some people will feel more comfortable writing letters than making asks in person. Sending letters can be an efficient use of time. You can include a reply card and return envelope (also called reply devices) to make it easier for the donor to return their payment.

- Cons: You lose some of the interpersonal exchange with the letter (although you can regain some of that with a follow-up phone call). It also takes time to craft individual messages. Once the donor has received the letter, they choose when (and whether) to respond; the fundraiser's role is more passive.

## TIPS FOR WRITING AN APPEAL LETTER

- Write simply and straightforward. There's no need to use fancy words and long, complicated sentences. Keep your paragraphs short and to the point. Don't use a small font (not less than 12-point type; shoot for 14). Make your letter easy to read and make a specific ask (ideally for a specific amount).
- Make it personal. You want your letter to be donor-centered. Maximize the number of times you use the words "you" and "we" (the organization and donor together) versus "we" (the organization alone).
- Focus on outcomes rather than needs. It's okay to talk about your organization's needs, but tie those closely to benefits or positive outcomes for the people you serve, and by extension, to your donors.
- Make the ask. Even in a letter you still have to make the ask. Some experts recommend asking in the beginning, middle, and end of the letter. Do what feels right for you and your donors, but make sure there's a call to action. Ask for a gift and tell your donors exactly what to do next ("Return your gift in the enclosed return envelope today").
- Entertain. Engage your prospective donor with a compelling story or share a bit of news. Try to create a personal connection between the person you're writing to and those you serve.
- Highlight your SMIT (single most important thing). Donors frequently just skim through letters. What's the most important takeaway for them? How can you make that stand out (and possibly even compel them to read the whole letter)? Where should you put that sentence? Can you use bold text or underline it?
- Include a reply device. Make it easy for your donor to respond. Include a reply card and pre-addressed envelope. Provide your online donation page web address. If someone regularly answers the phone (or checks messages) and can process gifts and memberships, give them the telephone number.

## Personalized emails

Although letters are more formal, an email may be as effective (or more so) in some situations. Again, this is an email written explicitly for the intended recipient, not a customized mass email. Email can be especially useful for following up after an initial conversation. Whether to send an email or letter will depend on the situation, and the fundraiser will probably have a pretty good feel for which is most appropriate.

- Pros: Email can be an excellent way to convey additional information through internet links (such as directing a prospective donor to a page on your website dedicated to a particular program). It's convenient for donors who prefer to process their payment online to access a link to your online donation form. Unlike in-person conversations and letters, emails capture conversations between the sender and receiver and can be used for reference if needed.

- Cons: Emails can feel less personal (as opposed to holding a piece of stationery in your hands). Messages are also easily overlooked and can inadvertently end up in a junk mail folder (especially if the prospect isn't expecting the email).

## Less personal letters and emails

These letters are also known as direct mail. One note is written for a larger group of recipients. As a result, the message is less personalized (although address blocks and salutations in letters should be personalized using your word processing software's mail merge function; email salutations can also be personalized). To make the process easier, save direct mail samples from other nonprofits for future inspiration, and make a note of what you do and don't like about the solicitations you receive. Consider adding text to your outer envelope to catch your potential donor's attention and motivate them to open your letter.

As funds come in, track your appeal responses in your database, and be sure to look at your open and click-through rates for your emails. (A click-through rate is the ratio of users who "click through" links in your email or advertisement as compared to the total number of people who see it.) This can tell you what types of emails are most likely to be read. This information should be readily available if you're using a third-party email platform.

- Pros: Direct mail can be a good way to reach large groups of constituents. Using information from a spreadsheet and the mail merge function, they can be further customized to include details such as how much the donor gave last year or the date their membership expires. Direct mail also presents opportunities to further

### TIPS FOR EMAILS

- Use emails to build relationships. Most emails will serve a cultivation role by providing information through e-newsletters, offering program updates, sharing resources, or inviting participation. It's commonly suggested that you should have three to four cultivation emails for every one solicitation email. Find the formula that works best for you.
- Provide a way to opt-in and opt-out of email communication. Get permission before adding someone to your email contact list. Consider adding a "join our mailing list" option on your website or through a sign-up sheet at events. You must also provide a way for them to "unsubscribe" from your email communications.
- Most readers will skim your email. Make the most of the parts they're likely to look at: email subject, first sentence, pictures, headlines, bolded or underlined words, and a P.S.
- Less is more. Keep emails shorter than letters. Ideally, they should be less than four hundred words.
- Give readers a chance to learn and do more. Include links to your website where they can get more information and make online donations
- Don't forget the ask. If the point of your email is to ask people to join or renew their membership, or to motivate them to support you with volunteerism or a monetary gift, don't forget your clear call to action.

refine your message by segmenting your donor database. You can also include reply devices or send donors to your online donation page to increase response rates.

- Cons: Bulk mailings can be expensive when you factor in printing, postage, and time spent folding and stuffing. It can also be time-consuming to track responses and make database updates (although most would probably argue that improving your contact list's integrity is well worth it). Some people feel they get too much mail in both their physical and virtual mailboxes. Sometimes, letters are opened over the trash, and emails never get opened at all.

## Peer-to-peer fundraising

Peer-to-peer fundraising happens when a volunteer raises money from their friends and family on behalf of an organization. We frequently see this in charity races or "thons" (think dance marathons or book-a-thons).

- Pros: The organization reaches new audiences by leveraging volunteers' networks. These may be donors the organization would not have contacted on its own, and these contacts come with the volunteer's endorsement. It's an excellent way to engage volunteers and help spread fundraising work among many people with a lower entry barrier. It can be a particularly productive way for board members to become engaged with fundraising. Many people are comfortable asking friends and family for smaller amounts of money to support an important cause.
- Cons: There is some upfront coordination and training that must take place to prepare volunteers to be good ambassadors for the organization. You want everyone to convey consistent messaging about your mission and goals. Someone from the organization should also be available to answer questions throughout the campaign and motivate volunteers to continue raising money. Peer-to-peer fundraising is often done through an online platform, which will take some investigation and implementation, and then volunteers and staff must be trained to use it.

## Impersonal

### Online giving

Online giving might be more of a donation channel (or method) than an appeal. Still, it's an integral part of fundraising success as online transactions continue to grow, especially among younger generations. You will likely employ various tactics to drive potential supporters to your website to make online donations. However, having a "donate button" can serve as a passive appeal, reminding anyone who visits your website that they can support your work. Digital giving (including online, social media, and text/SMS) increases each year while giving by mail decreases (down from 49% in 2010 to 23% in 2018).[1] These response rates will vary from one organization to the next, so your best bet is to track your organization's appeal methods to determine your donors' preferences.

- Pros: Online giving, from traditional channels like your website to social media and mobile giving, has surpassed conventional direct mail giving among some donors, mostly Generation X, millennials, and Generation Z. In one 2018 study, online donations made up 37 percent of reported contributions.[2] Because philanthropy is often a reflection of one's stage in life, organizations may need to move into these donation channels to keep up with changing donor demographics. With advances in smartphone technology, donors can make gifts from anywhere. Younger donors, whose philanthropic choices tend to be more impulsive, expect charities to have online and even social media giving options, and they're willing to leverage their social networks to promote causes they support.

- Cons: While there are many options for online donation platforms (the behind-the-scenes back end part of your website that allows you to process these donations, which will require an outside vendor), researching the best solution for your organization may take some time. The many available choices can seem a bit overwhelming. You will pay fees to use these platforms and to process credit card payments.

## TIPS FOR ONLINE GIVING

- Look at other donation sites. Do a little homework. Pick a handful of charities you'd like to support and work your way through their online donation forms to process your gift. Take note of what you did and didn't like about the experience. Was their form easy to find? Did it ask for the appropriate amount of information? Was the form intuitive? What happened after you made your donation? Keep these comparisons in mind as you build (or refine) your online donation process.
- Research online fundraising software vendors. There are a lot of fundraising platforms to consider with several variables that will influence your choice. In addition to price, you will also want to think about things like ease of use and integration with your CRM, as well as customer support and training. You can find many online tech reviews and comparisons (usually updated at least yearly), but some of your most useful (and honest) information may come from conversations with other small nonprofits about what they're using.
- Make sure your donation form is easy to find. Don't make prospective donors hunt for your form. Add a donation button that is easy to see from your homepage and include it in your navigation bar. They should be able to get to your form in one to two clicks.
- Minimize required information. You don't want donors to lose interest (or worse, become frustrated) by your donor form. Collect the information you need to process the gift—first and last name, email address, physical mailing address, and billing information—and let donors complete their transaction before asking additional questions about communication preferences or volunteer opportunities.
- Create a simple and straightforward donation page.[1] Make sure your membership fees and giving tiers (if you're using them) are clearly identified on the form so supporters can verify how much they expect to pay. If you want to use donation tiers, stick with four to six and add your suggested donation amount. You might put your average donation amount in the middle and add a few suggested amounts on either side of that. Many organizations use symbolic gift levels, such as $50 to cover the cost of ten student field trips, $125 to celebrate a 125th anniversary, or $1,900 to commemorate the year the organization was established. You should also give people the option to designate their own amount.

---

1. Tina Jepson, "The Essential Elements of an Online Donation Form," Causevox, accessed October 26, 2020, https://www.causevox.com/blog/online-donation-form.

(continued)

**TIPS FOR ONLINE GIVING** *(continued)*

- Use a trusted, secure payment processor. In order to accept online donations, you will need a payment processor to take payment from your donor's account and put it into yours. You will want to make sure the company you choose uses Payment Card Industry Data Security Standards (PCI DSS). A few other things to consider are whether the payment processor integrates with your CRM (so you don't have to manually enter every transaction) and whether it accepts all major credit cards (and possibly ACH direct debit payments from the donor's bank account). There are a lot of articles online to start your research on this topic, and don't forget to talk to other nonprofits about the systems they have in place.

- Make sure you have a mobile-responsive donation page. Approximately 25 percent of all online giving was done via a mobile device (smartphone) in 2018 and this number has increased steadily (up from 13% in 2014).[2] Make sure your supporters and visitors can access all pages on your website via their mobile device—including your donation pages.

- Offer an automatic, recurring gift option. Sustaining donations can increase your revenue and donor retention rates. By offering a recurring donation option, your donor can set up monthly contributions that are processed automatically. This will be handled through your fundraising management software, so check their website or ask one of their sales representatives for more information.

- Take your donors to a thank-you page. Make sure your donation process ends with a thank-you landing page (preferably one with links to continue exploring your site). This page does not serve as your official "thank-you," but rather helps donors know their contribution has been processed.

- Provide donation receipts. If your fundraising software allows it, set up an automatic donation receipt. This sends an email confirmation, along with the charitable giving receipt, to your donors as soon as their gift is processed. This can cut down substantially on back-end work for your staff and volunteers if they don't have to generate and send these receipts individually. However, this receipt should not take the place of a personalized thank-you letter.

- Test your form. Make sure you take your form for a test run. Ask friends and family to do the same. You want to identify anything that is not intuitive or seems redundant. This also gives you a chance to look at the screens and messages your donor will see throughout the process.

---

2. Steve MacLaughlin, "Charitable Giving Report: How Fundraising Performed in 2018," Blackbaud Institute for Philanthropic Impact, February 2019, https://institute.blackbaud.com/wp-content/uploads/2019/02/2018 CharitableGivingReport.pdf.

## Impersonal letters or emails

These are messages that go out to your contact list on behalf of the organization but are not personalized with the constituent's name or contact information. Examples could include newsletter (either printed or email), brochures, or any other piece of information or marketing material designed for a general audience.

- Pros: These pieces can be less complicated to print and mail, and the chance of getting the wrong letter in the wrong envelope is diminished. When done well, newsletters bring donors joy and confirm their donations are making an impact and can be effective fundraising pieces on their own. By making your newsletters "skimmable" with good headlines and short articles and using more "you" more than "we," you can create an effective fundraising piece. (Be sure to include a reply card and return envelope in direct mail, or include links back to your online donations page in emails.)[3]

- Cons: Less personalized mailings are likely to get less notice, unless they contain information that speaks to the reader's wants or needs. (Make them targeted and eye-catching to get their attention). Email communications often end up in people's junk mail files and can have abysmally low open and click-through rates. This is partly due to the sheer number of emails people receive in a day; inboxes get very congested.

## Social media

Social media has its place in the nonprofit world. People share a lot of information (and comments) on these platforms, and they have become second nature for most of the population (especially with younger generations). Coordinated social media campaigns can be incredibly useful.

- Pros: Unlike combing through a full email inbox, scrolling through social media can seem like less of a chore. Your posts can attract attention through a combination of photos, videos, and text, allowing you to showcase everything from events and programs to pieces from your collection. There are opportunities to engage with your followers by responding to comments and answering questions. Users can help you promote your organization by sharing your content with their friends.
- Cons: You have to build a following and create good content to use social media to raise funds effectively. The person (or people) in charge of social media has to regularly update the posts; stale content is worse than no content, so only engage on the social media platforms you can maintain. This includes ensuring that comments and especially questions receive attention. Social media algorithms change frequently and can be challenging to understand.

## Events

Events are frequently the "safe" fallback option for many small nonprofits. Events are an essential component of friendraising and fundraising, but most organizations cannot rely on events alone to raise enough money to sustain their organization (especially if they have staff to pay or buildings to maintain).

- Pros: Events are fun and provide a venue for people to gather, network, and build camaraderie. They offer a good opportunity to recognize and thank supporters publicly. There are ways to add on "extra" fundraising opportunities such as silent auctions, competitions, and sponsorships to boost revenue. They can increase visibility in the community. If done well, signature events can become part of the organization's brand, giving attendees an exceptional experience that they look forward to each year.
- Cons: Events are a lot of work, and unfortunately, that work usually falls to the same few people. When event expenses (including staff and volunteer time) are

subtracted from revenues, it can be a letdown when the profit is not proportional to the amount of work that went into the event. It can take several years to build and grow an event to achieve a high ROI (return on investment, and by that time, staff and volunteers may have abandoned the idea in search of something else. There are also many uncontrollable variables with events, such as weather, speakers or performers, and competing events. Finally, people are busy. It can be a challenge to find the right event to catch their attention and motivate attendance.

## Crowdfunding

Crowdfunding is based on the idea of many people giving smaller amounts to raise money for a cause. You could say that the charity jar next to the checkout register or the radio or TV telethons are the original crowdfunding methods. Still, nowadays, crowdfunding efforts are frequently digital and highly dependent on social media and online communication.

- Pros: Crowdfunding can be especially useful for project-based fundraising. It provides opportunities for the organization to reach new audiences and promote its brand. It can lead to new followers and can expand the organization's constituency circles. With crowdfunding, you can motivate donors to give without asking them for a considerable commitment.
- Cons: Crowdfunding campaigns tend to be project- or situation-focused. They have to be well-planned and executed, and they are more effective when you already have a broad audience to engage and help share your message. You will need to push out compelling stories and images and provide regular updates to keep the campaign from losing momentum. Finally, most crowdfunding websites will take a percentage of your revenue to cover service fees, so you have to figure that into your fundraising goal.

# Cold Calls

## Traditional media and advertising

Feature spots on TV, radio, or in the newspaper are good for raising awareness, but they don't often generate a lot of money. Consider ROI here; press releases may be worth your time if you have someone who can write them (and news outlets that are receptive to them), but paid advertising will cut into any revenue you generate as a result.

- Pros: Positive news coverage is good publicity. It may motivate someone to visit your website, plan a trip to your museum, look for volunteer opportunities, or possibly even consider donating. These things all contribute to bringing people closer to your center constituency circles, which is good.
- Cons: Advertising space is usually expensive, and whether you are paying for it or getting it in exchange for something else, you have to be strategic about how you use it. The most effective advertising campaigns tend to be the ones that generate an immediate call to action, encourage giving because of a natural disaster or other dire situation. This can be especially effective for those who tend to be more impulsive with their giving.[4]

## Door-to-door canvassing

Although you may see the occasional political campaign team going door-to-door, most nonprofits don't frequently use this canvassing style of solicitation.

- Pros: This method allows for face-to-face conversations with targeted audiences (if you can get someone to open the door).
- Cons: Many neighborhoods have regulations against door-to-door solicitation (or require preregistration), and many residents consider it intrusive. This is also a time- and labor-intensive effort.

## Telemarketing (phone calls and texts)

Aside from universities who employ students to call constituents, phone-a-thons tend to be resource-intensive for most organizations. It either costs the organization a lot of volunteer and staff time to make the calls or costs a lot of money to hire a company to make the calls. In a recent study about donor engagement, only 7 percent of donors identified a preference for phone calls (9% for text messages), and only 34 percent said they were okay receiving a solicitation call "every once in a while" (35% for texts).[5]

- Pros: Phone calls can be a good way to follow up with donors after letters are sent or to remind donors about pledges they have already made. They are also an effective way to say thanks, gather feedback, and verify contact information.
- Cons: In the age of caller ID and voicemail, many people simply don't answer calls from someone who is not in their contacts list, so even talking to a real person can be challenging. Making phone calls is labor-intensive, and callers may need a good deal of training to be effective. Most people are unwilling to give their credit card numbers over the telephone, and those who make pledges over the phone don't always honor them. Furthermore, organizations need to respect the requests of any donors who do not want to be contacted by phone.[6]

Sometimes, the best way to ensure you serve your supporters throughout the entire donation process (including the ask) is to put yourself in their shoes. Spend some time reflecting on your expectations and experiences as a donor yourself. Make a note of your preferences and turn-offs. If it's helpful, use the "When You're the Donor" worksheet to help guide you through this thought process. You could even use it to get feedback from some of your top supporters if that feels right for your organization. The goal is to approach your fundraising asks with an open mind and consider how you can continue to improve.

There is no perfect recipe for soliciting funds. The "right" way to do it is unique to each organization and, in fact, to each situation. It's okay to plan for some trial and error (although you'll learn more if you track and analyze your results). Just remember that no fundraising "expert" knows your supporters like you do, so never underestimate your gut instincts. Commit to learning as much as you can about your constituents and building authentic relationships with them. In the next chapter, we're going to talk about stewardship and how caring for your donors extends beyond the ask.

## WHEN YOU'RE THE DONOR . . .

What organizations do you give to (time, talent, treasure)?

Why do you give to those organizations?

How do the organizations you support ask you for gifts?

What is your preferred "ask" method as a donor?

How do you prefer to give?

How do you like to be thanked?

# Notes

1. Mark Rovner, "The Next Generation of American Giving: The Charitable Habits of Generation Z, Millennials, Generation X, Baby Boomers, and Matures," Blackbaud Institute for Philanthropic Impact, April 2018, https://institute.blackbaud.com/wp -content/uploads/2018/04/2018-Next-Generation-of-Giving.pdf.

2. "The Next Generation of Giving," 17.

3. For more information about creating effective newsletters, see Tom Ahern, *Making Money with Donor Newsletters* (Medfield, MA: Emerson and Church, 2013).

4. Henry Rosso and Meg Gammage-Tucker, "The Annual Fund," in *Achieving Excellence in Fundraising*, ed. Eugene Tempel, Timothy Seiler, and Eva Aldrich (San Francisco: Jossey-Bass, 2011), 62.

5. Rich Dietz and Tad Druart, "Donor Engagement Study: Aligning Nonprofit Strategies with Donor Preferences," Abila, 2015, https://www.netatwork.com/uploads/2015/05/Abila-DonorEngagementStudy_NetatWork.pdf.

6. Rosso and Gammage-Tucker, "The Annual Fund," 61.

# Stewardship

If you're part of a collections-holding organization like a museum, stewardship may already be a familiar concept. When someone donates a cherished item to your collection, there is a mutual understanding that the museum assumes responsibility for the care and safekeeping of that object. There is also an expectation that the organization will do this for the good of the general public. As such, it will make the item accessible to the community to the best of its ability. The same general principles apply when it comes to fundraising. By accepting monetary gifts, a nonprofit organization promises to carry out worthwhile, mission-focused service work on the donor's behalf. Put another way, "Stewardship is the sacred trust that nonprofit organizations accept in their role as servants of the public good."[1]

## Stewardship Strategies

Stewardship is equal parts gratitude and accountability. It is the practice of expressing sincere and thoughtful appreciation while also diligently managing gifts that have been entrusted to your care. Four stewardship strategies that are frequently cited in research can also be applied in practice.[2] As outlined in *Achieving Excellence in Fundraising*, they are reciprocity, responsibility, reporting, and relationship nurturing.[3]

1. Reciprocity: Expressing gratitude
2. Responsibility: Acting in a socially responsible way
3. Reporting: Keeping the public informed about developments
4. Relationship nurturing: Paying attention to the organization's constituents

According to research from the U.S. Trust Study of High Net-Worth Philanthropy, donors in the study expressed some expectations that are clearly in line with these stewardship strategies.[4]

- Ninety-one percent wanted the organization to demonstrate sound business and operational practices.

- Ninety percent expected the nonprofit to spend a "reasonable amount" on general administrative and fundraising expenses.
- Eighty-six percent wanted the organization to acknowledge donations by providing a receipt for tax purposes.
- Eight-five percent wanted the nonprofit to honor their requests for anonymity.
- Eighty-five percent did not want their names sold or distributed to others.
- Eighty-one percent expected the organization to honor their requests for gift use.
- Fifty-seven percent said that they would like to receive a thank-you note.

What should we take away from this data? First and foremost, donors want the organization to operate effectively and not overspend on nonprogrammatic expenses. (This is not to say that you should undercompensate paid staff, but it does underscore the importance of figuring out how much time staff spends on essential programming.) If you are already doing these things, how are you letting your current and prospective donors know about them? (More on that in just a bit.)

Second, we need to listen to our donors regarding how they want their generosity to be recognized. Undoubtedly, we can express appreciation through a thank-you note. However, we also have opportunities to demonstrate our gratitude by honoring their requests for gift acknowledgment and designations.

Like all aspects of fundraising, stewardship is best done deliberately. Take some time to figure out what this means for your organization. Although you'll want to consider the strategies above—reciprocity, responsibility, reporting, and relationship nurturing—you also have to factor in your capacity. Some stewardship activities take more time, people, and money resources than others. Focus on what you're trying to achieve through good stewardship. Now that we've connected the donor's interest with our cause, stewardship will help us retain them as donors with the possibility of upgrading or increasing their commitment. In the best-case scenario, we can also count on some of our donors to refer others to us, helping to build and expand our network of supporters.[5]

## Accountability

As mentioned above, stewardship is both accountability and gratitude. The nice thing is that stewardship is built on common courtesy; you're probably already doing many of these things organically, or you could implement them without too much trouble. Let's look at a few simple strategies to help you cover the logistics of accountability, and then we'll cover some thoughts on the art of gratitude.

1. Sound financial accounting: If you're going to accept donations, your finances must be in order. As discussed in section 1, get help from a financial guru, such as a professional bookkeeper or a certified accountant, if you could use some guidance to manage your financial accounting and reporting. Make sure your board understands basic nonprofit accounting, including how to read and analyze those financial statements. If they don't (or you just want to make sure everyone is on the same page), arrange to have a few training sessions for your board and any staff or volunteers with financial responsibilities.
2. Fundraising policies and procedures: Make sure policies and practices are written and in place to help safeguard donor information and ensure you can uphold their

wishes. This is everything from respecting their "do not call" designation on their donor record, to heeding their wishes to remain anonymous, to ensuring their gift is used as designated. These things are easier with fewer donors in your database. As your fundraising efforts expand and your donor base grows, you will want to have procedures in place that will help you manage your supporters as a whole while still being able to treat each of them as individuals.

3. Gift processing: The amount of time from when the donation comes in until the thank-you note goes out says a lot about your organization's ability to receive gifts gratefully and gracefully. If you haven't done so already, take some time to formalize (and write out) your gift processing procedures. You want others in the organization to replicate the process in the event "the person who takes the checks" isn't available for some reason. Your goal should be to process gifts quickly. This also includes making immediate updates to donor records, if needed (you don't want a bunch of record changes piling up). Finally, you want to generate the appropriate gift receipt and thank-you and mail them in a reasonable time. Ideally, thank-you letters should be sent within forty-eight hours of receiving the gift. If it's helpful, feel free to use the worksheet to think through your current gift processing procedures and determine whether there might be room for improvement.

## A DONATION STORY

A young, history-minded couple moved to a new city. Each with degrees and careers in history, they did what seemed natural after getting settled in their new home—they joined their local historical society. They looked forward to new exhibits and event invitations; they even thought they might be interested in volunteer opportunities. Check in the mail, they waited to hear back from the local group. One month passed. Then two. Finally, after a year of carrying the uncashed check forward on their bank register, they wrote it—and the organization—off.

It's possible the check got lost in the mail. It's also possible that it got misplaced, lost in the shuffle of disorganization. This couple, with history knowledge and nonprofit experience, could have given that historical society much more than money. They would have been excellent ambassadors, possibly even future board leaders. Instead, they found different organizations to receive their time, talent, and treasure. The moral of the story is to never let a check—or a donor—fall through the cracks. Make sure you have processes in place to demonstrate accountability and gratitude.

4. Donor acknowledgment: This is a two-part process. The first involves sending the donor a gift receipt. You should send gift receipts for all donations, but for tax purposes, your donor undoubtedly expects to receive one for gifts over $250. The second part involves building in a fail-safe way to ensure that you can uphold the donor's recognition exceptions, particularly those who want to remain anonymous.

5. Transparency through reports: Many organizations issue annual reports to highlight their achievements and help donors and community supporters understand the value of their work. Although many will include eye-catching photos and graphics, it's perfectly acceptable to work within your capacity. Even just a brief executive report can be a helpful way to give supporters a big-picture view of what you've achieved. Another option is to provide more frequent updates to donors. This is particularly effective for project-based work. It helps donors keep tabs on

# IRS GUIDELINES FOR CHARITABLE CONTRIBUTION ACKNOWLEDGMENTS

According to the IRS website:[1]

"The written acknowledgment required to substantiate a charitable contribution of $250 or more must contain the following information:

- Name of the organization;
- Amount of cash contribution;
- Description (but not value) of non-cash contribution;
- Statement that no goods or services were provided by the organization, if that is the case;
- Description and good faith estimate of the value of goods or services, if any, that organization provided in return for the contribution; and
- Statement that goods or services, if any, that the organization provided in return for the contribution consisted entirely of intangible religious benefits, if that was the case."

There are also situations, called quid pro quo contributions, where the organization must provide a written disclosure to the donor. This happens when the donor makes a payment more than $75 to the organization that is partly a contribution and partly for goods and services. For example, the donor pays $100 for a gala ticket, but $45 of that goes toward their meal. A disclosure is necessary because the donor may only take a contribution deduction for the amount of their payment that exceeds fair market value of the goods or services they received. In our example, only $55 of their payment would be eligible for deduction.

For more information and guidance, refer to IRS Publication 1771, "Charitable Contributions,"[2] and check in with your tax professional if you have questions.

---

1. "Charitable Contributions—Written Acknowledgements," IRS, February 13, 2020, https://www.irs.gov/charities-non-profits/charitable-organizations/charitable-contributions-written-acknowledgments.
2. "Charitable Contributions: Substantiation and Disclosure Requirements," Publication 1771 (Rev. 3-2016), Catalog Number 20054Q, Department of the Treasury, Internal Revenue Service, accessed October 27, 2020, https://www.irs.gov/pub/irs-pdf/p1771.pdf.

**Worksheet 10.1**

Consider your gift processing procedure:

1. How do donations come into your organization? List all the ways.

2. What procedures are currently in place to process these gifts? How do they differ depending on the gift type and method? For example, what's your process for dealing with gifts that come in online versus checks that come through the mail?

3. Who is responsible for processing these gifts? List each person and their role. Who is their backup?

4. Are there any inefficiencies in the process? Could it be improved? If so, how?

5. What other ideas does the team have for recognizing and thanking donors?

the progress you're making, which can be effectively demonstrated through before and after photographs. Be creative and take advantage of opportunities to show off the good work you're doing. Your donors will appreciate knowing they've played a part in your success.[6]

## Gratitude

1. Personalized thank-you: A proper thank-you shouldn't be optional. In addition to sending a gift receipt, donors deserve a note of thanks. (A letter with language from the IRS guidelines can serve as a thank-you and a record of donation.) If you haven't done so already, consider formalizing how you will thank donors at different levels. Under what circumstances should a donor receive a handwritten note or phone call from the executive director or a board member above and beyond the standard thank-you form letter? Or perhaps it's more situational. Maybe someone's first donation or membership triggers a special welcome. What makes sense for your organization, given your constituents and your capacity?

### TIPS FOR THANK-YOU LETTERS

- Personalize your thank-you letters. Make your language simple and sincere, like you're writing a friend. If you're printing form letters, have the sender sign each one rather than inserting their digital signature. (I actually know people who turn letters over to see if the signature is indented from the pressure of a pen!) Including a handwritten note is a great way to make your letter more personalized.
- Industry best practices will tell you to have your thank-you in the mail within forty-eight hours of receiving the donation. This is a good goal, but it may not be feasible for your organization (especially if you have an all-volunteer staff). Decide what is a reasonable turnaround time and build in processes to meet your own goal. If you can't get a letter out in forty-eight hours, consider making a thank-you call.
- Your thank-you letter can also serve as your gift receipt if you follow the IRS guidelines and include the required tax-deduction information. In addition to personalizing the letter with the donor's name and address, be sure to reference the gift amount and date. (And don't forget to include standard language about the exchange of goods and services as applicable.)
- If the gift was designated for a particular program or initiative, cite what the gift was given toward and what you are going to do with it. This helps tie the donation back to the work you're doing in support of your mission and also reinforces your commitment to using the gift as the donor intended.
- Include direct contact information in case the donor has questions. If that contact is not the sender, be sure to provide the person's first and last name, as well as a telephone number and email address.
- A "PS" at the bottom of the letter may be the last thing a donor looks at, so leave them with a call to action. This can be a good place to invite them to visit soon, remind them to check your website for updates, or to ask them to follow you on social media.
- Involve your board members and volunteers. Ask them to help you with thank-you calls and letters. This is a great way to involve them in fundraising.

2. Donor recognition: We've all seen the big university buildings (and even some history centers) bearing the name of generous donors who made substantial contributions for construction. Everything from auditoriums to conference rooms is named these days, but naming rights are just one way to recognize a donor's generosity. Consider how else you might publicly thank your supporters. Many institutions have a donor wall in their facility or publish the names of donors and partners in their annual report. Event programs often spotlight sponsors. Organizations "tag" their donors in social media posts. Start paying attention to how other nonprofits recognize their donors; their creativity may inspire you (and of course, you can always go to the internet for more ideas).

3. Donor appreciation events: Perhaps it makes sense to recognize your donors and volunteers at a special occasion if that fits your organization's culture (and budget). Outside of a formal event designed explicitly for that purpose, there are other ways to show appreciation to your supporters by giving them exclusive or first access to your programming. Could you host a member- and donors-only preview night before opening a new exhibit or provide them access to a special speaker? Perhaps you can host an offsite tour or invite them to go behind-the-scenes at your museum. Even offering a member discount for your events and programs can help your donors feel appreciated. Good stewardship is also good cultivation. Taking care of your donors sets the stage for future gifts.

4. Tokens of appreciation: Some organizations use part of their marketing budget to offer small tokens of appreciation, such as lapel pins or car window clings. Sometimes this can be an effective way to demonstrate your appreciation and get some additional outside exposure. However, this can also backfire if the donor perceives you are spending too much (of their) money on trinkets. Ideally, you want someone to support or join your organization because they back your mission, not because they can get a "free" coffee mug or poster for their office. (What would they need to receive next year in exchange for their renewal?) Thoughtful, signature tokens of appreciation can contribute to your brand; just choose wisely. (And refer back to those IRS guidelines again as well because there are thresholds for valuing these "goods.")

5. Donor societies: Outside of different membership levels, some organizations have also designated giving societies. These often have more than one level based on different giving thresholds. Proponents might also advocate that these societies recognize sustained donors who may not meet an annual threshold but are loyal and consistent supporters. Other societies include founders, planned gift donors, businesses, or young professionals. There are often exclusive benefits tied to each giving level. Some fundraisers like using giving societies; others don't. Research the pros and cons, and talk to other organizations that offer this option to get some of their lessons learned. As you consider whether giving societies are right for your organization, don't forget to factor in your capacity to provide the promised benefits at each level. You don't want to make your giving societies more complicated (and labor-intensive) than they're worth.

# Tailor Your Approach

You want to make the most of your stewardship efforts. Like so many other fundraising areas we've discussed up to this point, you will see the most fruitful results when you spend a little bit of time getting organized and putting together a plan. The good news is that your stewardship plan will fit nicely into your overall annual fundraising plan, which we will discuss in the next chapter. Work on your stewardship plan now, and you'll be ahead of the curve!

This plan has to work for you. In other words, it needs to match up with your capacity, resources, and expectations of your supporters. Also, like so many things we've discussed, it's a living document, subject to improvement. All you have to do is get started and shepherd its evolution. So, where to begin?

1. Take stock of your donor categories. Just as with cultivation, your stewardship approach can and should vary depending on the group of constituents you're addressing. This is an excellent opportunity to segment your donors (or members) for improved communication tactics. Consider these groups:

   • New donors
   • Loyal donors (What does this list look like? That's totally up to you. How do you define "loyal?")
   • Major donors (Again, the definition here is totally up to you. You might choose a gift amount threshold or use the top 20 percent of donors, for example.)
   • Project donors (Those who have designated gifts to a particular initiative.)
   • Lapsed donors (You will want to reengage with these folks before making a funding request.)
   • How else might you segment your donor groups? By event attendance? Geography? Age?

2. Decide which stewardship strategies you will use for which groups. What's your takeaway for each? Refine your messaging to ensure it's nuanced for each group.
3. Determine how you will implement your planned techniques. Who will be responsible for each task? What kind of materials will that person need to be successful? What's the timeline?
4. Consider how you will gauge each strategy's effectiveness. What data will you track? Donor retention and an increase in donations are two useful metrics to consider. Are there others? How frequently will you analyze the information? Who should get a copy of your findings? (Remember: don't collect data you don't intend to use at some point.)
5. Always be on the lookout for additional opportunities to make personal contacts and build relationships with supporters. Planned stewardship activities are important, but nothing can beat the unplanned, personalized actions that come from building genuine relationships. Examples might include forwarding articles you think could be of interest to a particular donor, making a note of significant personal events in their lives, or inquiring after their family, a recent vacation, or anything else of significance to them personally.

Donor relationships are just like any other significant relationship. They are all about give and take. From identification, through cultivation, asks, and stewardship, fundraising is about people. If your work is focused outward on the people you serve, and you keep your fundraising donor-centered, things that used to seem like a chore (like asking people for money) can turn into a calling.

We've made it through the fundraising cycle and covered a lot of material! Hopefully, you've picked up a few ideas you'd like to try. In the next chapter, we're going to apply what we've learned and walk through the process of putting together a personalized fundraising plan for your organization.

## Notes

1. William G. Enright and Timothy L. Seiler, "The Practice of Stewardship," in *Achieving Excellence in Fundraising*, ed. Eugene Tempel, Timothy Seiler, and Eva Aldrich (San Francisco: Jossey-Bass, 2011), 269.

2. Richard Waters, "Measuring Stewardship in Public Relations," *Public Relations Review Journal* 354 (2009): 113–19.

3. Enright and Seiler, "The Practice of Stewardship," 269.

4. "The 2018 U.S. Trust Study of High Net-Worth Philanthropy," Bank of America Private Bank in Partnership with the Indiana University Lilly Family School of Philanthropy, 2018, https://scholarworks.iupui.edu/bitstream/handle/1805/17666/high-net -worth2018-summary.pdf.

5. Sandy Rees, "15 Tips to Build Donor Relationships Through Stellar Donor Stewardship," *Get Fully Funded* (blog), May 12, 2015, https://getfullyfunded.com/15-tips-to-build-donor-relationships-through-stellar-stewardship/.

6. For more information about using your annual report to help boost fundraising efforts, see *Nonprofit Annual Reports*, National Council of Nonprofits, accessed March 13, 2021, https://www.councilofnonprofits.org/tools-resources/nonprofit-annual-reports; "Nonprofit Annual Reports: Complete Guide and 6 Best Practices," DonorSearch, accessed March 13, 2021, https://www.donorsearch.net/nonprofit-annual-report/.

# Annual Fundraising Plan

Now that we've gone through some nonprofit basics and spent some time on the fundraising cycle, we need to start thinking about your organizational plan. Like so many other things in fundraising, developing an annual fundraising plan is more art than science. There's no right way to do it; you want to personalize it to be most useful to your organization. In this chapter, we'll go over some basic considerations and components to get you started. Just remember that this is your plan, so make it work for you.

## Why Bother?

Remember, we started this book with an important goal: to make fundraising proactive, rather than reactive. A fundraising plan (also sometimes called an annual development plan) can help you do that. With your written strategic plans (or summaries from your less formal brainstorming activities) and your budget, the fundraising plan serves as a useful guide. It's your opportunity to take everything you've learned about fundraising, combine that with your current resources and new ideas, and put it on paper. But maybe you're wondering if it's even worth the effort to put together a formal fundraising plan. Here are a few considerations:

1. Your fundraising plan can serve as a to-do list that spreads regular, intentional fundraising efforts over the entire year. This allows you to be proactive and strategic because you have a chance to think through each campaign to create consistent measures that will maximize your cash flow and help you avoid clusters of activity followed by lengthy gaps. This helps build consistency and confidence and allows you to seamlessly weave fundraising into your daily operations.
2. A fundraising plan encourages better board, staff, and volunteer engagement. Everyone has a role to play in fundraising, and your plan will help them see the big picture and decide where they feel most comfortable and productive. Expectations are more transparent, and there are fewer surprises.
3. When you have a written plan, it serves as a to-do list for your organization. As a result, mailings and email communications go out on time. There's room built

in to test new technologies or program ideas. Events have plenty of lead-up time. Grant deadlines aren't missed, and tangible opportunities to engage prospective donors are created. It helps you avoid slapdash fundraising that burns out staff and volunteers.

Notice I said it needs to be a *written* plan. This is where it's tempting to slack a little. We might have good ideas—we might even have good conversations—but if we don't write it down, we don't have a plan. If you're serious about committing to better, more proactive and productive fundraising, you have to write things down. But here's the thing—it doesn't have to be perfect! Don't worry if you've never done a fundraising plan before; it's okay if you don't know what you're doing. Even if you've never had any formal fundraising training, you can still write a good plan. Something is better than nothing, so even if you start with a good-enough plan, you can refine it as you go. Just get it down on paper and make it real. Even if you feel a little overwhelmed by the process, I think you'll be pleased with what you've created when you come out on the other side.

## Assess the Situation

In addition to being proactive, we want our fundraising plan to be realistic. It needs to meet us where we are right now. What works for the state historical society across town or the school PTO down the street is not necessarily going to fit everyone's needs. We need to take stock of our situation. To do that, we need to answer a few questions.

What do we want to fund? How much money would we like to raise? Because the budget process and fundraising plan are so interconnected, you may want to work on them simultaneously. Your budget is going to inform your plan and vice versa. Your answers to these first two questions will likely come from the annual budget as you're trying to balance income (revenue) and expenses.

As you're developing your revenue section, be sure you're not using your fundraising goals as "plug figures" to fill gaps and balance the budget.[1] Your fundraising goals have to be doable. It's fine to have a stretch goal, but if you get a sinking feeling every time you think about those charitable giving line items, you may have to go back, focus on the "must-haves," and trim your expenses to meet the realities of your income. That's okay. It's better to be realistic and a little conservative than to overestimate and have to dip into reserves or assume unnecessary debt.

How much have we raised in the past? As you consider the amount you'd like to set as your fundraising goal, take a look at your track record (ideally over several years). How much have you raised in the past, and perhaps more importantly, how did you raise it? Differentiate charitable giving from other sources of revenue like earned and investment income. List all your past fundraising sources and how much money the organization received from each. You might look at membership, annual giving, major gifts, special events, bequests, and grants, and then classify them by category. While you're at it, look for giving trends in your data. Are your online donations increasing? How do your renewal rates look? Take it one step further and note any dates for specific campaigns such as annual appeal mailings, specific programming, or even grant deadlines.

What are our likely sources? After looking at how you've raised money in the past and making a note of each effort's success, ask yourself which of these you would consider doing again. Think about what worked well and what didn't go quite to plan.

## CAN NONPROFITS INVEST MONEY?

The board must protect the nonprofit's assets as part of its fiduciary responsibilities. For some organizations, this means stewarding financial reserves through investment. A nonprofit is allowed to invest the organization's cash in stocks, bonds, funds, and other investment vehicles. While the organization will want to maintain adequate and accessible emergency reserves, additional assets can be invested to build a nest egg for long-term goals such as capital projects or endowments.[1]

According to the National Council of Nonprofits, leaders must consider three (potentially conflicting) investment goals:[2]

1. Protecting the value of the initial invested assets.
2. Growing those assets to increase their value.
3. Maintaining access to assets in the event the nonprofit needs to tap into the investments for cash-flow needs.

In order to meet these obligations, the board should adopt an investment policy and designate who will be responsible for day-to-day management of investments (whether an outside fund manager, board committee, or the full board as a whole). As always, it's a good idea to consult with a trusted financial adviser for guidance if you're considering investments for the first time or if you have questions at any point in the process.

---

1. The Motley Fool, "Can a Nonprofit Organization Invest in Stock?" Nasdaq, January 15, 2016, https://www.nasdaq.com/articles/can-nonprofit-organization-invest-stock-2016-01-15.
2. "Investment Policies for Nonprofits," National Council of Nonprofits, accessed May 6, 2021, https://www.councilofnonprofits.org/tools-resources/investment-policies-nonprofits.

Could you revamp an effort that ended up being less than successful? Were there any that might be considered "successful" at first glance but that actually had a low return on investment. (In other words, was the amount brought in worth the resources expended?) For example, did the expensive four-color brochure bring in that much more money than a simple letterhead appeal? Was the 5K walk you hosted worth all the staff and volunteer time?

Next, consider new ideas. If you have a membership program, are you sending out membership renewal reminders? Are you planning special members-only programs? If you aren't currently doing an annual appeal, this might be a good time to start. If you already ask for general operating funds once a year, would your donor base support two a year? Do you have any initiatives that would be a good fit for a new major gift prospect? Have you been considering applying for a grant? Are you looking to consolidate multiple smaller events into one signature program? Use worksheet 11.1 to help you think through potential sources of revenue. After you've had a chance to brainstorm, refine your list to your most promising ideas.

While you're at it, take a look at your current processes. Think about how donations come into your organization. Do you accept credit cards? Can people make donations online? If so, is your mobile site friendly in case they're using a smartphone? Can you help donors set up monthly giving so that their credit cards are charged a certain amount each month?

As you consider *where* your fundraising dollars might come from, think about *who* will be responsible for leading the effort to introduce a new appeal or giving option. Do they have time to research and implement a successful campaign? It's all about balancing your resources, which goes beyond money to include people and time. And you may be able to raise the money, but can you process it effectively? Will you be able to manage it once you have it? Will you be able to honor donor or funder restrictions and timelines?

What's a realistic goal for this year? After you've evaluated your past and potential giving strategies, decide on the ones you think will be most viable for the coming year and start estimating how much you think each will bring in. Remember, you don't have to do everything all at once. It's perfectly acceptable to identify three to five focus areas based on your goals and an assessment of your best, most realistic fundraising options. As you're sketching out a plan, play to your personal and organizational strengths. (Maybe even go back to that SWOT analysis.) If you have a well-connected staff or board member who is especially comfortable making face-to-face asks, it might be worthwhile to spend some time identifying major gift prospects. If a volunteer knows how to write grants (or is willing to learn), plan to identify your most grant-ready projects and build in some grant research and writing time.

As you're refining your plans, think back to chapter 6 and our discussion about the fundraising pyramid. To maintain momentum and grow our fundraising programs, we have to identify activities that will attract, renew, and upgrade our donors' support for our work. Refer back to chapter 8 on cultivation and address each of these areas in your plan so you can be sure you're reaching donors in all three categories.

Remember, this plan will take a couple of passes and some back-and-forth before you reach the final version, and even then, it will probably still be subject to edits and updates as you progress through the year. Consider your plan a living document, open for adjustments as you go. Be sure to note any assumptions you're making as you set your goals and include them in the written plan. This will help you remember why you made the decisions you did and possibly make future planning more manageable.

Next, assign a realistic fundraising goal to each campaign (put it in writing) and gauge how well your total lines up with your budget. From here, we're going to orient your fundraising plans with your organizational calendar so we can get a big-picture view of a year in the life of your organization.

## Create a Calendar

You probably know how critical a "save-the-date" announcement can be for planning purposes (especially if you've ever been in a graduation/wedding/baby shower phase of life). Consider your development calendar as one big save-the-date. Once you plug board meetings, special events, fundraising campaigns, newsletter mailings, exhibit openings, grant deadlines, educational programs, and staff vacations into a master calendar, the rest of the year practically plans itself. Well, okay, maybe it's not quite that simple. However, you may just find that your master calendar becomes the linchpin for your fundraising success.

Use whatever format you like for your calendar. Put together a spreadsheet or table. Use an old-school paper calendar. You could even stick Post-it notes on a timeline around the room. The objective is to create a balanced year with different touchpoints for your members, donors, and visitors. Time is one of your most valuable resources, so you want to make good use of it. By planning out your entire year, you can help ensure that you aren't too heavy in programming or communications at one point and then too light at another. Your goal is consistent engagement that is manageable for your staff and volunteers.

How do you get started? I would advise first looking at the big picture (i.e., the whole year) and then narrowing your focus to individual months. First, let's start with the dates we know.

1. Plug in your organization's events, programs, and meetings with set dates. Do you have an annual membership meeting? Do you know your board meeting dates? Is your harvest gala fundraiser always held on the second Saturday of October? Do you close your museum for a few weeks or months in the winter? Put those significant events on the calendar first and plan around them.

2. Add dates that are important to your community. Do you have town- or county-wide festivals or significant events that occur annually? What about the local schools' schedules? Do their breaks affect your programming? Have you taken major holidays into account?

Next, let's fill in with things we know we want to do, but that maybe haven't been assigned a specific date yet.

3. If you're planning to introduce any new programs or events, try to pencil them in now. Do you want to launch a quarterly speaker series? Or maybe showcase local artists in an art show? Do you have special programming for youth, families, or seniors you'd like to offer? (Before you put these new events on the calendar, it might be a good idea to check your local community calendars. You want to avoid overlap with other events and programs that might draw the same audience or cause logistical challenges.)

4. Include any fundraising campaigns or appeals that can be added. Are you planning an end-of-the-year annual fund appeal? Are you thinking of doing a membership drive in the spring? Will you launch a campaign for a specific funding initiative such as a new roof or historic landscape restoration?

5. Note consistent communication efforts. Is there a specific day of the month that membership renewals go out? Do you send a monthly or quarterly newsletter? Or always do a social media post on Wednesdays? Do you send holiday cards, and if so, when do they go out?

By now, you should start to see some gaps in your calendar (and maybe also whether there are times you're overprogrammed). Once your yearly plans are on a master calendar, you can also add deadlines for registrations, printing, contracts, and other activities that will support your programs. You want to have frequent, meaningful opportunities to engage with your constituents and provide relevant content. Your planning and execution process will reduce scrambling and stress, giving you more time and energy to work on building meaningful relationships.

## Line Up Your Goals and Plans

Now that you can see the big picture of your plans for the year and have identified some fundraising opportunities, it's time to get specific about those campaigns. How much money do you reasonably expect to bring in with each of these efforts? Will it be enough to cover your budgeted charitable giving goals? Would it be possible to make up any gaps with earned income? If not, should you look for opportunities to raise more money, or should you put a "nice to happen" from your budget on a back burner?

Consider all the fundraising vehicles we've discussed so far. Hopefully, a few of them stick in your mind as potential good ideas for your organization. But it's still a lot to wade through. If you need help, use the funding source planning document in this chapter to help you work through the possibilities. As you decide where to focus your efforts, here are a few considerations:[2]

1. What's the potential financial payoff?
2. Does this provide opportunities to build new relationships or strengthen current ones?
3. Will this help us attract, renew, or upgrade supporters?
4. Do we have that capacity to invest our resources (specifically money, time, and people) in this?

## Measuring Success

Before you move forward with your fundraising plans, let's talk a little bit about what success looks like and how you'll know if you've achieved it. You will need to line up your fundraising goal and your bottom line. If you're in the black, you're good to go, and if you're in the red, something fell short. But measuring success doesn't have to be a yes or no question, especially when there's so much to learn just by tracking a few simple metrics. Fundraising success isn't measured only by total dollars raised. Other factors contribute to your present-day fundraising and your long-range goals to improve and grow.

Of course, your resources are finite, and there's no reason to track data you don't need. So, let's consider what type of fundraising information might help you as a small nonprofit heritage organization leader. In her article written for *Network for Good*, Barbara O'Reilly suggests that small shops with at least a decent donor database should consider tracking three things: donor behavior, financial returns from your fundraising costs, and board engagement.[3] Let's break those down a little more.

### Donor Behavior

1. Baseline statistics: How many members do you have? How many donors? How many members are also donors? Have these increased or decreased from last year?
2. Renewal rates: How many of your current donors also gave last year? The average renewal rate is 46 percent. How many of your current donors have given for three or more consecutive years? What about your members?
3. Donation levels: If you were to break your total giving into different groups from your smallest to largest gifts, how would that look? Do donors tend to cluster around certain dollar amounts? Is that based on their capacity or your asks? Look for patterns that can give you clues.
4. Donation timing: Similarly, if you were to plot your donations over a calendar year, do you notice any patterns? Do big changes correspond with events happening outside of the organization, such as a big employer leaving town, a financial

**Worksheet 11.1.** Potential Sources of Revenue.

| | CURRENT SOURCE | SHOULD PURSUE | MIGHT PURSUE | NOT RIGHT NOW |
|---|---|---|---|---|
| **Individuals** | | | | |
| Memberships | | | | |
| Annual giving | | | | |
| Major giving | | | | |
| Board giving | | | | |
| Planned giving | | | | |
| In-kind donations | | | | |
| Fundraising events | | | | |
| Other | | | | |
| | | | | |
| **Foundations** | | | | |
| Community foundations | | | | |
| Local family foundations | | | | |
| Regional foundations | | | | |
| Corporate foundations | | | | |
| National foundations | | | | |
| Other | | | | |
| | | | | |
| **Government** | | | | |
| Local/county grants | | | | |
| State grants | | | | |
| Federal grants | | | | |
| Contracts | | | | |
| Other | | | | |
| | | | | |
| **Corporations** | | | | |
| Employee gift matching | | | | |
| Community grants | | | | |
| Employee volunteer grants | | | | |
| Sponsorships | | | | |
| In-kind donations | | | | |
| Other | | | | |
| | | | | |
| **Earned Income** | | | | |
| Admissions | | | | |
| Programs/events | | | | |
| Retail/merchandise | | | | |
| Food and beverage | | | | |
| Facility rental | | | | |
| Other rental income | | | | |
| Other | | | | |
| | | | | |

recession, or even a global pandemic? Again, look for clues that might give you new information and spark new ideas.

5. Revenue source: How do your donors like to give? Are they more likely to respond to direct mail with a check or an email appeal and online giving?

6. Donor acquisition: How do donors connect with you? Are they visitors? Do they learn about your work through your website or social media channels? Through community partnerships or volunteering? This information might not be as readily available through your database, but a short, informal survey might provide a wealth of information.

## Financial Returns on Fundraising Costs

1. Cost to raise a dollar (CTRD): This is a standard metric in fundraising. To find it, divide your fundraising expenses by fundraising revenue. You want to maximize your return on investment (ROI), so it's a good idea to look at this number not just as a whole but also broken down by each of your fundraising efforts. For example, printing that fancy brochure in full-color will cost more than printing a letter in black and white. If you do both, track and measure your CTRD to find out which had a lower expense-to-revenue ratio.

2. Gift sizes: What was your average gift last year? What about your largest gift? Are these going up or going down? What factors are influencing this?

## Board Engagement

1. Percentage of board giving: We've talked about this number before. What percentage of your board is financially supporting the organization? There are many good reasons why this should be 100 percent. If it's not, how can you make it an attainable goal?

2. Amount of board giving: What percentage of your total funds raised comes from your board? While board giving is essential, if your number is too high, it could signal that you need to diversify your fundraising efforts and grow your donor base.

3. Percentage of board participating in fundraising. There's a job for everyone. Not every board member needs to make direct asks, but certainly, each has a role to play in advancing the organization's fundraising goals.

Don't underestimate the importance of baseline data. Take a little bit of time right now to gather and examine the metrics above if you think they make sense for you to track and measure. Once you have them, include them with your fundraising plan. You can go back and refer to them throughout the year if need be, but if nothing else, rerun them at the end of the year. This will allow you to track trends, gather insight about your donors, and make more informed decisions. Not only will you be able to decipher whether your fundraising went as planned, but you'll also be able to make an even better plan next time. And offer yourself and your colleagues some grace; you don't have to meet every goal to be successful.

With your fundraising plan in hand and your appeals, events, and campaigns on the calendar, you're ready to get out there and tell your story. In the next chapter, we'll go through a "recipe" to help you build a strong case for support in your fundraising.

# Notes

1. Gail Perry, "Do's and Don'ts for Your Annual Fundraising Plan", *Fired Up Fundraising* (blog), accessed August 19, 2020. https://www.gailperry.com/dos-donts-great-annual-fundraising-plan/.

2. To see other funding source planning documents and templates, see Steve Lew, *Creating an Effective Fundraising Plan*, Oakland, CA: CompassPoint Nonprofit Services, 2016, https://www.compasspoint.org/sites/default/files/documents/CreatingFRplan%20manualrev8.16.pdf.

3. Barbara O'Reilly, "Create a Fundraising Plan: Defining Fundraising Metrics, *Network for Good* (blog), October 16, 2015. https://www.networkforgood.com/nonprofit blog/fundraising-metrics-for-nonprofits/.

# Case for Support

Fundraising rarely happens by accident. Even the most out-of-the-blue gifts are probably the result of planning and preparation somewhere along the line. You took the time to create a wish list, you segmented prospective donors by their interests, or you knew what to say at the right time because you practiced your elevator pitch. One of the most deliberate things you can do to boost your fundraising effectiveness is to develop your case for support. In this chapter, we're going to look at both internal and external cases and talk about how you can make yours stronger.

## What Is a Case?

The work your organization does is important and worthy of support. While it would be great if each person we met recognized that immediately and stepped in line to help, in reality, it usually takes a little more explaining and perhaps a bit of persuasion. Whether you're building relationships with donors, recruiting volunteers, or identifying potential board members, you're likely making the case for your organization repeatedly. In this chapter, we're going to talk about making it a little more formal.

### CASE DEFINITION

According to *Achieving Excellence in Fundraising*, a case is:[1]

"Carefully prepared reasons why a charitable institution merits support ... including its resources, its potential for greater service, its needs, and its future plans."

1. Eugene R. Tempel, Timothy L. Seiler, and Eva E. Aldrich, *Achieving Excellence in Fundraising* (San Francisco: Jossey-Bass, 2011), 465.

So, what is a case? As you probably suspected, it's a general argument for why your organization deserves support. You use it to explain your position and persuade people to support what you're trying to accomplish. Specifically, you are explaining

1. the need you seek to meet;
2. how you plan to meet it; and
3. what you will achieve.

You're looking to persuade your audience that it's the right time and place for their support and that it will have an impact beyond the organization and into the community.

You will sometimes hear fundraising professionals refer to a case statement. Although *case for support* and *case statement* are frequently used interchangeably, to me, they just feel different. A case statement is like a multitiered wedding confection. In contrast, a case for support is an old-fashioned, homemade chocolate cupcake with frosting and sprinkles—both equally delicious and useful in their own situations. If you find yourself in a capital campaign seeking major donors, you will probably want a wedding cake case statement. For our purposes, we're talking about cupcakes cases. Our goal is to create something simple and accessible—something we can do on our own, with no pastry chefs needed.

## The Good Case Base Recipe

When my son was younger, he was a big fan of TV cooking shows. As a seven-year-old, he would come into the kitchen before dinner and remind me of mise en place. In case you're not familiar with this cooking term, it is the idea of getting your ingredients ready ahead of time—"everything in its place." What I like about this phrase is the fact that it is both a noun and a verb. As a noun, it's the setup of ingredients needed for the recipe— spices measured, egg whites separated. But as a verb, it is both the process of preparing and a state of mind. It refers to someone who knows to be well-prepared. A good, basic case for support is mise en place. Your resources are assembled, and you know you're ready. So, where to begin?

1. Compile what you already have. You know the saying: time is money. Your first step in making a good case for support is to get organized. I'm not kidding when I tell you I have a file on my computer called "Random Stuff I Keep Having to Look Up." You will find as you're filling out grant applications, writing appeal letters, or crafting text for brochures, you frequently add the same information over and over again. There's no need to re-create the wheel or waste time searching for material. This is what's in my file:

   • Our mission and vision
   • An annual program and event calendar
   • Our Employment Identification Number (EIN)
   • The date our nonprofit was incorporated
   • Admission numbers for the last three years
   • Board contact information
   • W-9 and tax status determination letter

- Most recent audit and financial statements
- Updated staff and volunteer roster
- A background overview of the history and purpose of the organization
- Boilerplate language that goes at the bottom of our press release
- The most recent strategic plan
- Graphic files of our logo
- A blank logic model template (more on that to come)

Your file may look different from mine, and that's fine. Tailor it to suit your needs. Remember that for now, these are internal documents, so you don't have to shine them up and make them look pretty just yet. The goal is to get your institutional knowledge and information in one place, prepared, and readily available when you need it (mise en place!).

2. Create an internal document that reflects institutional priorities. In addition to your mission and vision, make sure you have your top goals and priorities written in one place with some context for each. Depending on whether you have a formal strategic plan, or if you wrote down your priorities from our earlier exercises, you may already have this in some form.

3. Next, go ahead and make a note of any current programs and services you offer. A few sentences should do it. This helps you take stock of how you're serving your community and can be a useful reference when you're looking to match donors with funding opportunities.

4. Document your people resources. Write up a paragraph or so describing your board. How many people serve? Can you talk about their backgrounds and diversity? What about their experience and credentials? Next, do the same for your staff and volunteers. If you have bios or résumés for your team, put those in one place as well.

5. Talk about your physical space. If you have a building, summarize what those facilities are and how they are used. How many square feet on how many acres? Who owns and maintains it? Do you have separate gallery and collections spaces? Have there been any recent updates, or are there any on the horizon? Make sure to also gather up any facilities reports, structural assessments, or historic structures reports and keep them in one place.

6. Consider your planning and evaluation processes. These may vary by project, but try to give a general overview of how you know whether you're successful. How do you set goals and benchmark results? Do you regularly collect certain types of data such as zip codes or feedback from event surveys? Make a note of that.

7. Summarize your organization's history. Note when the organization was created (incorporation date is a standard grant question). Include relevant information about founders and other influencers. Detail any significant changes such as mission shifts, building moves, or significant new initiatives.

8. Create an overview of major accomplishments that have happened over the last few years. Detail your successes and why they were essential to the organization's mission. List things like awards, assessments, new programs and exhibits, new partnerships, and building upgrades.

9. Make sure others on your team who might also need access to the information know how to find it.

10. Pat yourself on the back. It's a lot of work to pull that information together, but the time you save (and hopefully the money you raise) will come back to you tenfold.

Although assembling and creating all this information may seem overwhelming, you can likely accomplish it in a few blocks of writing time. And yes, it will have to be updated. But you're still saving yourself time in the long run because you're creating boilerplate language that can be referenced repeatedly. And this information can be used for more than fundraising. Integrate it into staff and board training. Adapt it to provide content for your website, brochures, social media, newsletters, grant applications, and yes, even for more formal case statements for prospective donors. It's also helpful in other planning documents; it gives more context for organizational transitions and may help identify ups and downs in the institution's history. Furthermore, if your organization's spokespeople are familiar with everything that makes up your internal case for support, they are going to be much more effective during one-on-one conversations about the organization.

## CASE EXPRESSIONS

Where do you make your case?

- One-on-on conversations/solicitations
- Appeal letters
- Capital campaign materials
- Grant applications
- Brochures
- Website content
- Social media
- Press releases
- Newsletters

## Internal to External Case

So, let's say you have all of this info—your internal case documents—together. Now what? How do you morph these into an external case for support that is going to help you raise money? Let's talk about two significant challenges that come up when you're talking about your organization's fundraising needs and then how your internal case for support provides a starting point for all communications. But first, the challenges: you have different audiences and you still want consistent messaging.

Every time you communicate on behalf of your organization, you have to consider your audience. Who might end up being on the receiving end of an appeal, email, or social media post? If you recall the constituency model from chapter 7, you can probably envision a situation where you might need to speak (either in writing or in conversation) to any one of the groups in the concentric rings. Although we often think in terms of fundraising, you might find yourself putting together a case statement for board member recruitment or as a sponsorship or partnership proposal. In many cases, you'll be trying to meet the needs of more than one audience at a time. How can internal case documents help?

If we go back to the kitchen again, we can understand that the components of our internal case are like the ingredients in a recipe. You might vary how much of one thing or the other you add, depending on who will be eating what you've prepared—less salt here, more pepper there. The same is true for preparing your external case for support. You are going to want to adjust what you use and how you use it according to your audience. This comes, in large part, from your understanding of what they want, need, and expect from your organization. With a solid internal case, you can be sure that you're always using the same top-quality ingredients. (Actually, when used correctly, you can ensure that everyone in the organization is using the same ingredients.) And you can expect consistent results because you're using consistent messaging.

When it comes to communicating a funding need, the internal case resources inform the external case for support to address four objectives:

1. Explain why funding is needed.
2. Propose a solution for the need (problem, situation, opportunity).
3. Build confidence from past accomplishments.
4. Detail the results that will come from investment in the organization.

If the external case is supposed to accomplish these things, what else do we need to consider besides the internal resources we've assembled? We need a compelling need and a persuasive request for support.

## Compelling Need

Some funding needs are more attractive to certain donors than others. And some may, quite honestly, not be all that attractive to any donors. Why is that? One of the first questions you can ask is whether you're dealing with a compelling need. But how can you tell? If there are so many different audiences and interests in the world, how do you know your need will catch their attention? It's part situational and part personal. A donor might be more interested in giving to a disaster relief charity right after a major storm or fire. Someone else might naturally gravitate toward supporting a local county museum near their old family homestead. Different people have different giving priorities, and even those change. We can still identify a few common characteristics of any compelling need.

### COMPELLING NEED

What makes a need compelling?

- A critical but solvable problem
- Objective data and personal testimony
- Expansion of services or capacity
- Public benefit
- Right time, right place

Critical but solvable problem: There are two parts to this, and they are equally important. First, the need has to be critical. In this case, critical means important, obvious, understandable—and also fixable. It will take more than just saying something is important; you will need to demonstrate why and be able to provide details about how you reached that conclusion. The other part of this equation is that the problem needs to have a realistic, reachable solution. Donors want to know that their money is being put to good use to make a difference. This is where data-informed needs can be especially helpful. For example, a collections assessment or building report can help you identify your needs and provide realistic solutions.

Objective data and personal testimony: Think of this as a combination of data and storytelling. You want objective information—statistics, benchmarks, and projections—in the form of quantitative data. You also want personal stories and themes identified from people's experiences or qualitative data. (We'll talk more about this in the chapter about evaluation in the next part of the book.)

Continuation or expansion of services or capacity: People want to be part of a good thing. They want to see successful programs continue, and new ideas come to fruition. Part of what gets a donor excited about a particular project or opportunity will be your ability to share your vision and explain why it's essential. Not every need is inherently exciting. (I once had a funder tell me that shelving isn't sexy.) In these cases, we have to talk about how addressing specific needs in one area can lead to more exciting opportunities down the road. (Remember the springboard effect?) To use our baking analogy, flour might not be very exciting, but we need it before we can have cake.

Clear public benefit: Sometimes it's easy to get too focused on the work we're doing inside the organization. We lose track of the fact that everything we do is for the benefit of those outside the organization. As nonprofit charities, we have public missions. We exist not for the sake of the organization but the community at large. In the case of museums and others with collections-based institutions, we hold and care for these objects in the public trust. Sometimes we do have internal needs (such as staffing, professional development, or updated security). Our goal is to help prospective donors understand that even requests for operational needs still support our mission and service to the community.

Right time, right place, right person: Timing is everything. Just as we mentioned "the right ask" a few chapters ago, we are most successful when we can demonstrate a high level of situational awareness and sensitivity when it comes to matching potential donors to needs. This comes down to building relationships with current and potential donors to identify which need is right to pitch to which person. You and I may differ on which projects we find interesting or compelling, and even that will depend on what's going on in our personal lives and the world around us. We also need to demonstrate a high level of institutional readiness. We want to build confidence that our case for support is firmly built on the premise that we are the right organization for the job. This may require a little finesse in the form of persuasion.

# Persuasive Request for Support

Funding requests are linear: Need + Solution = Outcomes. Once you've addressed the compelling need, you want to convince the prospective donor or funder that you have identified a logical, necessary solution that (with their help) will lead to achievable, measurable outcomes. We already know that to do this, we need

- a realistic budget;
- well-planned activities; and
- people-focused results.

But how can we use the power of persuasion to help people connect to our case for support? Look no further than "the persuasion triad," a lesson from Aristotle passed down from your high school speech teacher. Even two thousand years later, using these three appeals can help you strengthen your case and gain support. As you build and write your external case for support, be sure to consider each of these "artistic proofs" (Aristotle's term for them).

## LESSONS FROM ARISTOTLE

- Logos: Reasoned argument
- Ethos: Credibility
- Pathos: Emotional appeal

Logos—Persuade with Logic: When developing your logical argument in your case for support, you want people to nod their heads and say to themselves, "Yes, of course. That makes sense!" Consider three tactics:

- Play to the linear, cause-and-effect nature of your project. A great way to do this is to use "if-then" reasoning. This helps donors understand their important role in how the dominoes fall. Remember my example above about the nonsexy shelves? I used if-then reasoning in my funding request for this project. "If we can purchase new, museum-quality cabinets for our trophy collection, then we won't risk having the trophies, which are currently stored on high shelves, fall on staff and volunteers, potentially injuring them and damaging the object." If-then statements are a powerful way to express logical cause and effect relationships. They also tend to help with visualization, which makes the situation more real to people.

## LOGOS TIP

Although you generally want your proposals to be positive and upbeat, sometimes it doesn't hurt to address what might happen if you don't get funding for a particular project. If-then statements can be used in this case too. For example, "If we don't remediate the mold in our archives now, then it might spread through the HVAC system to the museum at large." (And no one wants that!)

- Appeal to logic with evidence-based facts. We've already talked about using data to inform your need. The same is true for further developing your case to gain support for your solution and outcomes. Make sure you rely on facts. Site statistics. Relay results from any data you have been collecting or that has been noted by experts in the field. This is where assessments and outside reports can be hugely beneficial. My request for new trophy shelves was based on a collections care assessment done by the Conservation Center for Art and Historic Artifacts. This provided not only recommendations from a preservation specialist but data readings from her site visit. Consider what kind of metrics you're currently collecting, as well as any you could or should be gathering to help make a stronger case.
- Make sure your objectives and outcomes are tangible. When talking about what you want to accomplish, make sure you are specific and realistic. Talk about it in a way that is relatable and easy to understand. If you are digitizing a portion of your collection, build confidence by describing your reasoning, the process, and the expected results. As you get into more detail about those results—what you're planning to achieve in the given time frame—make sure they are trackable and measurable. How will you know when you've achieved success? Convince your prospective donors that the project is well-developed, and they have an essential role to play.

Ethos—Establish Credibility: Each person responsible for any aspect of fundraising—whether they're making face-to-face asks, writing grants, or just speaking as a champion and advocate—needs to establish personal credibility as a spokesperson for the organization. How can that be done?

- Define your character. People want to feel like they understand the situation before they agree to commit their resources to change it. Trust plays a significant role, and it's fostered in genuine, authentic relationships. Make sure facts are accurate, honest but not overblown, and that you communicate any actual or potential negatives or risks as early as possible.
- Demonstrate intelligence. Make sure your thoughts are clear and organized, whether they are in writing or being delivered verbally. If you're unsure, enlist the help of someone you trust to provide feedback. Consider your audience and avoid using unfamiliar references and acronyms, or explain them with enough context to be understood. Finally, watch for spelling and grammatical errors. You don't want them to take focus away from the message you're trying to convey.
- Show goodwill. Your prospective donor or funder has giving priorities that may or may not line up with the need you're trying to meet. Your professionalism and respect, even in the face of rejection, still contribute to your credibility and could turn "no" into "next time."

Pathos—Appeal to Emotions: According to a study, three of the top reasons people make charitable donations are altruism, trust, and social connections.[1] In other words, they are motivated by kindness and compassion, confidence in the organization's ability to make a difference, or opportunities to make donations that will matter to someone they know and care about. Philanthropy is an emotional business.

- Know your audience. People often follow their hearts when it comes to embracing causes and charities. Respect their needs and values, and appeal to their emotional sensibilities. Consider an appeal that asks them to send in their favorite memory of a particular location or situation. Add images that elicit emotions. Include relatable testimonials.
- Share your passion. If you're dedicated enough to your cause that you are willing to embrace fundraising *and* read a book about it, I don't doubt your passion. If fundraising makes you uncomfortable, try funneling your enthusiasm from other areas. I met with a local history leader a few years ago who was lamenting over her discomfort about asking people for money. Moments later, she enthusiastically invited one of my colleagues to come to their annual festival, and she was nearly bursting with pride for the organization. "You'll just love it!" she said. After this, I gently pointed out that if she approached fundraising with the same passion and enthusiasm, she would probably be pleasantly surprised with the results.
- Tell good stories. For most heritage organizations, storytelling is their specialty. This is another example of taking something you already know how to do and applying it to your fundraising practice. Provide potential donors with context using good descriptions and help them get a visual for what you're asking of them. Use specific examples of people who have been impacted by your programs and help supporters understand why the work you do matters.

A solid case for support can take many forms. These are called case expressions. Whether you make your case through campaign material, brochures, letters, grant applications, or over coffee in a face-to-face meeting, you want to be sure you're prepared to speak about the organization's (compelling) needs. You also want to explain your plans for addressing those needs and persuade the donor to be part of the solution to create co-ownership of the results. Any work you put into gathering your internal case resources and developing external case statements will reap exponential returns.

# Note

1. Sara Konrath and Femida Handy, "The Development and Validation of the Motives to Donate Scale," *Nonprofit and Voluntary Sector Quarterly* 47, no. 2 (April 2018): 347–75. doi:10.1177/0899764017744894. See also Sara Konrath and Femida Handy, "5 Reasons People Why People Give Their Money Away—Plus 1 Reason They Don't," The Conversation, November 26, 2017. https://theconversation.com/5-reasons-why-people-give-their-money-away-plus-1-why-they-dont-87801.

# REFINING YOUR APPROACH

# Involving Your Board

If you think your board should be doing more to help with fundraising, you're not alone. According to a national index, nonprofit CEOs and board chairs ranked fundraising as their boards' biggest challenge.[1] This chapter will look at ways to get the board more involved—and believe it or not, most of what we're going to cover doesn't have anything to do with asking people for money!

## "Pinch Points"

It's human nature to avoid things that make us feel uncomfortable. When it comes to fundraising, we often see only the possible pinch points, and then try (sometimes subconsciously) to steer clear of them. What are some excuses you've heard (or perhaps even thought of yourself)?

- "I don't want to twist peoples' arms."
- "If I ask them to give, then they're going to hit me up for a donation to their charity."
- "I don't know what to do or what to say."
- "People are busy. I don't want to bother them."
- "I will be embarrassed if they say no."

These are all valid concerns. You don't have to try and talk people out of them. You can, however, help your board and staff colleagues see around them.

Fundraising is a continuous team effort. To effectively engage your board in the process, you have to help them overcome some of their misgivings and embrace their fundraising roles. And before you do that, you may want to reflect on your own comfort level with fundraising and how it affects the board's perception of solicitations. We've already spent a lot of time working through this in previous chapters, but here are three takeaway truths for you and your board:

- Truth #1: The work you do is important and worthy of support.
- Truth #2: Without money, your organization can't carry out its mission or programs.
- Truth #3: You can do more and still (mostly) stay in your comfort zone.

# Standards of Conduct and Attention: AKA "Legal Duties"

Before we talk about how the board can contribute to the organization's fundraising success, let's make sure everyone is on the same page about a board's standards of conduct and attention, also known as "legal duties," to the organization they represent. These are duty of care, duty of loyalty, duty of obedience, and the board's fiduciary role.[2]

## Duty of Care

To execute their duty of care, board members must demonstrate an expected level of competence. This includes ensuring that the organization's resources are used responsibly in ways that are consistent with the mission. In other words, they

- exercise reasonable care in decision-making as stewards of the organization;
- actively participate in planning; and
- demonstrate a level of care that an "ordinarily prudent person in a like situation would exercise under similar circumstances" (as outlined in several state codes).

## Duty of Loyalty

The duty of loyalty is a standard of fidelity that requires undivided allegiance and faithfulness when making decisions for the organization. Board members are expected to always act in the organization's best interest and never use information obtained from their position for personal gain. This includes avoiding potential conflicts of interest. For this reason, many organizations require their board members, volunteers, and staff to complete conflict of interest disclosure statements each year.

You can find sample disclosure forms online, including some from museums, and adapt them to fit your needs. If you are leading a collections-based organization, it's especially important to use museum-specific forms that can help you address situations where an individual's personal collection interests may overlap with the museum's collecting initiatives.

## Duty of Obedience

Board members should uphold the organization's bylaws and mission and make progress toward the organization's central goals. The organization was established for a public-serving purpose, and the board is expected to make decisions that will help the organization fulfill that purpose. They are also responsible for ensuring compliance with all applicable federal, state, and local laws and regulations. Finally, and most specifically for fundraising, they are to uphold the public's trust that the organization will manage donated funds to fulfill that mission.

## Fiduciary Role

In addition to the legal duties, a nonprofit's board of directors is expected to maintain oversight of the institution's finances. This includes evaluating financial policies, approving annual budgets, and reviewing financial reports. They must also ensure the organization has the necessary resources to carry out its mission. In some cases, this means working through staff to accomplish this objective. In smaller organizations, the board may take a more hands-on role. In either case, the board must always remain accountable to donors and the general public.

## Service as Ambassadors

In addition to their legal duties to the organization, boards should also serve as ambassadors, networking on behalf of the organization within the community. They should be the organization's spokespeople and most dedicated advocates. They provide personal and professional links in the community and should take it upon themselves to make connections that can advance the mission. Nonprofit boards have an essential role to play in fundraising, but there's some groundwork to lay before this can happen. You need engaged, willing board members who understand their responsibilities and take them seriously. To be well-prepared and effective, they need support through proactive education and good communication.

If your organization doesn't have a representative (either staff or volunteer) to initiate, plan, and implement board training, there's no time like the present to designate someone for this role. It's easy to push this work to the backburner, but if you want your board to spearhead fundraising, you have to provide them with the right resources to be successful. Redouble your efforts to prioritize professional development for both board and staff members.

## Education

Whether staff or board-led, the organization will benefit from concerted efforts to increase knowledge and competency, especially when it comes to fundraising. This can be self-directed education, or it can come from outside facilitators. While fundraising training can be helpful, the board first needs to look at its internal processes. From recruitment and onboarding to committee work and leadership roles, everyone will benefit from transparency and clearly defined expectations.

## Recruitment

Board education begins in the recruitment and onboarding stages. Unfortunately, this is one of the most neglected areas when it comes to board relations. I've talked to more than one heritage organization leader who has lamented how difficult it is to find new board members. It's often the same people rotating through the same roles year after year. Maintaining this status quo doesn't generate the momentum needed for board members to become more engaged with governing the organization in general and with fundraising specifically.

If you want your organization to be better at fundraising, start with recruitment. Sometimes just "cleaning up" this process will create the structure and enthusiasm needed to attract new candidates and help current board members better understand and embrace their roles. Here are a few suggestions for improving your board member recruitment strategy:[3]

1. Try to see it from the outside looking in. How do people perceive your organization, and more specifically, your board and volunteers? Are there any hints of exclusivity? Could people possibly view your group as more of a club than a public-serving charity? If you're not sure, ask for insight from those outside the organization. Sometimes getting a read on this can make all the difference because it may affect your messaging and recruitment approach.

2. Set and honor term limits. Many boards have term limits, but some choose not to enforce them. We probably all know of at least one nonprofit board whose work has become stale because they've been recycling the same people through the same few roles for years (and sometimes longer). Even worse is when a longtime board chair refuses to give up the post despite long-expired terms. In cases like these, complaining there is "no new blood" becomes a self-fulfilling prophecy. Commit to honoring term limits, especially if they are part of the group's bylaws, and then hold people accountable. (And remember, the board does have a legal duty to follow the bylaws.) If you'd like to retain the service and expertise of long-serving board members who have exhausted their terms, you can consider whether emeritus status might offer an appropriate transition. For example, a board chair emeritus might still participate in board meetings and committee work as a non-voting member.

3. Get new people involved. Create volunteer roles that appeal to people from different backgrounds with different skills. Also, look for ways to involve remote volunteers to work on tasks outside of your museum or site. Examples might include editing your newsletter or indexing online documents. Consider inviting qualified nonboard members to serve on subcommittees to help develop their commitment to a leadership position. You might want to review your member and donor lists and consider longtime supporters or those who have significantly supported specific areas related to the positions you're trying to fill.

4. Define your needs and seek out candidates with those skills. Assess potential growth areas, as well as project needs. What type of expertise could help you realize your goals? Put those skills in writing and start looking for prospects. If you need expertise to help achieve a specific task with a clear beginning and end, consider recruiting someone's service for a finite period of time. For some, a one-term commitment may seem more manageable. It's probably also worth noting that sometimes people don't want to replicate their professional responsibilities in their service activities. For example, a professional fundraiser might not want to chair your fundraising committee (or she might see it as a conflict of interest to actively solicit for another nonprofit), but she might be willing to facilitate your board training or providing strategic direction.

5. Publicize board recruitment in new ways. Take stock of how you currently get the word out to recruit new board members. Is it entirely word of mouth? Do you only communicate it within your ranks? If you want to broaden your appeal, identify some partners who can help you get the word out. Talk to your local community foundation, chamber of commerce, service organizations, and local businesses. Contact school and university officials. Find out if there are regional or state newsletters that advertise volunteer opportunities. Reach out to your state Field Services office. Pitch a story idea to your local newspaper. If you're serious about recruiting new prospects, you may have to get creative to reach them.

6. Prioritize diversity. One community or organization's idea of diversity may look very different from another's. A heritage organization operating in a small, rural midwestern town will serve a very different audience than one located in a coastal urban city. Ideally, you might try to establish a board that represents the community you serve. But remember that there's more to diversity than race and ethnicity (although those are both important). Diversity also addresses culture, gender, age, sexual orientation, religion, disability, and military status, just to name a few. If you say that your community isn't very diverse, you aren't looking hard enough.

7. Create and maintain a list of potential board candidates. Your spokespeople—the ones nearest the center of the constituency circles—are meeting new people every day. Some of those people might make good board members, but it's easy to lose track of them if you don't make a note of it until you need their names. Encourage your organizational leaders (whether paid or volunteer) to always be in "recruitment mode" and designate a spot for everyone to add prospective board members to the list or ask each person to keep their own.

8. Define board roles and service expectations. Put these in writing. In addition to the legal duties we discussed above, outline commitments for meeting and event attendance and committee work. Be sure to include expectations for fundraising involvement and personal contributions.

## BOARD EXPECTATIONS

Still feeling hesitant to talk about fundraising with your board? Consider this data from BoardSource: when fundraising expectations are clearly communicated during the recruitment process, 52 percent of CEOs reported that their boards were actively engaged in fundraising, as opposed to only 12 percent when this expectation was not communicated.[1]

---

1. Tips on How to Address the Board's #1 Challenge: Fundraising," BoardSource, 2017, https://boardsource.org/tips-address-boards-number-one-challenge-fundraising/.

9. Create job descriptions for general board members and each officer position. People like to do work that is satisfying and meaningful, especially when it comes to community service commitments. If you want board members to treat their responsibilities seriously, put them in writing. Without a job description, it's difficult to know if they're a good fit for a position. You owe it to your board members, officers, and volunteers to establish parameters for their service and demonstrate a thorough understanding of their responsibilities, especially for officers serving as leaders.

10. Follow a proper nomination process. Appoint a specific nominating committee whose work is ongoing. (They should be looking for new board members all the time, not just in the weeks leading up to a vote.) Consider adopting a formal screening process and conduct two-way interviews with candidates, even if you have three openings and only two applicants. The prospective board member needs to see that the organization takes the process seriously. And perhaps most

importantly, candidates need a forum to ask questions and decide whether the organization is a good fit for them. You want leaders who are committed and engaged. It's far better to find out there's no love match at the beginning rather than after the onboarding process.

## Onboarding

Once you've successfully made it through recruitment, you're ready to bring on your new board members. Because you've already laid a good foundation during your recruitment process, new board members understand their commitment. You don't have to worry that they will be caught off-guard because you've already identified fundraising as one of their primary responsibilities. That is the benefit of fair, two-way recruitment and screening. Education and communication create a mutual understanding you can build upon. Now let's consider what other information will help new board members better understand their positions.

### UNDERSTANDING

According to BoardSource, "Boards with a strong understanding of their roles and responsibilities are better at fundraising than those who have a weaker understanding."[1]

_____

1. "Tips on How to Address the Board's #1 Challenge: Fundraising," BoardSource, 2017, https://boardsource.org/tips-address-boards-number-one-challenge-fundraising/.

## Board Manual

Before your new board members attend their first meeting, consider providing them with reference material in the form of a board packet. This can be a paper version in a binder or digital through an external storage device or shared file service. Include information such as:

- Organization history
- Copy of the bylaws
- Descriptions of key programs and initiatives
- Staff and board contact lists
- Board member, officer, and committee role descriptions
- Financial statements
- Strategic planning documents
- Annual fundraising plan and calendar
- Brief summary of past fundraising initiatives and ongoing fundraising projects
- Collections plan
- Conflict of interest disclosure form
- Other forms you think they may need for reference

## Industry Standards, Ethics, and Best Practices

Depending on your organization's specific heritage work, you may want to include information about industry standards, ethics, and best practices. You ask board members to make decisions that will affect how your organization does this work, and you're going to expect them to raise money to support these efforts. You want them to understand that there are professional guidelines to help them make the best decisions in governing and good cases for support in fundraising. Organizations such as the American Alliance of Museums and the Association for State and Local History are good places to start.

## Face-to-Face Orientation

Another critical aspect of the onboarding process is a face-to-face orientation with a staff or board member. This is helpful because most board members aren't going to read the manual front to back. It would be great if they did, but we have to accept that it's mostly for reference. A sit-down meeting with someone from the organization is the best way to draw their attention to the most critical pieces of information, and it gives them a chance to ask questions in the moment. Further, it establishes an open line of communication for future inquiries and discussions. These meetings allow you to cover the high points and direct them to resources, either in the board packet or on your website, that are available when they need more information.

## Board Self-Evaluation

If you haven't done so before, you may also want to ask your board to complete a self-evaluation questionnaire. This is a useful tool not just for new members but also for board veterans. An assessment can help identify strengths and weaknesses while providing an overall read on board performance. It builds the framework for continuous improvement that can inform a board development plan. Each person can take the assessment anonymously, with the results going into an overall board summary.

It's recommended that boards go through this process every year or two to benchmark their progress and build in professional development opportunities to address areas for improvement. Maybe that schedule is realistic, maybe it isn't. If you think it's something that might work for your board, there are templates available online. There are companies and independent consultants that will provide paid assessments and analysis. You can also look for organizations in your community to assist. Try contacting your local community foundation or Field Services office for recommendations.

# Fundraising Training

Organizations often start talking about fundraising training as they approach a capital campaign or other big fundraising push. Someone says, "The board doesn't do much fundraising. We'd better teach them how if we're going to raise any money." While it's always a good idea to provide extra training for staff and board members while preparing for a major fundraising push, don't wait for a big campaign. In fact, your board's ability to fundraise will have a major impact on whether a capital campaign is even feasible for your organization.

If fundraising is a priority, it should be discussed at every board meeting. You can use many of the worksheets and activities in this book for short brainstorming sessions to help your board think and talk about fundraising. If you want a more thorough, organized approach, seek a qualified trainer to facilitate a board retreat. You can use your board self-assessment feedback to identify any preconceived notions, gaps, or areas where the board may need more resources.

Including fundraising training in meetings doesn't have to take a lot of time. Encourage board and staff members to practice their elevator pitches for each other or do a "show and tell" of fundraising materials from other organizations to discuss what you do and don't like. Even ten minutes spent on a brainstorming activity can yield positive results by keeping fundraising top of mind.

# Communication

One of the essential roles a board member can play is that of a spokesperson. They are frequently your eyes, ears, and mouth in the community. How do you know what they're saying? How do you know they're communicating your funding priorities? Have you provided them with the support and information they need to get your message across? They need to know the whats, whys, and hows to be effective public representatives for the organization.

## The Big "So What?"

I talk a lot about The big "So What?". It's a phrase I started using while coaching organizations through grant applications. If you think back to our chapter about making a case for support, you may recall we talked about having compelling, people-focused needs. Your spokespeople need to be prepared to talk about these needs and why your organization is best positioned to meet them. They need to be able to answer the "So What?" question. This means understanding not only what your organization does but also how and why. According to a 2017 Leading with Intent survey, "Strong understanding of programs is linked to stronger engagement, strategy, and external leadership—including fundraising."[4]

As spokespeople, advocates, and eventually fundraisers for your organization, your board members need a few critical pieces of information to speak intelligently and effectively about the organization's work. Specifically, they need to

1. Know, understand, support, and be able to articulate the organization's mission. Your mission drives the work you do. That work—and the outcomes you're trying to achieve for those you serve—dictate your funding needs. Your board members need to be able to speak about mission-driven initiatives. If they're not doing this, you need to find out why and remedy the situation.
2. Know program and project basics. Your board needs to have a handle on major initiatives supported by the organization. It may be easier to keep tabs on this at smaller institutions where board members are also implementing programs, but that doesn't mean small organizations are immune from the silos that often form around individual departments, projects, and events. My general rule of thumb: if it's on the website, everyone on the board should be able to talk about it.
3. Understand how initiatives fit into the bigger picture. This is where The big "So What?" comes in. Board members should be able to talk about how programs (and funding requests) support the mission. Why is that work necessary?

4. Know the price tag. When discussing new or improved programs and projects on the list for funding, board members should know the price tag to make them a reality. This goes back to prioritizing the organization's wish list and assigning costs to each initiative. For example, in addition to understanding the total project cost for a new roof, the board should also have a good idea what you spend each year for collections care.

5. Create a personal statement about why the organization and its mission matters. Spokespeople need to have an elevator pitch. These statements should be unique to the individual, not a memorized, canned version. And it needs to go beyond just relaying the mission. Each board member should craft and practice their summary of why the organization and its work are important.

To help your board work through how to talk about The big "So What?" you might want to start with a conversation about your organization's value proposition. This is how you communicate why the work you do is important.

## VALUE PROPOSITION

Value proposition: how you communicate why the work you do is important.

Questions to consider:
- Who do we serve?
- What needs do we fill?
- Why is it important to address these needs?
- How do we address these needs?

Bonus questions:
- How do we know we're delivering positive results?
- Why are we different from others doing similar work?
- What does success look like for us?
- What impact do we hope to have on our community?

## Frequently Asked Questions (FAQs)

What does your audience (donors and the general public) want to know about your organization? Identify some frequently asked questions you and your board members receive, and then compare answers to ensure everyone is relaying the same (correct) information. You could spend five or ten minutes at the beginning of a board meeting identifying these questions and then prepare answers for the next meeting. A few areas for consideration are:

*Operational Basics*
- Open hours
- Admission costs
- Seasonal closings
- The organization's website

- Contact information (name, phone number, email) for at least one representative at the organization who can answer more complex questions or provide more detailed answers

*Volunteer Opportunities*
- Needed skills
- Scope of commitment
- Contact information for the person in charge of coordinating volunteers

*How to Donate*

Not every gift, whether object or money, comes from an outright ask. Sometimes questions about donations are unsolicited. Board members should know the basics about the processes and refer the prospective donor to someone who can help them make the gift.

Objects:
- Scope of collections and specific collecting initiatives (what type of objects the organization does and does not accept)
- Donation process (what happens from the time someone offers an object until it becomes part of the collection and beyond)
- Contact information for someone who can help them make their object donation

Money:
- Membership and giving levels
- Ways to donate (in person, mail, online, sponsorships, gifts-in-kind)
- Contact information for someone responsible for processing gifts of money

## The Board's Role in Fundraising

Fundraising grows and evolves organically at each organization. What works for one might not work as well for another. Spend a little time discussing how you and other leaders envision fundraising working at your organization. What role does the board play now, and what role do you hope they play in the future? If you have staff, how should that interaction work? Are there fundraising volunteers? If so, how should they be integrated?

If you're serious about getting your board more involved in fundraising, put your goals and plans in writing. That's what makes them real. Then seek out the resources that can help you address any deficiencies you've identified.

## The Development Committee

Many organizations establish a development committee to provide oversight for fundraising efforts. This committee helps keep fundraising on track by supporting the board and staff. But don't let the name fool you. This committee is not solely responsible for raising money. That is everyone's responsibility. Instead, they help engage other board members in the fundraising process, coordinate individual initiatives and campaigns, and encourage 100 percent board giving. They are not, however, a special event planning committee. If your organization hosts large fundraising events, consider establishing a separate subcommittee to manage those events. This allows the development committee to focus on "driving the train" for the greater fundraising effort, which may include smaller events for donor cultivation and stewardship.

How you engage the rest of your board in the fundraising process is up to you. It will be dependent on your goals, as well as your resources. Take stock of what you want to accomplish in the short-, middle-, and long-term range, the willingness (and comfort level) of current board members, and your prospects for new recruits. Here are a few ideas to get your started.

## TEN NO-ASK FUNDRAISING IDEAS

1. Make a personal financial commitment. It's easier to ask someone else to give when you've already invested in the initiative.
2. Host small, personal no-ask events at your home or a unique venue. Spotlight the good work the organization is doing, but no checkbooks or pledge cards necessary.
3. Make thank-you calls. Call your members and donors and thank them for their support with no associated asks.
4. Write personal thank-you notes. Use your own personal stationery and tailor each note for the individual recipient.
5. Speak at other nonprofits. Volunteer to speak at another organization's meeting. Be prepared to tell them how to get involved and about possible collaborative opportunities.
6. Make infinite connections—network, network, network. Carry business cards for the organization. Follow up with new contacts.
7. Evaluate and plan earned-income ventures. If fundraising isn't your thing (yet), explore alternate avenues to generate revenue. For example, work with a local screen printer to develop logo items, sell a few local products on commission in your museum, or design at-home activity kits to sell online.
8. Recruit in-kind donations. Not every donation has to be cash. Do you have connections to secure needed goods or services for free or at a reduced rate? Make a wish list (and don't accept donations you don't need).
9. Talk about the organization. Tell your friends and colleagues (and maybe even strangers) about your service to the organization and why you love it.
10. Stretch (a little) past your comfort zone. If you're not ready to do a face-to-face ask, consider taking on a letter-writing campaign or setting up a peer-to-peer platform.

There's no magic recipe or quick fix for board success with fundraising. However, chances are good that if you identify areas to boost education and communication, you will also see fundraising results improve.

## Notes

1. "Tips on How to Address the Board's #1 Challenge: Fundraising," BoardSource, accessed November 19, 2020, https://boardsource.org/wp-content/uploads/2017/10/Tips-Challenge-Fundraising.pdf.

2. For more information, please see the following resources: "Board Roles and Responsibilities," National Council of Nonprofits, accessed November 19, 2020, https://

www.councilofnonprofits.org/tools-resources/board-roles-and-responsibilities; "Funda-mental Topics of Nonprofit Board Service: Roles and Responsibilities," BoardSource, accessed November 19, 2020, https://boardsource.org/fundamental-topics-of-nonprofit -board-service/roles-responsibilities/; Herrington Bryce, "Nonprofit Board Responsibil-ities: The Basics," *Nonprofit Quarterly*, August 21, 2017, https://nonprofitquarterly.org/ nonprofit-board-governance-responsibilities-basic-guide; Jeremy Barlow, "Nonprofit Board Legal Responsibilities" (blog), *BoardEffect*, August 12, 2016, https://www.board effect.com/blog/non-profit-board-legal-responsibilities/.

3. For more information, see "Developing a Board Recruitment Process," Wild Apri-cot, accessed November 19, 2020, https://www.wildapricot.com/articles/developing-a-bo ard-recruitment-process#find-candidates.

4 "Leading with Intent: 2017 BoardSource Index of Nonprofit Board Practices," BoardSource, 2017, https://leadingwithintent.org/.

# Members and Donors

If you and I were to sit down over coffee to discuss fundraising at your organization, I would want to know how you fund your programs and special projects. I would ask how you pay for your building expenses and purchase new equipment. But what I would be most curious about is how you pay for your everyday expenses. How do you pay the mortgage, keep the lights and heat on, keep your office supplies stocked, and pay for staff? Do your donors provide support through unrestricted giving? Do you have a membership program that supports general operating? Do you actively ask your supporters to join or give money? Do you send members renewal reminders and ask donors once or twice a year for ongoing support? This chapter will look at two different, but related, ways that many heritage organizations raise money for their operating expenses: membership programs and annual giving campaigns.

## General Operating Funds

According to a survey conducted by the American Association for State and Local History and the Field Services Alliance,[1] 72 percent of heritage organization respondents (specifically historic houses or sites, historical societies, and museums) identified membership as a funding source, and 81 percent reported they receive money from donations. However, for all three types of organizations, local government funding was most frequently given as their top source of income. These results may not be surprising, but there is a significant distinction between these three sources. Namely, memberships and donations are within the organization's control, whereas local government funding usually is not. Not surprisingly, 39 percent of respondents cited lack of financial sustainability as their number one most pressing issue. As more and more heritage organizations see decreases in municipal and county funding, proactive fundraising from memberships, donations, or both, becomes even more critical for general operating support.

Funding for everyday expenses often comes from unrestricted dollars in our general operating fund. Why are these funds so vital? Because we can direct unrestricted money for core operating support wherever the organization most needs it. This offers tremendous flexibility to meet immediate needs and builds capacity to reach our goals. Many nonprofits rely on regular requests for memberships or donations in response to this need for operating revenue. These programs can serve as the foundation for our fundraising efforts. They are often the first programs we implement because they help us establish our base of supporters. If managed well, they can provide a regular, predictable source of unrestricted income.

## Membership and Annual Giving: Similar and Different

We'll get into other types of fundraising in future chapters—including large or "major" gifts, grants, and special events. In this chapter, we will limit our scope to memberships and donations that go to the annual fund. To make sure we're all on the same page, let's define these two things:

Membership: Memberships generally provide benefits in exchange for payment of dues, although some organizations do offer free memberships. This exchange of money for benefits is called quid pro quo (more on that later).

Annual giving: The name is misleading. This is an ongoing process to raise money for yearly expenses (general operating), not something you focus on only once a year. It's kind of a catch-all term that includes different types of asks, from direct mail and email solicitations to online giving and face-to-face asks.

On paper, the distinctions between members and donors seem simple. Members receive tangible benefits dependent on a continued (usually annual) payment or renewal of their membership. Donors don't receive ongoing tangible benefits (other than a possible write-off on their taxes), and there is no set timeline to define their relationship with the organization. For some organizations, these differences are clearly defined. However, for others, the distinction between these two groups is less clear. Why is that? Members might also be donors. Or donations at a certain level might include a membership. Some donors might receive benefits (such as special invitation-only events, behind-the-scenes access, and early notification of important announcements). And at some institutions, membership benefits are negligible (or nonexistent), creating a situation where members are more like donors on a timeline.

What does your member/donor program look like at your organization? I'm going to go out on a limb here and guess that your current member/donor activities fall into one of four categories:

- No memberships, no donations
- Only membership
- Only donations
- Memberships and donations

Before we dissect these programs any further, I want to mention that there is no right or wrong answer. Our goal is to look at these programs, weigh the pros and cons, consider your organization's unique circumstances, evaluate whether you could be doing more, and if so, what. First and foremost, you should decide what you can do well. Lean into what makes sense for your organization and get good at it. Develop a process and streamline it. Then when you're ready, gradually build in other areas. This applies not only to membership and annual giving but to all the other fundraising techniques we'll talk about in subsequent chapters. That said, I think you will find that the methods we apply to recruit and retain members are similar to those we use for annual donors because it's all based on relationships. There's a lot of crossover. If you can do memberships well, you can do annual giving well (and vice versa).

## Similarities and Differences

For all my genealogy friends out there: membership and annual giving are basically first cousins. They don't share all the same traits, but they are definitely related. Let's take a look at some of the similarities and differences.

**Membership**

- Creates expectation of benefits in exchange for dues
- Must consider "cost" of benefits
- Set on a timeline that requires renewal to remain an "active" member
- May support natural affiliation with the organization
- Creates a sense of belonging
- Can serve as an entryway for annual giving

**Builds base of loyal supporters**

**Barriers to entry are low**

**Retaining is more cost effective than recruiting**

**Can be advocates for the cause**

**Must be actively managed**

**Annual Giving**

- Likely giving for the sake of philanthropy
- Gift is 100% tax-deductible (no quid pro quo)
- Promotes focus on mission of service to community
- May involve giving once a year or more frequently (or less, but likely still consider themselves donors)
- Can create regular patterns of giving
- May help identify those interested in monthly giving, larger gifts, or legacy giving

**Figure 14.1.** Membership vs. Annual Giving

First, let's talk about some characteristics membership and annual giving both share:

- They present a low-barrier entry for building relationships. Entry-level memberships are usually reasonably priced, and initial annual giving contributions are generally modest. This gives supporters a chance to get to know the organization. Their loyalty builds the foundation for fundraising.
- You want to acquire new members and donors but focus on keeping the ones you already have. Donor retention averages around 45 percent, which means most charities lose more donors than they retain each year.[2] It costs less to retain a

donor than to acquire a new one. Suppose it takes $1.00 to acquire a new $1.00 donation but only $0.25 to renew a $1.00 donation; your ROI for retaining the donor is $0.75. In that case, it's easy to see why you should direct time, energy, and money to stewarding the supporters you already have, whether they are members or donors (or both).[3]

- Your loyal members and donors have opted-in as supporters. They are an obvious audience for outreach and communication efforts, and they can also be advocates for your cause. If they have good experiences with you, they may want to tell friends and family, share your posts on social media, and even become involved as volunteers.
- Whether we're talking about membership or annual giving, staff or volunteers must actively manage these programs. You need to communicate with these supporters. This also means consistently and actively asking them to renew their commitment. Send membership expiration reminders and renewal requests. Plan one or more annual giving appeals. And in-between asks, provide them with member/donor-focused messaging and opportunities to interact with your organization (in other words, stewardship).

From here, let's look more closely at each of these programs. First, let's talk about a few characteristics that are unique to membership. At the end of this section, I will offer a few extra points for your consideration.

# Membership

Membership programs are relatively common among heritage organizations, although they are all managed and maintained a little differently. Here are a few things to think about when it comes to membership:

- Memberships create an expectation of benefits offered in exchange for payment of dues. This is called quid pro quo. If you provide tangible benefits as part of your membership program, your organization incurs a "cost" for each member. For tax purposes, this cost is equal to the value of the benefits—the goods and services—offered. The total fair market value of those goods and services can be subtracted from the membership fee. Any funds left above and beyond this value can be considered a charitable contribution. If it sounds confusing, that's because it is. Your best bet is to review the IRS guidelines on quid pro quo and discuss them with your accountant if you have more questions.[4]
- A timeline usually defines memberships. Sometimes this can be beneficial if the member is looking for a clearly defined commitment, but organizations must proactively encourage people to keep their memberships active. This is why you will frequently see one, two, or even three membership renewal reminders sent from organizations trying to retain members.
- Memberships fit the culture of museums and other visitor-serving organizations. People who frequent these sites are probably already familiar with the concept of membership, and it provides a natural way for supporters to affiliate with the organization. It can also help promote visitation and participation in programs and events.

- Members are often joiners. They seek out opportunities that create a sense of belonging, so look for ways to help them feel the love. Once they are part of the organization, they may be open to learning more about your mission and work. This can sometimes serve as an entry into charitable support through annual or sustained (monthly) giving.

## Member Motivation

A membership program's success is influenced not only by how it's formalized and managed but by what motivates members to join the cause. People have different reasons for joining organizations, and sometimes those reasons vary over time. Think about the organizations where you have memberships (both for-profit and nonprofit). Why do you belong? What's your motivation?

Generally, we can look at members by two categories, depending on motivation: value and affinity.

- **Value members** are motivated by benefits associated with membership in the organization. They want access to something appreciable that they can only get through that membership. For example, people with young children might join a zoo or children's museum if membership includes free admission. They know they only have to go a certain number of times before the membership more than pays for itself. Another example would be event rental space that is available at a discount to members. If someone wants to use that space, they can subtract the value of that discount from the membership fee.
- **Affinity members** are motivated by the organization's mission. They like the work that's happening, and they want to support the continuation of programs and services. These members have altruistic reasons for joining; they want to be part of something they view as valuable and beneficial. In some cases, they may be members because that's what the organization asked of them. (In other words, your affinity folks will likely join to support the organization, but they would also probably donate if asked.)

One of these members is not "better" than the other. Value members are the reason some organizations work so hard to create solid benefits programs. We know they like the perks: discounts, insider knowledge, early access, and other members-only benefits. Many organizations will have good reason to continue dedicating resources to this type of member. Affinity members are more like donors hiding in the membership rolls. Their motivation to support the organization is similar to what we expect from donors, and they might respond well to the same type of cultivation and stewardship tactics.

## Member to Donor Mindset

I am a big fan of membership programs for local history organizations. I think they are an excellent, low-barrier way to recruit and engage supporters. Leaders at some organizations may be more comfortable asking for memberships than donations when they're first starting (or perhaps restarting), and sometimes it just makes sense to focus on membership. That said, I do think there is one potential pitfall to memberships. There is a possibility that some organizations are training their members to believe that membership is all the organization needs from them.

If you think this might apply to you and you have a decent CRM, try running some numbers to get a better feel for who is in your member/donor rolls. Here are a few things to look for:

1. How much income do you average from memberships?
2. How many of your members are also donors? (In other words, they maintain active memberships and give extra on top of that.)
3. How many of your donors aren't members? What's the average gift size for this group? Are they contributing more or less than your members?

If you find that your membership revenue far outpaces your donations, your members may think their membership fee is all you need from them. Are you asking them for donations beyond their membership? If your answer is no, and these tend to be affinity members who genuinely support your mission and the work you're doing, you may have fallen victim to the number one reason people don't give: you never asked. Allow these supporters to assist you beyond membership. Reinforce how important they are to the people you serve.

If you're just starting to move from a member to a donor mindset (and hoping your supporters come along with you), consider a few ideas:

• Offer a benefits waiver option with your memberships. Explain each benefit's value and give people the chance to take a pass on some or all of them. They will begin to understand that the organization has a cost for each member.
• Add the option for an additional donation to your membership form (even if they direct it toward a specific program, which restricts the gift). This gets supporters used to going above and beyond, even if just a little bit.
• Decide whether giving societies or donor clubs might be an option for you. They create that sense of belonging and loyalty while still encouraging progressive giving. While we might most readily think of dividing these groups by giving amounts, consider special recognition for sustained or monthly giving. Another option would be to create a level for those who have given to your organization consistently for years—these are your most loyal, time-tested givers. You may also find that communication with these groups is more consistent and systemized.
• Don't be afraid to include your members in your annual giving appeal. If you don't tell them that you need their help funding general operating needs, they may never know.

## Annual Giving

From here, let's spend a little bit of time looking specifically at annual giving. After we talk about some characteristics that make annual giving different from membership, I'll offer a few extra considerations and tips that will, hopefully, be helpful.

• Donors to annual fund campaigns are likely giving for the sake of philanthropy. There's no quid pro quo, no expectations for goods or services exchanged. While some donors are motivated by tax deductions, most want to know that their money is making a difference.

- Donors want to make a positive impact on the communities you serve. They use your organization as a pass-through to accomplish this goal. Your mission—and stewardship of their money—is important to them.
- As mentioned above, annual giving does not necessarily mean giving once a year. Many organizations make several direct mail/email appeals (or what are called "soft appeals" through newsletters, for example) throughout the year. Some people like to give once at the end of the year, and others will donate more frequently.
- If you can set an annual giving appeal schedule (for instance, spring and fall appeals combined with summer and winter newsletters), your donors get used to hearing from you. They may even come to expect it. This can create regular patterns of giving. I know many donors who have a list of charities they support at the end of every year. How fortunate we are when we're on that list—but it likely came about through consistent appeals and stewardship!
- Most of an organization's donors contribute to the annual fund. They aren't giving huge gifts, but they are our base, our fundraising foundation. As we come to know and understand these donors, we should better identify those who might be interested in becoming sustaining donors through monthly giving. We might build relationships with donors who could potentially have the interest and capacity to make more significant gifts. Or we may have conversations with supporters who want to include the organization in their wills.

## An Annual Giving Appeal Process

We've talked about a few characteristics that make annual giving different from memberships, but we probably need to spend a little bit of time looking at how to make annual fund asks and what strategies we might use to be more successful. (Although we will be talking about annual giving in this section, you will probably notice some crossover; we can use many of these tactics for membership appeals as well.)

When we are ready to reach out to current and potential donors to ask for annual fund support, we can employ a range (and even a combination) of fundraising channels. These might include direct mail appeals, newsletters, phone calls, emails, online donation pages, social media, in-person asks, and special events. We're not going to detail each of these here because they are covered elsewhere in this book. It's also worth noting that many (many, many) books and online resources talk specifically about annual giving. (Actually, entire books focus solely on one giving channel, such as direct mail, for instance.)

## Creating Your Annual Giving Process

We will walk through a process that can help you get an annual giving piece out the door. The most important takeaway here is to remember that annual giving is an Ask, Thank, Report, Repeat process.[5] That's four easy steps to remember. (I'm going to give you a few additional action items to consider before and after these steps, but they are more behind-the-scenes. When it comes to the donor, Ask, Thank, Report, Repeat is the most important.)

1. *Set a realistic fundraising goal*

In an ideal situation, you would feel comfortable setting a number goal based on your current operational budget. You'd consider your income, as well as expenses, and weigh those against past fundraising success to gauge a realistic goal. If you can do that, great! If you don't feel like you can rely on those numbers and you want to make an educated guess, that's fine too. And if you've never done this before and you just want to get your first appeal letter in the mail and see what happens, make that your goal. The point is, don't be paralyzed into inaction worrying about how you "should" be doing it.

2. *Analyze your current and potential communication methods*
   Take stock of any outreach you're already doing, even if you're not explicitly asking for money. Experts estimate you need between four and seven "touches" before a prospective donor is ready to give a gift, so account for efforts already in progress. This might include newsletters, email updates, blog posts, or social media engagement, as well as events and programs (in-person and virtual). Understand all the ways you reach your supporters, but don't forget to look for gaps.

3. *Build your plan into a calendar*
   Take what you know (or even suspect) about your current supporters and translate that into your appeal plan. Determine when and how you will ask for donations. Will you do one big mailing or tailor different messages for segmented groups? Will you follow up direct mail with email? Will you give people the option to make online donations? Do you have any prospects that warrant face-to-face asks for more significant amounts? Start putting dates on your calendar. For instance, I usually start with my drop date (the date I want letters to go in the mail) and work backward to ensure I have enough time to write, design, edit, print, and process the mailing.

4. *ASK*
   There are many different tips about what makes "the best" annual giving mailing. Some organizations will rely on direct mail, while others may find that email or even social media outreach works for them. Luckily, several best practices have been tested (and again, whole books about this topic are available).[6] Plan some time before your next appeal to do some research on your own, but watch out—it's a rabbit hole! For now, here are a few suggestions to get you started:
   • Think of your direct mail as a packet rather than just a letter. Consider what will motivate the recipient to open the outer envelope. Keep in mind that most readers will skim your letter to decide whether or not to read more closely. Enclose a reply device that is easy for the donor to complete without too many extra choices. Include a preaddressed envelope to make their response easier. (And don't forget to mention your website if you offer online giving.)
   • Write a personal, conversational correspondence, not a formal business letter. Indent your paragraphs. Use "You/I" instead of "We." Use a serif font of at least 14 point for easier reading, and don't worry about it being more than one page. If you're using email, keep it brief, use shorter paragraphs, and draw attention to the SMIT (single most important thing).

- Make the ask. Make it more than once. Make it at the beginning, in the middle, at the bottom of the first page, and again at the end. Make it in the P.S. Say things like, "I am writing you today to ask . . ." Make the ask.
- Consider your timing. Many organizations do their annual giving appeals in the last quarter of the year. November and December are big months for giving; nearly 30 percent of giving occurs in December alone.[7] Many people are accustomed to donating at the end of the year, but do what makes sense for you, your staff/volunteers, and your budget.

5. *THANK*

Send gift receipts and thank-you letters as soon as possible once donations start coming back. You can do them in batches, but don't sit on them too long. Donors expect and deserve a quick turnaround on these. (Best practice says to send a thank-you within forty-eight hours. If this isn't a reasonable goal for your organization, define a realistic turnaround time, so the response time is not open-ended.) If you offer online giving, make sure your donor gets immediate confirmation that their gift has been processed and then follow up with a thank-you letter. Consider whether first-time donors or those who give larger gifts should receive a phone call or a personal note from a board member or the executive director. And then recognize and thank your donors every chance you get going forward.

6. *REPORT*

Donors want to know how you're using their money. Use your communication channels—from newsletters, social media, and your website to phone calls, personal notes, and formal reports—to demonstrate how the organization is making a difference to people because of the donor's generosity. If you're wondering what tone to take, consider how you can inspire *joy* for your donors.

7. *Track your results*

Put plans in place to code and track appeal responses in your database. More data can equal better strategy. Ideally, you'd like to be able to take into account factors such as how many years a person has given (longevity), the number of gifts given in a year (frequency), the dollar value (amount), as well as when the last gift was given (recency).[8] By tracking this information, you can start identifying patterns, including total giving and average gift ranges.

8. *REPEAT*

You will learn something new every time you do an appeal. You might uncover something new about your donors, or you might pick up new tips and tricks to add to your fundraising toolkit. Regardless, take what you learn and apply it to the next one. The important thing is to be consistent, listen to your donors, and trust your instincts.

## Leaning Toward Your Cause

If you're just starting your membership or annual giving programs, or you're looking to revamp what you've been doing, there's no time like the present. One or both of these efforts could provide the solid base your fundraising needs. Don't be discouraged if you have a slow start. People are busy and distracted, and let's face it, some of us just have poor memories and follow-through regarding things like returning membership and donation forms. Also, remember that it may take four to seven "touches" before someone makes a gift. Give them multiple channels for information and make it easy to join as a member or donate, so when they do carve out time to focus on you they can have a pleasant, convenient experience.

Pace yourself. You don't have to do everything all at once. Focus on being good stewards to your current members and donors (and get feedback from them—it can affect some of the decisions you're trying to make). Put your process in place and refine it as needed. Demonstrate value, polish your messaging, and don't be afraid to take creative risks. Follow up on every gift and new membership because they represent a person leaning toward your cause.[9] Take every opportunity to let your members and donors know how much they mean to you and the people you serve.

# Notes

1. American Association for State and Local History and the Field Services Alliance, "Cultural Heritage Organization Survey," 2020, unpublished survey.

2. Bill Levis, Ben Miller, and Cathy Williams, *2018 Fundraising Effectiveness Survey Report*, Growth in Giving Steering Group, April 12, 2018, https://afpfep.org/wp-content/uploads/2018/04/2018-Fundraising-Effectiveness-Survey-Report.pdf.

3. Clair Axelrad, "[ASK AN EXPERT] How to Measure Donor Acquisition Costs," *Bloomerang* (blog), May 22, 2020, https://bloomerang.co/blog/ask-an-expert-how-to-measure-donor-acquisition-costs/.

4. For more information, see IRS Revenue Procedure 90-12 at https://www.irs.gov/pub/irs-tege/rp_1990-12.pdf and Revenue Procedure 90-49 at https://www.irs.gov/pub/irs-tege/rp92_49.pdf.

5. For more information, see Jim Shapiro, "Why Does Ask, Thank, Report, Repeat Work," *The Better Fundraising Co.* (blog), November 19, 2019, https://betterfundraising.com/ask-thank-report-repeat-work/.

6. For more information, look for research from Adrian Sargeant and Jen Shang at the Philanthropy Institute, https://www.philanthropy-institute.org.uk/; John Lepp from Agents of Good, https://agentsofgood.org/; Gail Perry, https://www.gailperry.com/; and Tom Ahern, https://www.aherncomm.com/ to get started.

7. "The Digital Giving Index: 2015 Year in Review," Network for Good, accessed November 23, 2020, https://www.networkforgood.com/digitalgivingindex/.

8. Henry A. Rosso, "The Annual Fund: A Building Block for Fundraising," Lilly Family School of Philanthropy, IUPUI, accessed May 29, 2021, https://philanthropy.iupui.edu/files/course_resources/annual_fund_building_block_for_fr_by_rosso.pdf, 11. Originally from Hank Rosso's Achieving Excellence in Fundraising (ISBN: 0787962562). Copyright © (2003) by John Wiley & Sons, Inc.

9. My thanks to Tom Ahern for this concept: "there's no complicated formula, people either lean TOWARD you or not." Tom Ahern, email to Jamie Simek, April 28, 2021.

# Major Gifts and Targeted Project Funding

Major gifts. Chances are, when we're thinking about fundraising, this is what comes to mind—big asks. But before you make those big asks, maybe you have a few questions: Who am I supposed to ask? Do I ask, or should someone else? How do I know how much to ask for? How do I start the conversation? Do I just come right out and say it? What if they say no? These are all fair questions. It's about building relationships and being organized enough to strategically maximize your resources, but it certainly helps to understand the process ahead of time. In this chapter, we are going to see how to use the fundraising cycle for major gift fundraising and consider tactics to help fund special projects.

## WHAT IS A MAJOR GIFT?

A major gift varies from organization to organization. What might be considered "major" for one organization may not be for another. Generally, your major gifts are the largest donations your organization receives. To better understand this amount for your organization, go back through your donation history and get a feel for your average and highest gift amounts (graphs can make this helpful). It might be worth noting that, generally, 80 percent of your money comes from 20 percent of your donors (major gifts) and 20 percent of your money comes from 80 percent of your donors (annual fund gifts).[1] In other words, while small in number, major donors are mighty! Their support is essential for reaching your fundraising goals.

---

1. Andy Robinson, "What Are Major Gifts—And Where Do I Find Them?" Guide-Star, February 13, 2019, https://trust.guidestar.org/what-are-major-gifts-and-where-do-i-find-them.

# Major Gifts: A Team Sport

An organization needed to raise a sizable amount of money for much-needed renovations to their building. They decided the answer to their problems was to hire a fundraising consultant. They thought that person would come in, make all the asks, and raise the money they needed in short order. It was the perfect solution to what they perceived as the uncomfortable business of fundraising. Except it wasn't.

They failed to realize that fundraising—especially for major gifts and special projects—is a team sport. If an organization has the resources to hire a fundraising consultant for guidance, that person can be a great addition to the team. However, even the best consultant can't replace the critical relationships that must be built for long-term fundraising success (although they can help you develop a good cultivation plan). Don't worry if your organization can't afford to hire a fundraising consultant. You can still create a successful major gift program with buy-in and commitment from your team (even if that is just you and a small cadre of volunteers).

Major gifts tend to be above and beyond a donor's usual annual gift. You're more likely to ask for something specific—a predefined amount for a particular project or program, capital improvement (such as building construction or equipment), a gift to help build an endowment, or a capital campaign contribution (more on that near the end of the chapter).[1] While there should always be a clearly defined relationship manager for each donor prospect, a good major gift program results from the combined effort of multiple people, even if just a few. It's good to brainstorm with others. Ideally, you will have volunteers (such as board and committee members) who will help you identify prospects, screen lists, make introductions, host events, and possibly even help with solicitations.

## The Fundraising Cycle

If you remember back to our section on the fundraising cycle steps, some of what we're going to talk about below will be familiar. Major gift solicitations provide the perfect opportunity to apply what we know about identifying, cultivating, asking, and stewarding donors.

### Identify

Let's address the first question from the opening paragraph: Who am I supposed to ask? You need to create a list of prospective donors to decide where and how to focus your efforts. The list will be your jumping-off point, but it's helpful to consider a few things:

- Each person on your list represents an individual, unique relationship that will progress at its own pace. Some may make gifts relatively quickly, while others will remain prospects for an extended time. Not every person you add to the list will make a gift, and that's okay.
- You're never "done" prospecting. While you may create lists for specific initiatives, your master prospect list will never be complete. You and your fundraising team should continue to add new prospects as you identify them.

## BE ACTIVE

If you're looking to grow your list of contacts, partners, and donors, there is no substitute for networking. Be active as a representative of your organization in your community. Attend meetings, serve on committees, attend community events, and volunteer to give presentations for other nonprofit and municipal organizations. Don't be afraid to reach out to people and organizations that may not seem to have a natural connection at first glance. Carry business cards, refer people to your website and social media accounts, and encourage visitation. These connections are critical whether you live in a small, rural community or a large, metropolitan area.

## Inside your database

The best place to find prospective donors is among your current supporters. These are people nearer the center of your constituency model, and chances are, you may already know something about them. To start your list, look through your donor rolls for

- anyone who has given a significant gift in the past;
- donors who have contributed several gifts over a year;
- loyal, long-term donors who've made gifts year after year;
- current and former board members with the capacity to make a significant gift;
- midlevel donors who may need more cultivation; and
- members who have upgraded membership levels.

Review your donor lists with stakeholders (such as staff, board and committee members, and key volunteers) to identify who needs more research or outreach in your database.

## Outside your database

Next, make a list of individuals from outside your database to add to your prospect list. Involve your support team by asking for recommendations. When determining whether to add someone from outside the organization to the prospect list, we still want to consider LIA (linkage, interest, and ability). Don't add someone to the list simply because they're wealthy. However, if someone who happens to be close friends with a board member (linkage), has a history of giving to arts and culture organizations (interest), and the capacity (ability) to make a gift, he or she might be a good prospect.

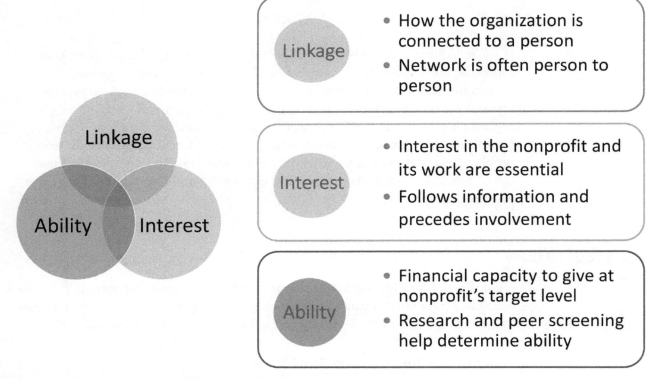

**Figure 15.1.** Linkage, Interest, and Ability

## Prioritize

After you've developed a solid list of prospects, it's time to prioritize where you should focus your efforts. Every relationship is important, but your resources are limited. When it comes to major gift fundraising, you want to focus your attention on those who are most likely to give sizable gifts according to their linkage, interest, and ability. You also want to make sure you're working with the prospective donors who are most interested in having a relationship with your organization. (This is known as qualifying the donor—deciding whether to keep them on your active prospect list. More on this in a bit.)

Next, sort your list according to priority. Those at the top will be the focus of your initial outreach efforts. There are many different ways to prioritize who to contact first.[2] Consider

- donors who have expressed interest in doing something more significant for the organization;
- donors who have given more than your average gift;
- someone referred by a current major donor;
- someone referred by a board or staff member; and
- someone from the community who has demonstrated a genuine interest in or passion for your cause.

You may also want to use data points such as recency (how long it's been since the donor made a gift), gift amount, capacity, and relationship with the organization.[3] To determine capacity, some organizations seek a "wealth overlay" from an outside company. This entails running your prospect list through an in-depth screening of public information to determine your wealthiest prospects using indicators such as real estate ownerships, stock holdings, business affiliations, and past giving to other nonprofits and political causes. As you can imagine, this is often too costly for small organizations, and an indication of wealth does not necessarily translate to an inclination to give. There are other valuable data points to consider, and many organizations can use their workforce to do necessary prospect research.

In addition to the information gathered from your donor records and simple internet searches, you can also use peer screening to learn more about your prospective donors. Ask their peers (such as board and committee members, and possibly even current major donors) to review your list and provide feedback about anyone they know. You'll be doing more research on your most promising prospects, but peer screening can help you prioritize your list.

## Qualify

Chances are good that you will be able to look at your prioritized prospect list and know with relative certainty that some of the people on that list are interested in further engagement with the organization. You will know this because you're already in frequent contact with them. That relationship development is already well underway. However, there may also be a few on your list who are less familiar with the organization. To qualify these folks as major gift prospects, you're going to need to reach out to gauge their interest.

You can determine the prospective donor's interest through a series of low-pressure touchpoints. There are different recommended "formulas"—various combinations of letters, emails, phone calls, or face-to-face meetings. If you were a major gift officer at a large organization, and if your prospect list was new to you, there might be more pressure for you to follow one of these formulas (e.g., lead off with an introductory letter, followed by a phone call before the letter gets "cold," then a personal note, a survey, another phone call, and a final letter). You may find that some or all of these work for you, or you may feel more comfortable establishing your routine. Just remember the goal of qualifying your prospect list. You want to confirm that each of those people wants to be on your list. In other words, they are open to developing a relationship that will likely result in a gift supporting the work you do.

As you work your way through your lists, you may feel pressure (from yourself or from others in the organization) to produce immediate results. Just remember that this is a process. Qualifying and then cultivating donors (our next step) takes time. Be consistent, but don't rush.

## Cultivate

As you work through your prospect list and identify donors who qualify to receive your major gift time and effort, you can begin creating a cultivation plan for each person. While you may have some cultivation activities that reach your entire major gift prospect list, your objective is to get to know your prospects better and understand their interests, values, and priorities. You want to learn about the donor's life mission, help them learn more about your institutional mission, and decide where they overlap. You want to listen to what they're saying and reflect on what you're learning about them so you can look for matches between their interests and your initiatives.

We covered cultivation strategies in-depth in chapter 8. To refresh your memory, you can use the Four I's to engage with your current and prospective donors proactively and further develop relationships:

- Inform: Do they have enough information about us?
- Invite: Have we invited them to participate in ways that would be meaningful to them?
- Involve: How can we take them beyond participation to genuine involvement?
- Inquire: What could we learn about ourselves from them?

## QUESTIONS TO ASK DONORS

Below is a list of ten potential questions to ask your current and prospective donors:

1. Tell me about your life.
2. How would you describe your personal mission?
3. How did you first hear about us?
4. Do you have a personal connection to our mission?
5. What is your impression of the organization?
6. What interests you most about the organization?
7. What would you like to see improved or changed?
8. Why did you first give to the organization? What inspired your gift?
9. What are the most critical outcomes you expect from us?
10. Could you see yourself becoming more involved with our organization?

For more suggestions, a simple internet search for "potential donor questions" will provide more than enough ideas.

## Ask

Next to "Who should I ask," "How much should I ask for" is probably the most mulled-over question in major gift solicitation. Remember, your goal is to find the intersection between what your organization needs and what your donor wants to accomplish.[4] Determining that magic number can seem like a tall task. Ask for too much, and you risk the sting of rejection. Too little, and you could leave money on the table. It's tempting to speak in more vague terms, asking instead for "help" or "support" in hopes your donor will offer the exact amount you need. Unfortunately, it doesn't usually work like that. You need to be prepared to ask for a specific amount based on data points available for your consideration.[5]

## Researching financial capacity

Gathering information to help you gauge an appropriate amount for your request will take some detective work. However, even without a research team or wealth screening services, you can still gather useful information about your prospective donor to inform your ask.

Before we progress, let's go ahead and acknowledge that sometimes there's a certain "ick factor" that goes along with researching people's financial situations. Considering potential wealth indicators like what someone does for a living or how much their house is worth can seem impolite at best and invasive at worst. Scouring another nonprofit's annual report or donor wall for prospective donors can feel a little like cheating. You may start to feel better about the process the more you do it—especially as you see how helpful the information can be in formulating an appropriate ask. That said, while it's good to stretch yourself a little, don't feel pressured to go too far outside your comfort zone here. If combing through this type of information isn't your thing, feel free to recruit another trusted researcher to help you. (Just underscore to everyone involved that this information should be kept confidential. Refer back to the Donor Bill of Rights and your fundraising policies for guidance.)

It may also be helpful to keep in mind that women and people of color may give differently than their white, male counterparts. As you review your sources of information, consider whether you might be missing opportunities to develop more diverse relationships. Women and people of color are most certainly among those with the capacity to make significant gifts to charities, but sometimes fundraisers fail to cultivate these relationships and make donation requests of them at the same rate or level. If your organization has prioritized diversity, put strategies in place to ensure your fundraising also reflects this commitment, which will likely extend into prospect research.

In addition to the information you find through formal searches and inquiries, you will also want to keep track of pertinent details shared through building relationships. Tracking things like kids graduating from college or the decision to sell a business can give you clues about financial capacity, as well as appropriate timing for a request. Life transitions such as weddings, divorces, retirements, and caring for aging parents can all play a role in someone's philanthropic inclinations. It's also important to keep tabs (when possible) on significant commitments to other nonprofits. If someone just gave a stretch gift to an organization down the road, they may not be ready for a similar request from your nonprofit, even if they have the capacity. Timing is as important as the amount when it comes to asking for money.

## Determining a starting point

Fundraising resources will often offer formulas to use as a starting point for determining your ask amount. Some recommend choosing a baseline amount from past donations and multiply it by three or five for a face-to-face ask. This might work for you, and if nothing else, it can serve as a starting point from which you may move up or down depending on the situation. Consider how you feel about that amount and what you've learned about the prospective donor. Is it in line with what you know about them from the relationship you've built? How do extenuating circumstances in their lives influence it? Does it make sense in relation to what you're trying to accomplish? Is it enough to allow you to demonstrate good outcomes with the investment in your organization?

Always factor past giving to your organization into your request. While giving to other charities should be considered in determining capacity and interests, it does not necessarily equate to inclination. Your donor likely has relationships with other nonprofits, and some of those may be deeper and more connected. That's why giving to your organization informs your baseline number, if possible. It's also helpful to realize that your ask amount (or range) is just the start of negotiations.[6]

## Don't surprise your donor

As you progress toward an eventual ask of your prospective donor, you need to set the stage, ensuring both you and your donor are prepared. You want both sides to be well-informed, and you certainly don't want the ask to come as a surprise to the donor. If you think it will be helpful, consider a "premeeting" to discuss the organization's mission, initiatives, and plans and to determine the donor's interests and priorities as they relate to your organization. By cluing the donor in to your intentions, this meeting also asks for permission to make the request. If the donor is on board, you should determine their interest and possibly answer any lingering questions about their involvement and potential commitment levels.[7] The result will be a well-informed, personalized proposal for their consideration.

An ask for financial support is an invitation. It deserves thorough preparation. Make sure you create a proposal tailored specifically for the donor. If they are numbers people, give them statistics and charts. If they prefer the more personal aspects of your organization's work, tell them stories about people who will benefit from their investment in your project. If they are visual, show them photos. Don't worry about stretching your budget to create flashy, expensive packets. The merits of the project, and the fact that you've tailored them to your donor, should speak for themselves.

When the time comes to schedule the visit, make sure you set an appointment and plan to meet with the prospective donor in a comfortable and private place (restaurants and other public places are not good choices). If an in-person visit isn't feasible, you can find out if the donor would be willing to meet via an online meeting platform.

If you are going to bring someone with you to the visit (such as a staff/board member team), make a special effort to coordinate the visit with that person. Make notes and rehearse who will say what. Brainstorm possible questions the donor may ask and take time to develop your responses. Decide how you will present your request and practice saying it out loud. Be sure your pitch underscores why the gift is needed right now and connect it to meaningful outcomes that demonstrate how impactful it would be to the organization's work.

## Wait for it

You're asking the donor for a significant commitment, so don't panic if they don't answer right away. It means they're considering many factors. They're probably doing some mental math and possibly thinking who else needs to be involved in the decision (such as spouses, children, or financial and legal advisers). It's tempting to try and fill the (uncomfortable) silence, but do your best to wait. Let your donor speak first. Their reaction will gauge where the conversation will head from there. They may say yes, they may say no, or they may want to negotiate. If you think through each of these scenarios ahead of time, you will feel more comfortable about your response in any of these cases.

Regardless of their response, make sure you follow up with the donor after the visit. If they respond favorably to your proposal, be sure to send them all the necessary paperwork or information. If they say no, thank them again for their time and circle back to update your cultivation plan. Unless they've indicated a preference not to receive future solicitations, you can request permission to continue building the relationship, keeping them abreast of new developments and opportunities. Once you're back in the office, make sure to update their donor record and initiate your stewardship plan.

While major gifts may play an important role in helping you meet your annual fund goals, they are also often directed toward specific project goals. Now that we've reviewed how to apply the fundraising cycle to your larger gift requests, let's take a look at some specific considerations for special project and capital campaign requests.

## Raising Funds for Specific Projects

Although some generous donors and foundations will provide funding for general operating expenses—such as staffing and overhead—many prefer to fund specific priorities or projects. Whether these are public programs, special events, capital building expenses, collections care projects, or some other contained initiative, they generally have a predefined timeline with specific target audience outcomes.

## Design, Develop, and Deliver Your Projects

When you decide to pursue major gifts, you need to have well-defined, impactful projects to pitch to potential donors. Spend some time prioritizing your projects so you're ready to talk about your opportunities (and make sure your spokespeople can do the same). Here are a few suggestions that can help with project design and development and delivery once you secure the funding you need.

*Base projects on data-informed needs*
Be able to answer the question, "How do you know this is needed?" and back it up with data. You can use survey results, a report from a building study or collections assessment, a comparison of museum best practices, or even benchmarking from other organizations.

*Understand the scope and cost of the project*
Work from a well-developed implementation plan that takes the project from start through completion. When you talk to a donor about your goals, you want to inspire confidence that (with their gift) you will have the capacity to complete the work.

*Designate a project manager*
Every kitchen needs a head chef, and the same is true for your projects. Designate a manager. It doesn't necessarily have to be the same person who is raising money for the project. Just make sure to keep the project manager in the loop about funding developments. You will likely also want to work with the project manager to develop your proposal when the time comes.

*Phase the project when possible*
Sometimes we have to undertake significant projects that aren't likely to be covered by one funding source. We may find that we need to combine major gifts with grants to accomplish our goals. In this case, it's helpful to break the larger project down into smaller, contained phases if possible. For example, a collections care initiative might involve a collections assessment in phase one, new storage units in phase two, hiring temporary help with cataloging and rehousing in phase three, and a public exhibit in phase four. Each of these phases might require separate (and possibly multiple) funding requests.

*Develop a project budget*

When you sit down to talk through a proposal with a potential major donor, they may want to know your numbers. They may want to see the project expenses broken down and learn about other income sources supporting the project. Don't forget to add staff or volunteer time to the budget so the donor can understand the people resources that will be needed to complete the project and achieve the desired outcomes. You should also anticipate that they may want to know what it will cost to keep the program going beyond their initial investment.

*Make a case for support*

When meeting with a major donor, go through the trouble to prepare a proposal to help you make your case. This might be a formal case statement with supporting documentation; it might be a little less traditional in other cases. You will likely have a sense of what's appropriate with each donor. The bottom line is that you will want to be prepared to make your case using whatever resources you have at your disposal.

*Bonus step: Find a matching donor*

Some donors (and foundations) are keen on matching gifts. Also known as challenge gifts, they are designed to encourage giving from others. In these cases, a donor offers to match up to a certain amount of other people's contributions. This can be an excellent way to encourage lower-level donors to get involved and double their donations using the major donor's leadership gift. This can be especially useful when kicking off new projects or making the final push to secure the last bit of needed funding.

## Capital Campaigns

You hear a lot about capital campaigns these days. It seems like nonprofit organizations are always either preparing for, in the middle of, or wrapping up a major campaign. While common among universities and hospital networks, other nonprofits—including heritage, arts, and culture organizations—also engage in campaigns. The most critical factor is not size or even years in existence but a well-developed network of supporters and a solid record of past fundraising success. A capital campaign is an advanced fundraising initiative that requires a great deal of planning, coordination, and most importantly, a strong fundraising foundation. Organizations work their way up to capital campaigns as they build stronger relationships and garner increasing levels of support from donors and funders. We're not going to spend a lot of time talking about capital campaigns because if you decide to pursue a capital campaign, you will need resources and reference materials beyond what this book is intended to provide. For now, this can serve as a jumping-off point to provide an overview.

Capital campaigns are extended, multiyear, coordinated fundraising efforts intended to raise significant sums of money for a specific project (or projects). Organizations frequently seek outside expert fundraising advice from consultants who specialize in capital campaigns. This often starts with a feasibility study to better understand people's perception of the organization and gauge their willingness to support a significant fundraising effort.

Capital campaigns are divided into two phases: the quiet phase, during which the organization raises a certain percentage of their goal with major gifts, and a public phase, where most of the remaining contributions come in smaller amounts from a greater number of donors. Usually, by the time an organization moves into the public phase by announcing their capital campaign, they have already secured a significant amount of funds (anywhere from 50%–70% of the total campaign goal).

As mentioned, capital campaigns are part of an advanced fundraising strategy. They require a solid foundation of past fundraising success. Organizations that undertake a capital campaign must invest many resources—particularly time, money, and people—to succeed. You don't want to *start* a major gift program with a capital campaign. They should be considered only after annual and major gift initiatives are well established and the organization can call on a cadre of dedicated staff and volunteers to help with planning, implementation, solicitation, and stewardship. When and if you think you are ready for a capital campaign, you will find many resources available online and through fundraising consultants, community foundations, and leaders with capital campaign experience at other heritage organizations.

## Notes

1. Jennifer Weber, "How to Determine the Right Ask Amount for a Major Donor," *Nonprofit Notes* (blog), September 2016, https://www.nonprofitnotes.com/how-to-determine-the-right-ask-amount-for-a-major-donor-a-5-step-process/.

2. Claire Axelrad, "Top Strategies to Kickstart Major Gift Fundraising," *Bloomerang* (blog), December 27, 2018, https://bloomerang.co/blog/top-strategies-to-kickstart-major-gift-fundraising/.

3. Richard Perry, "How to Qualify Donors," Major Gift Academy, accessed December 30, 2020, https://www.majorgiftacademy.com/wp-content/uploads/2018/06/How-to-Qualify-Donors.pdf.

4. Amy Eisenstein, "How to Determine an Exact Ask Amount for Each of Your Major Gift Donors, *Amy Eisenstein* (blog), accessed December 30, 2020, https://www.amyeisenstein.com/determine-exact-ask-amount-major-gift-donors/.

5. Weber, "How to Determine the Right Ask Amount for a Major Donor."

6 Weber, "How to Determine the Right Ask Amount for a Major Donor."

7. Weber, "How to Determine the Right Ask Amount for a Major Donor."

# Grant Funding

Grant funding can be a terrific boost to your organization. It can cover the expenses for an innovative new program. You can use it to provide a much-needed leg up for collections care initiatives or build capacity to help springboard your organization to its next big thing. It can also help you establish relationships with funders that can lead to increased partnership and investment levels. If you've never written a grant proposal before, there's one surefire way to change that: write a grant proposal. Will it be perfect the first time? Probably not. Will you learn something every time you write a new one? I know I certainly do. Much of what you can learn about writing good grant requests is transferrable, regardless of the amount or funder. This chapter will cover some of the basics to help you feel more comfortable and confident about your proposals.

## Being "Grant Ready"

Grant-funded projects should be a natural extension of the work you're already doing. They should align with your mission and fit strategically into what the organization is trying to accomplish. As we go through the grant process, it's important to remember that you should pursue grant funding that aligns with your objectives, not the other way around. Don't create programs or projects to fit grant opportunities. That's a recipe for disaster that can lead to overcommitment, poor performance, and mission creep. A big part of being grant ready means you know how grants can strategically fit into what your organization is working to accomplish.[1]

### WHAT IS MISSION CREEP?

"Mission creep" is a term borrowed from the military that refers to the gradual shifting away from original objectives. Also known as "mission drift," it occurs when an organization expands its focus beyond the original scope or goals. In other words, the nonprofit creeps or strays from its intended mission, often investing resources in an area outside of the original focus while diluting efforts that impact the organization's initial intent.

# Who Gives Grants?

Generally, foundations or trusts, corporations, or government departments offer grants to organizations to cover administrative or program expenses for a set period (known as a grant cycle). Foundations can either be private entities or grantmaking public charities.[2] In private foundations, their money comes from individuals, families, or a corporation, and they must meet a threshold for giving a certain amount of their assets each year. Grantmaking public charities, also called public foundations, get their money from several different sources. Examples would be community foundations and other grantmaking organizations such as United Way. If you want to learn more about a potential funder (in addition to what you find on their website), you can access their form 990s online. (GuideStar by Candid is a good place to start.) Many 990s provide a list of grantees and award amounts.

## Types of Grants

Grantmakers have the freedom to designate their funding priorities, specifying the types of activities they want to fund. Grants can be divided (and then subdivided) into two different categories: those meant for general purpose or operating support and those directed toward programs and projects.[3]

General operating support grants help the organization cover administrative and overhead costs associated with its daily business. This might include personnel, supplies, or occupancy expenses such as utilities and maintenance. Although general operating support grants are highly coveted by nonprofit organizations, they are usually very competitive and less common in the grant world. These types of grants may come as the result of relationships built between the funder and nonprofit over time, often after the successful completion of a project grant (or grants). Funders may also offer general operating support to start-up organizations or increase giving in this area in response to emergency situations.

Program or project grants are divided into several different subsets of grants. These might include funding for project planning or implementation, research projects, capacity building initiatives (including management training and technical assistance), or capital expenses, such as facilities and equipment.

## Where to Look for Grants

Several organizations offer grants specifically for museums and other arts and culture institutions. A few national examples worth checking out include:

- The Institute for Museums and Library Services (IMLS)
- The National Endowment for the Humanities (NEH)
- The National Historical Publications and Records Commission (NHPRC)
- The Costume Society of America
- The National Endowment for the Arts (NEA)

It's worth noting that some of these organizations—including IMLS and the NEH—offer grants specifically for small museums and heritage organizations. It is also worth mentioning that the registration, application, and reporting requirements for federal grants can sometime be rather (very) arduous. In order to apply for a federal grant, you must register in the System for Awards Management and submit your application online through the federal website (www.grants.gov). If you plan to apply for a government grant, start this process right away because it can take several weeks to verify and process your registration. Also, be sure you understand the reporting expectations should you receive an award. Depending on the grant, these could be a little more detailed and stricter than other grant reports you've filed.

You can also look for grants from state historical societies and humanities councils, as well as state and regional arts commissions. Don't forget to check closer to home by reaching out to area community foundations, as well as local private and corporate foundations.

There are many search engines and databases that can assist you in your search for grants. In addition to visiting the organizations listed above, you can use your state's association of nonprofits as a reference.[4] There are subscription-based search engines such as GrantStation or the Foundation Directory Online, but they can be costly for smaller organizations. Luckily, Candid, the company that offers the Foundation Directory Online, supports Funding Information Network locations. These are sites (often public libraries or universities) that offer free, on-site access to the Foundation Directory Online.[5] You can search for federal government grants (including those from the NEH and NEA) for free on the government grants website at Grants.gov. Finally, you might be surprised what you can learn from a good old-fashioned internet search and by word of mouth. Find out who is funding other local nonprofits and economic development groups, and don't be afraid to talk to funders about who else might be interested in the work you do.

## Finding a Good Match

After you've done your research and located a grant you think might be a good fit, you will want to visit that organization's website to get more information. Look for the grant guidelines or request for proposal (RFP), and be sure to read it carefully. There are several factors you'll want to consider to help determine whether to pursue funding through any particular grant program. You can also call program officers directly to talk about their funding opportunities. This is a great way to start building your relationship with them, and they can answer questions and provide direction that will save you time and probably make your proposal package more competitive should you decide to apply.

### SMALL FAMILY FOUNDATIONS

Many small family foundations do not have a robust website (or sometimes any website at all). In these cases, you may have to write or call the organization's representative directly to inquire about their grant opportunities. This may take some creative contact management, so don't be afraid to do some networking. If you have a community foundation in your area, that can be a good place to start.

## Eligibility

Most grant funders have established eligibility criteria. Many require 501(c)(3) tax-exempt status, although some (especially government grants) are open to public higher education institutions, state and local government agencies, and Native American tribal governments. Some grants are geographically focused on specific regions, states, or counties. Others target organizations of particular sizes (usually determined by the annual budget). You may also see specifications about the organization's mission and work. For instance, a grant funder may require a history or art-focused mission, or they may stipulate that the organization demonstrates a commitment to diversity and inclusion.

> ### WHAT IS A SMALL MUSEUM?
>
> According to the American Association for State and Local History Small Museums Committee, a small museum typically:[1]
>
> - has an annual budget of less than $250,000;
> - operates with a small staff with multiple responsibilities; and
> - employs volunteers to perform key staff functions.
>
> _____
>
> 1. "Small Museums," AASLH, accessed May 29, 2021, https://aaslh.org/communities/smallmuseums/.

## Funding priorities

Once you have confirmed eligibility, you must then consider the stated funding priorities. Like you, most funders are trying to make an impact in specific areas, so be sure to consider whether your proposed project fits with what they're trying to accomplish. It can be tempting to either contort your plans to meet their priorities or, worse, to create programming just to gain access to their potential funding. Resist. Your goal is to find a priority match between your organization and the funder, not force one where it doesn't naturally exist.

## Timelines

Make sure you understand the funder's timeline and steps to the application process. Look at due dates. Are they asking for an LOI? (Before they look at a full proposal, some funders will request an LOI—or a letter of intent (or inquiry or interest)—which can extend the timeline. More on this below.) Other funders may require you to contact a program officer to discuss the project before you apply. You will also want to consider the proposal deadline. Do you have enough time to create a high quality application? Next, look at the notification and award dates. Do they fit with your project timeline? Some grants (particularly government grants) have very long turnaround times. Finally, make sure you understand the duration of the grant cycle. Most are one-year grants, but some are shorter, and others are spread over multiple years. Make sure you can accomplish your proposed outcomes in the time allotted.

## ROI

When you find a possible grant match, it can be tempting to jump in with both feet. However, stop and consider your potential return on investment (ROI). Although it may be difficult to believe, there are some grants out there that just aren't worth the trouble. Be on the lookout for long, complex applications for relatively small grant amounts. Exceedingly long applications, complex budget templates, and additional requirements such as videos can take a lot of time to complete. Consider what your time is worth in relation to the potential grant award.

## Grant Proposal Format

While each grant proposal format is different, there are common elements that repeatedly appear in most applications. Whether you are answering questions in an online form or writing a freeform narrative, you may feel more confident with the entire process once you become familiar with the most common categories and questions.

## LOI

If the funder requires a LOI, they generally want a big-picture view of your proposed project. Your LOI will probably have two components: a project summary and some sort of confirmation of institutional readiness. For the project summary, make sure you identify your (hopefully compelling) need, propose reasonable solutions, and confirm that your anticipated outcomes will address the need. To demonstrate institutional readiness, you may want to share some history about your organization's accomplishments and detail aspects that contribute to your success, such as programming, community engagement, qualifications of key people, facilities, and external assessments and training. Be sure to address any specific questions required by the funder.

## Proposal

The grant guidelines or online application portal should provide additional information about how to structure your proposal. Be sure to read through each section carefully. Although each application will be different, funders are all trying to understand your need, why it's important, how you propose to address the need, what your intended results will be, and how you will make a difference to the people you serve.

### Data-informed need

You're requesting funding to address a particular need or opportunity. Explain that need, providing context so a grant reviewer can understand how it was identified and why it should be addressed. (You may want to discuss the consequences if that need goes unmet.) Data-informed means you have facts and evidence to support your claims.

### Project overview

You'll want to walk the reviewer through your project so they understand the linear cause and effect of what you're proposing. This can be divided into two parts: your planned work and your intended results

Many funders, program managers, and professional grant writers use logic models to help develop and explain projects. They are like road maps for your project. Logic models can seem a little daunting at first, but it's important to remember that there's no one right way to complete a logic model. It's a tool, not a test. Using a logic model can help you think through your project and better explain it to potential funders.

# LOGIC MODEL

| Objectives | Inputs | Activities |
|---|---|---|
| Define project goals and specific solutions that will address the need. Make them S.M.A.R.T. (specific, measurable, actionable, realistic, and timely). | Identify resources needed to implement the solution. Consider resources currently available as well as those you must acquire. | Describe the project's planned work. Consider implementation of the project "to-do" list. |

| Outputs | Outcomes | Impact |
|---|---|---|
| Describe the results, products, and services that will directly result from project activities. *Answer: "What will we do?"* _____ How will this be measured? | Detail the short-term changes or benefits the target population will realize from project activities. *Answer: "What difference will we make?"* _____ How will this be measured? | Anticipate the long-term changes or benefits the organization and broader community might expect because of the project. _____ How will this be measured? |

**Figure 16.1.**  Logic Model

As you can see from figure 16.1, your planned work consists of your objectives, inputs, and activities:

1. What do you aim to do (objectives)?
2. What resources (inputs) will go to the project?
3. What activities will be implemented?

Your intended results are your outputs, outcomes, and impact:

4. What will you do? What products, services, or activities will you create (outputs)?
5. What difference will it make (outcomes)?
6. How will it affect your audience(s) in the long run (impact)?

## LOGIC MODEL QUESTIONS

What problem, situation, or opportunity will your project address (NEED)?

What is the desired end-state? At the end of the project, what difference will it have made (OUTCOMES)? How will you measure this?

What specific solutions will address this need (OBJECTIVES)?

What is the work plan for this project? What steps must be undertaken to make this happen (ACTIVITIES)?

What resources are needed in order to successfully execute this plan (INPUTS)?

What products or services will come as a result of the project activities? What will have been done (OUTPUTS)? How will you measure this?

How will this project allow you to do something you can't currently do or allow you to do it better (IMPACT)? How will you measure this?

Logic models take a little practice, but there are many useful resources online to help you work through them. When you're faced with a limited character count and need to explain your project concisely in your application, logic models can be a great way to organize your thinking and help tie your proposed outcomes to the work you're asking the funder to support.[6]

## Implementation

Most funders will ask you to explain your implementation plan in detail, expecting you to detail how the project will be initiated, managed, and completed. You will need to set a timeline, outline project team responsibilities, and define critical project milestones. It can help to track your project using a project schedule (known as a Gantt chart) or an implementation plan template.

## Evaluation

Project proposals should address what success looks like and how you know when you've achieved it. Your funder will likely want to see how you plan to track, document, measure, and evaluate your project results. Thinking through this will also help you determine how you'll collect data for your final report and may help you determine whether you can meet the requirements of that report. Although you will want to demonstrate good results to your funder, assessment is critical for your internal understanding of your current project and the development of future initiatives. We're going to cover evaluation in more depth in chapter 19.

## Sustainability

Some funders will want to understand how your proposed project fits with your long-term goals. They will want to know how the outputs and outcomes will contribute to your organization's sustainability. In these cases, you may want to highlight your next logical steps (or phases) and demonstrate how you will continue the momentum generated by this project. If applicable, you may also want to discuss how it will increase your ability to attract diverse funding in the future.

## Attachments

Make sure to take note of the funder's requested attachments; it might be a good idea to create a checklist. Although the requirements will vary from one funder to the next, these are some of the most common:

- Annual operating budget: Depending on the application timing, the funder may want to see your organizational budget for the current fiscal year, last year, or the coming year (or even a combination of the three). Sometimes they want to see the entire budget, and sometimes they just want the number (which would be your budgeted expenses for the year). Double-check to see if your funder wants you to use a specific template for the budget.
- Project budget: The project budget is an essential piece of the application, as it demonstrates that you've accounted for the expenses related to your project

**Worksheet 16.2.**

## PROJECT IMPLEMENTATION PLAN

| DATE | TASK | DEADLINE | TEAM MEMBER | STATUS | NOTES |
|---|---|---|---|---|---|
| JANUARY | | | | | |
| | | | | | |
| | | | | | |
| | | | | | |
| FEBRUARY | | | | | |
| | | | | | |
| | | | | | |
| | | | | | |
| MARCH | | | | | |
| | | | | | |
| | | | | | |
| APRIL | | | | | |
| | | | | | |
| | | | | | |
| | | | | | |
| MAY | | | | | |
| | | | | | |
| | | | | | |
| | | | | | |
| JUNE | | | | | |
| | | | | | |
| | | | | | |
| JULY | | | | | |
| | | | | | |
| | | | | | |
| | | | | | |
| AUGUST | | | | | |
| | | | | | |
| | | | | | |
| SPETEMBER | | | | | |
| | | | | | |
| | | | | | |
| OCTOBER | | | | | |
| | | | | | |
| | | | | | |
| | | | | | |
| NOVEMBER | | | | | |
| | | | | | |
| | | | | | |
| | | | | | |
| DECEMBER | | | | | |
| | | | | | |
| | | | | | |
| | | | | | |

activities. It also helps the funder understand the cost of the individual parts that make up the project. There are several questions you need to consider as you work through your project budget:

1. Do they provide a template to use, or can I use my own?
2. Are my estimates based on reliable quotes?
3. If I include staff compensation, have I accounted for payroll taxes, and do I plan to track time spent on the project?
4. Should I include contingency funds? If so, how much?
5. Can I include indirect costs?
6. If there is a match requirement, will cost-sharing and in-kind donations count toward the match?
7. Is the budget balanced? Have I accounted for all of my expenses in the incomes section so that they zero out?

## INDIRECTS, COST-SHARING, AND IN-KIND: GRANT PROPOSAL BUDGET TERMS

When preparing a grant proposal budget, it's helpful to be familiar with the following terms:

- **Indirect Costs:** These are expenses of doing business that apply to more than one business activity. They are not assigned to a specific project or organizational activity because they benefit the organization as a whole. Examples include administrative salaries, rent, and utilities. Indirect cost rates for federal grants must be negotiated ahead of time, although you can usually charge the minimum rate of 10 percent. If the funder's guidelines do not specifically address indirect costs, it is appropriate to contact a program officer and ask for guidance.
- **Required Match:** Some funders will require organizations to match the awarded funds at a specific percentage or ratio. For instance, a funder may require a 2:1 match, meaning that the organization must provide twice as much money toward the project as the grant award (e.g., $20,000 to match a $10,000 grant). It's important to understand how that match can be achieved. Some funders may require a cash match, while others will allow matches through cost-sharing or in-kind donations.
- **Cost-Sharing:** These are contributions of resources that the organization makes toward the project outside of what comes from the funder. For instance, if the organization will dedicate staff resources to a project but does not ask for funding to cover these salaries, that can be classified as a cost-share. Sometimes cost-shares can be counted when the funder requires a match. For example, if the organization covers the salary of a project coordinator, they may be able to count that person's compensation toward the match for time spent working on the project. It's always a good idea to clarify the specifications with the funder's program officer.
- **In-Kind Donations:** These are noncash donations made to an organization, usually in the form of goods, services, time, or expertise. In some cases, in-kind donations can be counted toward a match requirement. For example, if a partner designs and creates interpretive signage for a grant-funded exhibit, the organization may be able to count the value of this in-kind donation toward their match.

- Budget justification: The budget justification might be part of the budget template or a separate section or document. The budget justification is a useful supplement to the budget because it allows you to further explain the line items in your budget, giving you an opportunity to "justify" each of your proposed expenses. The budget justification is a chance for you to "show your work" in terms of how you calculated each cost. For example, suppose you've proposed personnel compensation in your budget. In that case, you could use the justification to explain the hourly wage (or base salary), as well as payroll taxes and benefits, if applicable. It might also include how many hours per week that person will spend on the project. Similarly, if you're proposing the purchase of collections care furniture, your justification could detail the price of each unit, plus shipping, handling, and installation costs. You might also briefly explain why you chose one vendor over another.
- Board list with affiliations: Funders often want to see your board list with details about each member, including their professional associations (such as employer and job title) and possibly any other nonprofit leadership roles (such as service on other boards). Not only does this help the funder understand the leadership of the organization, but it helps them identify areas of potential conflicts of interest (such as one of their proposal reviewers also sitting on your board of directors).
- Confirmation of nonprofit status: You can usually achieve this by including a copy of your IRS tax determination letter. If you don't have the original letter, you can request a certified copy from the state office that handles nonprofit registration.
- Most recent fiscal year financial statements (or audit): Don't be surprised if a funder wants to see your financial statements and sometimes your most recent audit, especially for larger grant requests. Some funders will accept unaudited statements from smaller organizations. If you'd like to apply for a grant that requires audited statements and you don't have them, reach out to the funder to see if there is a workaround—it never hurts to ask.
- Additional supporting documents: Some funders may request (or give the option for) supplemental materials such as letters of support or agreement (from partners, landlords, or others who will be involved in the project). You may also have the opportunity to submit project-specific documents such as assessment reports, quotes, or "before" photos. Some funders also require or give the option for video submissions.

## Application Submission

Make sure you understand the submission process well before you start working on the grant application. If you're working from an online grant portal, make sure you log in ahead of time and get familiar with the format. If you wait until the deadline to do this, you may not reach a program officer to help you if you have technical difficulties. Check to see how the program saves your work. You may have to save manually before exiting the system, so make a note of this. There's nothing more frustrating than losing hours of work because you didn't hit "save." Also, note the required format for attachments; they often need to be PDF documents.

If the funder requires paper copies sent by the postal service or another carrier, be sure to note how many copies they need of each document. You will also want to pay attention to whether the deadline is set by postmark or delivery date. While it might be tempting to send the application package with a signature required, this is not always a good option for the funder. You risk having your application excluded from consideration if it gets redirected to the post office. It's better to send the application early, with plenty of time for delivery, and retain a tracking number.

# Reporting

It's easy to get caught up in the grant application to-do list and neglect to look at the reporting requirements should your proposal receive funding. Before you apply, you must understand the reporting expectations. Many foundations include a copy of their grant report form online. It's helpful to look this over to ensure that your organization can track the required information. If you don't find any information about the end-of-grant report, you can call the funder and ask about the reporting process. Just be aware up front that some grants, especially those from the federal government, can include detailed tracking and reporting requirements. It's better to know these expectations ahead of time so you can honestly evaluate your ability to gather data and meet the reporting requirements.

When you receive a successful grant application notification, you will likely also receive a grant agreement to sign and return. Make sure to note all agreement terms and requirements, and keep a copy of the signed documents. Plan ahead for reporting deadlines (for both interim and final reports). Notify your team about the terms of the grant and the expectations for reporting so you can identify what to track, how, and by whom. You will also want to put into place a system for keeping track of receipts and other paperwork. If the grant includes personnel costs, be very clear about how they should track their work on the project (clarify with the funder, if needed).

The project manager should follow the proposed project timeline and check in with team members to monitor their progress. You will also want to regularly update your project budget with actual revenue and expense amounts.

When it's time to begin working on the report, use the report template as a guide to gather feedback from team members. Allow plenty of time to create and collect the needed materials. Identify attachments required (such as financial statements, completed budgets, before and after photos, and sample materials) well ahead of time. Don't forget to build in time for review and revisions in addition to writing time.

In addition to securing much-needed funds for your organization, grant writing can be a great way to open dialogue between team members, organize your goals into a realistic plan, and continue building relationships with supporters. If you follow the tips from this chapter and continue to learn with each new proposal, you will find that you are more confident and comfortable—and likely more successful—with your grant writing efforts.

## GRANT CHECKLIST

_____ Set up a grant calendar to keep track of proposal submission and report deadlines.

_____ Read and understand the guidelines (if you have a question, call a program officer and ask).

_____ Review every page of the organization's website related to the grant process and read the entire request for proposal (RFP) or grant guidelines document.

_____ Access the online grant portal early on in the process to make sure you can log in. Get familiar with the format. Understand how to save your work.

_____ Work from a separate word processing document to create a master copy in case the online form doesn't save.

_____ Use formatting (such as bullets, bold type, and white space) when possible.

_____ Pay attention to character or word limits as well as specifications about font size and margins if you will need to submit separate documents. (Note whether you're working with characters or words before you begin writing!)

_____ Look for and follow writing prompts with each section or question. Be sure to address all requested information.

_____ Don't make your reviewers guess what you're proposing to do. Lay out your plan and be specific about how you will use the money. Make the ask.

_____ Remember that your reviewers may not be familiar with your organization or its community impact, so don't make assumptions about what they might know. Write for an educated stranger and avoid acronyms, jargon, and place references that are specific to your community or your work.

_____ Provide context for the need you're trying to address. Help reviewers understand the cause-and-effect relationship by tying need to past circumstances and future plans.

_____ Talk about people, not things. Make sure you're addressing community needs, not just organization needs. When discussing objects, collections, or buildings, always bring it back to the people you serve.

_____ Tell a story. Engage your reader with a "hook" and try to stir an emotional attachment to your cause. Create a memorable visual impression.

_____ Don't overlook implementation. Identify the project team's responsibilities. Present a complete timeline and clearly note project milestones.

_____ Edit, then edit again. Make every word count; if it's not relevant, leave it out. Try not to repeat yourself (and never use "copy and paste" to answer a question with the exact same answer you already provided in another section). Avoid spelling and grammar errors. Run your writing through your word processor's spelling and grammar check, or use a program like Grammarly. Some writers also use the "read aloud" function in their word processing program to help them catch errors.

_____ Recruit proofreaders from outside your organization to review your writing. Getting an outside perspective will help you identify areas that need more context or explanation.

_____ Determine whether you have to use the funder's templates (such as for organization or project budgets or the budget justification).

_____ Make sure your project activities, budget, and budget justification all align. Double check that your numbers match up in all these areas.

_____ Focus less on what you'll do and more on what difference it will make. Write outcomes from audience-change perspective: start with "Visitors (researchers, members, etc.) will. . . ." Consider short-, mid-, and long-term objectives.

_____ Don't make your organization part of the problem. Remember, it exists to serve the needs of others.

# Notes

1. For more information about getting your museum or heritage organization grant ready, see Sarah Sutton, *Is Your Museum Grant-Ready?* (Lanham, MD: Rowman & Littlefield, 2018).

2. "What Is a Foundation?" Candid, accessed December 18, 2020, https://learning .candid.org/resources/knowledge-base/what-is-a-foundation/.

3. "Common Types of Grants," Minnesota Council on Foundations, accessed December 18, 2020, https://mcf.org/common-types-grants.

4. For more information, visit https://www.councilofnonprofits.org/find-your-state -association.

5. It is sometimes challenging to find the Funding Information Network location page. As of publication, the current website is https://candid.org/improve-your-non profit/funding-information-network/, but an internet search for "Funding Information Network locations" should provide the most updated link.

6. For more detailed information about logic models, look at the W. K. Kellogg Foundation's Logic Model Development Guide at https://www.wkkf.org/resource -directory/resources/2004/01/logic-model-development-guide or the Institute for Museum and Library Services Tools & Resources section on Logic Models at https:// www.imls.gov/cci/tools-resources.

# Special Events

You've probably been to a charity fundraising event. Perhaps it was a gala with dancing, a silent auction, a community-wide festival, or a 5K fun run. Maybe you have an event (or several) of your own. Some of these events make good returns, and some of them go bust. While fundraising events are often an organization's go-to when trying to generate income, even successful, well-planned, and well-executed events aren't a quick fix for budget revenue gaps. In this chapter, we will talk about how special events fit into and compliment your overall fundraising efforts. We'll go through tips for preevent planning, review event-day strategies, and talk about postevent evaluation.

## ROI

Special events should complement a well-rounded fundraising plan. They can be an essential part of donor cultivation and stewardship. However, events should not serve as a replacement for membership, annual giving, and major giving initiatives. Unfortunately, too many organizations rely on one (or more) events to raise much needed funds, often at the expense of more personalized fundraising outreach.

Perhaps an enthusiastic volunteer is leading the event planning charge. Or maybe the organization is just doing what they always do, hosting a long-standing event out of habit without reviewing its effectiveness. I suspect the popularity (and sometimes, overreliance) on events may also have something to do with their contained, project-based nature. There is a beginning and an end with events, whereas developing and implementing a fundraising plan is an ongoing, continuous effort.

To be considered a success, your event needs a positive return on investment (ROI). On the surface, this means that ticket sales must cover costs before you can raise money from an event. But that's the problem with hosting events strictly to raise funds. On the input side, it only accounts for "costs" or money put into the event; it doesn't account for things like time and effort. On the outcomes side, it doesn't consider intangibles like greater mission awareness, goodwill, and "friend-raising."

Rather than looking strictly at the bottom line to determine whether an event is successful, consider the return on objectives.[1] In addition to covering your costs and then some, what else might you be able to accomplish with your event?

- Increased public visibility
- Public education about your mission and programs
- Volunteer recruitment
- New donor prospects
- Improved donor relations

As you begin to formulate (or reformulate) your unique event plans, consider laying out your objectives ahead of time, and then determine how you can track and measure your success at meeting them. This can help you gauge an event's success beyond the bottom line.

## Choosing the Right Event

Suppose you've determined that an event fits well with your overall fundraising strategy (and you have the resources to make it successful). In that case, it makes sense to think through a few questions before committing to any particular event. Consider:

1. What are you trying to achieve? What would make this a successful event? Would you base it solely on funds raised, or will you also look at new memberships, sponsorships, and prospective donors? Many events—especially those in their first year—don't generate as much revenue as planners initially hoped. Consider whether you're approaching the event as a "get rich quick" idea or if you're looking to build a signature event that may take a few years to reach its potential. Also think through how many times you will try an event if it's not as successful as you expected the first time.
2. How can you use your organization's strengths to capitalize on the event? Remember back to the SWOT analysis from chapter 4. Do your buildings or grounds lend themselves well for a particular type of event? Can something from your unique history translate into an intriguing theme? Do you have a large cadre of dedicated volunteers at the ready? How can you use these strengths to your advantage?
3. What events are in line with your mission? Events can take a tremendous amount of time and effort to plan and execute, sometimes at the expense of other organizational priorities. You want the event type, theme, and format to fit with your mission. Your goal is to reinforce your work's importance, so ensure every aspect of your event does this.
4. What will appeal to your supporters? Identify your likely and preferred audiences during preplanning. Will you host an appreciation event for current supporters, or are you looking to broaden your reach in the community? Identify who you want to attend your event and create a plan to reach each of these audiences.

## TYPES OF EVENTS

As you draw up plans for your event, consider what type you want to host. There are many factors to consider when determining the event's theme and location. You may even want to consider brainstorming a list of pros and cons once you've narrowed your choice to a few different formats. Common fundraising events include:

- Dinners, luncheons, breakfasts, chili cook-offs, ham and bean dinners, spaghetti nights, pancake dinners, fish fry, ice cream socials, etc.
- Auctions: silent, online, or live
- Fairs and festivals
- Lectures, exhibit openings, behind-the-scenes tours
- Benefit concerts, productions
- Home and garden tours
- Tournaments and contests
- Sporting events: golf outings, distance runs, softball games, volleyball tournaments, etc.
- Wine or whiskey tastings, pub crawls, brewery tours
- "-athons" (such as walk-a-thons or dance-a-thons)
- Raffles, casino nights, and other contests (You should check with your state gaming authority before implementing these types of events. States regulate games-of-chance and you may need to apply for special permits.)
- Garage sales, car washes, bake sales, etc. (Be careful with these types of events. They tend to be more in line with the "one-off" events we're trying to avoid rather than part of a strategic plan to professionalize our fundraising efforts.)

## A Comprehensive Fundraising Event

Fundraising events are more than money in, tickets out. A comprehensive fundraising event has several components that extend beyond the cash box. As you develop your objectives, consider how your event can contribute to your larger fundraising goals. There are many revenue options you can consider beyond ticket sales, including concessions, in-kind donations, table sponsorships, a membership table, and the option to donate instead of purchasing a ticket, just to name a few. Ask your committee to brainstorm ideas at the beginning of your planning process.

### Donor relations

Special events are ideal for building stronger relationships with current donors. Consider events as part of your cultivation efforts and be deliberate in making your current donors feel included and appreciated. Assign staff or volunteers to serve as hosts for major donors. Consider printing a list of current supporters and be sure to thank them publicly. Add membership status to their name tags.

## "Friendraising"

Extend invitations to potential donors. Even if the event doesn't generate a large number of funds, it may solidify friendships for your organization that will lead to monetary support in the future. Events are a great way to broaden your reach into the community, raise awareness, and start building relationships.

## In-kind gifts

Not every gift comes in cash. Events provide a unique opportunity to solicit and receive in-kind donations of goods or services. Local businesses may be willing to contribute silent auction items. Musicians might perform for free or at a reduced rate. Even a donation of large, disposable garbage boxes will keep you from having to rent or purchase them. Highlight these contributions at your event. This will increase the visibility of your partner companies. You will also want to consult with your accountant about how to record in-kind donations and provide a gift receipt to each in-kind donor.

## Marketing

Fundraising events should fit your brand and serve as a marketing opportunity to your community, donors, and potential donors. Spend a little time defining how you will market the event to ensure your message is professional and on-point. Don't forget to explore digital marketing through your website, email communication, and social media.[2]

## Public relations

You want to generate as much "buzz" for your event as possible. Although media opportunities vary by location, it never hurts to reach out and personally invite members of the media to your event. At the very least, take time to write and distribute a press release. You can also reach out to businesses and other nonprofit partners and ask them to help you spread the word. Don't forget to include your local tourism and events commission on that list.

## Sponsorships

Events provide excellent opportunities for sponsorships. This helps you generate funds and provides visibility and positive exposure for for-profit partners. Start talking to these companies well in advance of the event before they have allocated all their sponsorship and marketing resources.[3]

## Volunteer involvement

Use events to grow and engage your team by recruiting new and returning volunteers. Assemble a strong team of volunteers to help make your event a success (but make sure you're organized enough to give them clearly defined responsibilities that make it worth their time). If you have a presenting sponsor, find out if some of their employees might like to volunteer.

# Planning Your Event

Once you've decided on the type of event you'd like to host, there are many variables to consider as you try to balance your guests' experiences with your event budget. Let's consider a few factors.

## Audience

Who's on your guest list? Determine who you plan to invite and who is most likely to attend. Is this a family-friendly event or will it be adults-only? Knowing your audience will help you make decisions about theme, location, timing, and budgets. Will your target attendees prefer an early start? Are they more likely to attend on a weekend or weeknight? Will they expect plated meals and a hosted bar or hot dogs and popcorn? You'll never plan the "perfect" event for all your constituents, but it certainly helps to identify who you're trying to reach.

## Location, Location, Location

The location may be decided by default if you're planning to host the event at your facility. Other factors may narrow your choices if you have access to a low-cost location or if you are hosting your event in coordination with a larger community celebration. If your event location is still to be determined, here are a few considerations.

- Guest convenience: Consider whether the venue is easy to find with convenient parking or public transportation. Factor in whether the location is within a reasonable travel radius so that your guests don't spend more time driving than actually attending the event. If the site isn't necessarily a mainstream "event venue," will you be able to meet your guests' needs onsite?
- Services and amenities: This goes beyond just making sure you have enough restrooms for your guests and a place to hang their coats. Consider aspects such as parking, tables and chairs, a dance floor (if needed), and catering set-up space. Don't forget the more technical aspects such as WiFi and cellular service (especially if you will be running payments onsite), lighting, sounds, and other audio-visual needs (like electrical outlets). Don't forget about your guests with special needs. Inquire about accessibility accommodations for physical access, lighting, and other assistive technology needs.
- Cost: Create your budget ahead of time so you can identify all the little things that tend to add up. When you meet with facility rental representatives, make sure you find out what's included with the event rental. Fees for tables, chairs, linens, and tableware add up, as do extras like bartenders and security personnel. Where applicable, find out if fees cover delivery, set up, and teardown of equipment (and if they don't, determine whether you will have to pay someone to do this or if you can recruit enough volunteers to help). You may also want to consider liability when deciding between on- and off-site venues, especially if alcohol will be served.

**Worksheet 17.1.** Sample Budget Template

| VENUE COSTS | |
|---|---|
| Site rental fee (Hourly or flat rate? Is there a food and beverage minimum?) | $ |
| Parking | $ |
| Permits/license | $ |
| Additional labor | $ |
| SUBTOTAL | $ |
| **RENTAL COSTS** | |
| Tables and chairs | $ |
| Pipe and drape | $ |
| Flooring | $ |
| Heat/air units | $ |
| Tents/canopies | $ |
| Risers/staging | $ |
| Stanchions | $ |
| Labor (find out if your costs include delivery, set up, and teardown) | $ |
| SUBTOTAL | $ |
| **FOOD AND BEVERAGE COSTS** | |
| Catering | $ |
| Servers/attendants | $ |
| Beverages | $ |
| Bartenders | $ |
| Food service equipment (such as hot dog steamer or popcorn popper) | $ |
| Linens (tablecloths, skirts, napkins) | $ |
| Tableware (glasses, plates, utensils, etc.) | $ |
| Labor | $ |
| Gratuities | $ |
| Health permits/licenses | $ |
| SUBTOTAL | $ |
| **AUDIO-VISUAL AND ENTERTAINMENT COSTS** | |
| Lectern/podium | $ |
| Microphones | $ |
| Sound system/speakers | $ |
| Lighting | $ |
| Photographer | $ |
| Videographer | $ |
| Overhead projectors/screen/TV monitors | $ |
| Computers/tablets (make sure systems are compatible and/or you have the required connectors) | $ |
| Wi-Fi access | $ |
| Walkie-talkies | $ |
| Generator/extension cords | $ |
| Technical staff/labor | $ |
| Entertainment (DJ/band/other talent) | $ |
| Other | $ |
| SUBTOTAL | $ |

| UTILITY AND TRASH COSTS | |
|---|---|
| Water hookup | $ |
| Portable restrooms | $ |
| Trash cans/dumpsters | $ |
| Disposal services | $ |
| Cleanup crew | $ |
| Supplies | $ |
| SUBTOTAL | $ |
| **SECURITY COSTS** | |
| Facility | $ |
| Private | $ |
| SUBTOTAL | $ |
| **INSURANCE COSTS** | |
| General Liability | $ |
| Rider | $ |
| Specialized | $ |
| SUBTOTAL | $ |
| **DECORATION COSTS** | |
| Table/stage decorations | $ |
| Stage backdrop | $ |
| Flowers/plants | $ |
| Specialty linen (stage skirting, chair covers, etc.) | $ |
| Labor | $ |
| SUBTOTAL | $ |
| **PRINTING AND SUPPLY COSTS** | $ |
| Invitations | $ |
| Tickets | $ |
| Paper and envelopes | $ |
| Postage | $ |
| Advertising | $ |
| Media kits | $ |
| Registration packets | $ |
| Programs | $ |
| Directional signage | $ |
| Menus | $ |
| Maps | $ |
| Sponsor/signage | $ |
| Nametags | $ |
| Place cards | $ |
| Thank-you cards/letters | $ |
| Other | $ |
| SUBTOTAL | $ |
| TOTAL | $ |

Adapted from the Event Sample Budget from the Home for Little Wanderers, Boston, Massachusetts, http://www.thehome.org/site/DocServer/Event_Sample_Budget.pdf.

- Flexibility for contingency plans: Certain event times and locations may need more consideration. If you're planning an outdoor event, be sure to speak with facility rental representatives about whether there is an alternate indoor space or tent to provide shelter if it rains. Similarly, if you're planning an event where adverse weather could jeopardize your plans, understand your options for postponing the event and whether you will get any money back if you have to cancel it.
- Ability to return year after year: If you're hoping to make this an annual event and the venue fits your needs, find out how far in advance you can book if you want to have the event around the same time each year. A great location contributes to your guests' experience and can serve as a motivating factor to return the next year, so you don't want to lose out on your preferred date.

## Setting the Date

There are a few things to consider when picking the perfect date for your event. First and foremost, you want to give yourself, your staff, and your volunteers plenty of lead time. Create a timeline, starting with the event and working backward.[4] Decide how much time you will give your guests to RSVP (if needed). Then backtrack for invitation mailing, printing, and design. Be sure to account for details like media promotion and contracts with other vendors (such as caterers, entertainment, lighting, and sound). If you're planning to do a silent auction, allow plenty of time to collect auction items.

You should then factor in your community schedule. Be sure your event will not overlap with any significant events for other area nonprofits or have to compete with community festivals and fairs. Depending on where you live and who's in your target audience, you may also want to factor in local schools and sports teams' schedules. Religious and secular holidays also warrant consideration. Finally, don't forget to take a look at schedules for your staff and volunteers.

## Work with a Committee

As we've already established, large-scale events require many hands. Consider whether it makes sense to create an event committee to handle the finer details. If so, try to recruit volunteers of different ages, social groups, and professional networks. Depending on the tasks at hand and the number of volunteers you have, you may want to establish subcommittees to work on specific aspects of the event, such as entertainment, decorations, ticket sales, setup, cleanup, sponsorships, auction, and catering for example.

## Room Layout and Setup

Identify your space requirements ahead of time to determine if the venue meets your needs. Besides sizing up whether the location's capacity will accommodate your guests, consider your event logistics, and designate specific areas for each activity. You may want to consider the layout for:

- Registration
- Coat check
- Restrooms
- Table placement

- Food and beverage stations
- Trash cans
- Stage/podium/mic
- AV equipment
- Mingling and networking
- Dancing or other entertainment
- Silent auction

You may have other needs that are specific to your event. Once you've settled on your space, create a room layout diagram. Share this with staff, team leaders, key volunteers, and vendors for equipment rental, catering, and beverages.

## Catering and Beverage Service

Food and beverages are usually significant expenses when hosting an event. The first time you get a catering estimate, the bottom line can be surprising. The type of service you choose will also affect the cost, so be prepared to discuss different options with your caterer. You may choose to have meals plated, served through a buffet, or at service stations throughout the venue. The type of service you select will also likely dictate your required server-to-guest ratio. Gratuity will also probably be added to your food and service costs.

You may also have sticker shock for beverage service and associated costs. If you choose to offer alcohol at your event, you will find options to pay by person or consumption. You will also have to decide what types of alcohol you want to serve (beer, wine, and spirits) and what quality (economy, midtier, or top-shelf). Even if you choose a cash bar and expect guests to pay for their alcoholic drinks, you may still have to pay for ice, disposable drinkware, extra bartenders or barbacks, full bars, and additional insurance.

### FOOD AND BEVERAGE MINIMUM

If you're hosting your event at a venue that provides catering, you may run into a food and beverage minimum. This is the specific dollar amount that you must spend on food and beverage in their selected space. In other words, if you're at a venue with a $5,000 food and beverage minimum, the final cost will be at least $5,000 (even if you don't technically order $5,000 worth of food and beverages), and the minimum reflects the base price (exclusive of tax, service charge, and gratuity).

You may find that this amount varies even from room to room within the same venue. A larger or more sought-after space could have a higher food and beverage minimum. These also sometimes vary by day of the week and tend to be higher on the weekends. The food and beverage minimum will often take the place of a room rental fee or cause it to be waived if you meet a certain threshold. Make sure you examine your contract carefully and understand how a food and beverage minimum will affect your budget.

# Get the Word Out

How you promote your event will depend, in part, on what type of event it is and which audiences you're trying to attract. You may have to prioritize according to your budget and how much time you have for each form of outreach. It might help to brainstorm a list of possibilities and then rank them, so you know where to focus your efforts. Before you begin promoting your event, make sure you have worked out registration logistics. Team members with a hand in the registration process should know what's expected of them and have a plan to keep track of attendees (and their payments, if needed).

## REGISTRATION TIPS

- Determine how your process will work. A few questions to consider are:
  - Will you request RSVPs or will you be selling tickets? Or both?
  - If guests must register what are their options for doing so? Will you offer online registration or should they register by phone, email, or in person? (Note: email is not a good method for payment exchanges; financial information such as credit card numbers should not be sent through email.)
  - Who will be responsible for handling registrations, including processing payments and updating records?
  - If you're providing physical tickets, will they be printed and distributed at the point of sale or will the person need to provide contact information so the tickets can be mailed or emailed later? Who is responsible for will call?
  - Who will be responsible for selling tickets? Will they be available through multiple outlets?
  - If physical tickets will not be distributed, does the attendee know that they need only check-in on arrival? (Emphasizing this may decrease calls from people saying they haven't received their tickets yet.)
  - When will reminders be sent out and who will send them?
- If you mail invitations, include a reply device. Provide a way for people to donate to your organization if they are not able to attend the event.
- Determine whether you will offer early bird incentives for registration, such as different price points that increase the closer you get to the event. Before doing so, consider what this will do to your bottom line and whether you think the event is likely to sell out. If you haven't reached your registration goal, hiking the price may not be a good strategy.
- Print blank registration forms for phone-in and walk-in reservations. This ensures that all required information is collected at the point of sale.
- Make sure to track dietary restrictions, as well as the need for any mobility, visual, or hearing accommodations your guests may require.
- Put plans in place to handle on-site registrations and donations. Although onsite registration may not be possible for catered events, plan ahead for event-day snafus that may require last-minute changes to registrations.
- Have a backup plan in place in case the online system crashes.

## Your website

If your organization has a website, start there. Ensure that anyone looking for information about your event can find what they're looking for on your website. Even if you aren't offering online registration, create a page with details about the event, including date, time, location, and registration process (if necessary). It would also be useful to include a phone number or email where people can get more information. If you have social media accounts, you can also add details about the event there (creating an event on your Facebook page, for example). People are used to getting their information online, and they may go to your website as soon as they hear about the event, so don't wait to get it online. Do this before you do any other promotion.

## Invitations

Depending on the type of event, you may want to send printed invitations in the mail. Although direct mail can be a good way to get someone's attention, design, printing, and postage costs can add up, so consider your return on investment. Allow plenty of time for premailing tasks and give your invitees a reasonable amount of time to sign up.

If you plan to send invitations via email, consider using an email marketing service if you're not already doing so (Constant Contact and Mailchimp are examples). Although there may be a fee associated with creating an account, these services allow you to create professional-looking templates for emails and other promotional communications. They provide a way for you to email all your contacts at once and help keep your emails from being flagged as spam. They also help ensure that your emails follow expected standards, including a way for recipients to unsubscribe.

## Advertising

Paid advertising is another option to consider. Again, weigh the pros and cons to determine whether it would be a good investment. A well-placed ad in a newspaper or through a social media site could be just what your event needs to get the word out. Or you might have options for free promotion through an in-kind donation or sponsorship. It might be worth engaging with your local newspaper or tourism bureau to get recommendations. Many news outlets and arts, culture, and tourism organizations offer free promotion through community calendars. You can also use press releases and other media contacts to promote the event and possibly even score a feature story with one of the media outlets.

## Social media

As mentioned above, social media can be an excellent way to promote your event. In addition to creating a specific page for your event, consider other ways to promote it on social media. You might want to create a hashtag specifically for the event or run a contest leading up to the big day. You could also tap local "influencers" to promote your event with their social media accounts. Be sure to tag partners and sponsors in your posts so they can help make sure your posts reach their followers as well. If you feel like your social media knowledge lacks a bit, this is your chance to engage new volunteers. Don't be afraid to recruit someone to help you expand this area of communication.

### Postevent promotion

As you're outlining your promotion plan, consider whether there are opportunities for postevent promotion. Whether through traditional or social media, an article in your next newsletter, or a blog post on your website, you can let people know how your event went. Providing a summary and talking about positive outcomes (and maybe even offering a "save the date" for next year's event) can serve as a nice wrap-up. And don't forget to include fun photos!

## Risk and Liability

There are additional risks associated with hosting events, so you will want to limit your personal and organizational liability. Be sure to comply with all local and state laws governing your event and pay special attention to any permit requirements. (Double-check with your venue, catering, and beverage providers about permits and additional insurance.) It's probably a good idea to also contact your insurance provider. It may recommend adding event-specific insurance riders to your policy. You should also ensure that your organization has directors and officers (D&O) insurance to limit your board's personal liability. Finally, consider developing an event safety plan. If you're using a venue other than your own, the site may have one you can adapt for your event. If you're using your buildings and grounds, a venue safety plan should be part of your disaster preparedness and emergency response plan.[5]

# Event Day

## Run of Show

You may find it helpful to create what event pros call a "run of show." This provides a detailed (sometimes minute by minute) account of the event day schedule. By listing delivery times, setup details, and staff assignments, pre-event prep work goes more smoothly. As you get closer to kickoff time, a run of show can help people make sure they're in the right place at the right time, and no small detail is overlooked.

Double-check that speakers and entertainers know their time limits and include technical cues (such as when to dim the lights or turn microphones on). The run of show should have key phone numbers listed (especially cell phone numbers if you're not using walkie-talkies) and should be distributed to all key personnel. Start working on the run of show sooner rather than later in your planning process as it can help you visualize the flow of the event and make sure the team has accounted for all details.

## Packing for the Event

Whether you're hosting at your site or another venue, you will need supplies on hand. From decorations to registration, use checklists to help you keep track. You'll likely need more than one—at least a to-do list and a supply list. You may find it useful to pack an event supply toolkit for your onsite needs. Items to have on hand include tape, pens, markers, highlighters, a stapler, extra name tags, a first aid kit, and important phone numbers, although you will undoubtedly have other items to add. Be sure to also include notepads for event organizers so they can make notes during the event. This will not only help you stay focused when things get hectic, but it's also a great way to capture observations of what did and didn't work well so you can improve your processes for next time.

## Dry Run

A day or two before the event, plan a dry run. Walk the venue from the parking lot through the event space. Imagine what the guest experience will be from various locations. If you're using directional signage, take a copy of your sign list so you can confirm placement and determine if additional way-finding materials are needed. Locate the restrooms and emergency exits, and make sure your event team knows where they are (you can include this information with your run of show). If possible, test sound and visual equipment ahead of time.

## Registration and Check-In

Your guests' initial interactions with the site and host team will shape their first impressions. The registration and check-in process will be one of your early opportunities to make a good impression, so try to make it run as smoothly as possible. Use greeters and directional signage to help your guests feel welcome and cut down on confusion (this is especially important if there's more than one event taking place at your venue).

If you have an extensive guest list, consider separating your lines by last names and providing separate queues for VIP guests and sponsors. If you're using assigned seating, make sure you have access to your guest list in different forms, including one by last name and another by table number. Be prepared to accommodate lines and anticipate where people will stand if the lines become long. Finally, count on no-shows, walk-ins, and last minute changes because they will happen. Help your check-in team prepare for this by explaining how they should handle the situation. Generally, it's best to have one or two people tackle reservation troubles, so consider sending guests to a designated area to deal with issues as they arise.

Where you go from here really depends on what type of event you're hosting. Refer back to your run of show to determine what other aspects of your event may need extra attention. It's always a good idea to confirm (and reconfirm) expectations with outside service providers such as valets, caterers, florists, equipment rental and audio-visual technicians, speakers, entertainers, and anyone else who is playing a role in the success of your event.

## Paying for Help

You may want to consider using an outside event planning company to assist with details for larger, more complex events. There is a cost associated with this, but even small organizations have reported that having a pro handle ticketing and registration or online silent auctions can be invaluable. This is another area where it's worth asking around for vendor recommendations to find out who provides the best service at a reasonable cost.

If setup or teardown is exhausting your core volunteers, you can also look for community partners to help. Some organizations have great success enlisting the help of local youth groups to do part of the heavy lifting. Many school programs have community service expectations for their students. A modest donation to their group (and possibly a few thank-you pizzas) can make it a win-win for everyone.

## IDEAS THAT RAISE MORE MONEY AT EVENTS

As we've discussed, not every event is going to raise a lot of money, especially in the beginning before it's well established. Ways to maximize fundraising during events are:

- Remind guests why they're there. If you have an emcee, have them talk about the organization's mission and work. Don't let people forget that the purpose of the event is to generate funds to support that work.
- Recognize supporters/sponsors. Be sure to recognize and thank sponsors and donors publicly throughout the event, both verbally and in writing, if appropriate. (Requests from anonymous donors should be honored.)
- Look for matching gift opportunities. If you have a donor or funder who is willing, matching gifts can be a good way to compel others to give. For instance, if your lead donor agrees to match up to $10,000 in gifts, they give a dollar for every dollar contributed by others during the match period.
- Consider crowdfunding. Crowdfunding and peer-to-peer fundraising can be a good way to inform and involve new supporters outside your closest circles. With crowdfunding, the organization uses the internet to encourage small donations from a large number of people toward a particular project. The project is promoted mostly through word-of-mouth and social media shares. Peer-to-peer fundraising is a crowdfunding strategy that asks individual volunteers to fundraise on behalf of your organization by reaching out to their social network.
- Organize silent and live auctions. Auctions are a popular and often effective way to raise extra funds during events. Auctions can take place on-site or online and can even complement virtual events. It's helpful to know your audience for auctions; this can help you identify what might command high profits. Keep in mind that popular auction items are often experiences rather than tangible goods. You will probably want to work with an accountant to make sure you consider all tax issues. If you're working with a professional auctioneer or auction company, make sure to ask about extra fees.
- Make tasteful merchandise available. You don't have to relocate your entire museum gift shop to your event site, but you could consider making some of your more popular items available for event attendees, or you could allow attendees to place orders for something special that is only available through the event.

You want to be sure that event attendees don't feel nickel-and-dimed, so don't overdo it. However, a few extra well-planned (and fun) ways to help raise money for the organization can be well-received. If you're not sure how guests will feel about your ideas, talk to some of your most trusted donors and loyal event attendees to get some feedback.

## Postevent

You will need one more checklist to ensure your postevent tasks are complete. You may want to start with the following and add to your list:

- Pay outstanding vendor bills.
- Thank staff and volunteers.

- Thank sponsors and donors.
- Update constituent records.
- Follow up with new contacts.
- Send surveys to participants (if using).
- Schedule an after-action meeting and make notes ahead of time.
- Discuss what went well and what can be improved at your meeting.
- Write a final report and distribute it to stakeholders.

Events are part of a robust fundraising plan. Done well, they can increase visibility, draw new audiences, facilitate relationship-building, and contribute to fundraising success. Just be sure to use your events to complement your overall fundraising efforts rather than replace them.

## Notes

1. Michele Wade, "Special Event Fundraising," Learning to Give, accessed December 31, 2020, https://www.learningtogive.org/resources/special-event-fundraising.

2. For more information, see Sammy Lau, "6 Powerful Ways to Market Your Fundraising Event for Free," *Winspire* (blog), accessed December 31, 2020, https://blog.winspireme.com/6-powerful-ways-to-market-your-fundraising-event-for-free.

3. For more information about sponsorships, visit the National Council of Nonprofits at https://www.councilofnonprofits.org/tools-resources/corporate-sponsorship or Classy at https://www.classy.org/blog/corporate-sponsorships-for-nonprofits-the-basics/ to get started.

4. To see a special event timeline sample, visit the Texas Commission on the Arts at https://www.arts.texas.gov/wp-content/uploads/2012/05/Special-Events-Timeline.pdf.

5. For more information on the American Alliance of Museums Facilities and Risk Management Core Standard document, visit https://www.aam-us.org/programs/ethics-standards-and-professional-practices/disaster-preparedness-and-emergency-response-plan/.

# Volunteers

Many small heritage organizations already know the value of volunteers. Even those with paid staff often rely on the time and expertise freely given by unpaid team members. For more than a few organizations, volunteers are their lifeblood. They are the reason the organization can accomplish most, if not all, of its work. This chapter will focus less on volunteers as collections assistants or newsletter editors and more on the important role they play on both sides of philanthropy, as donors and fundraisers.

## The Value of Volunteers

If volunteers fill the halls of your small museum or historic house, you already know their service goes far beyond usefulness. When it comes to measuring the contribution of volunteers to nonprofit work in the United States, it helps to understand just how valuable their gifts of time and talent are to individual organizations and nonprofits as a whole. According to the Corporation for National and Community Service data, one in three American adults (30.3%) volunteered for at least one organization in 2017. That's nearly 77.4 million people donating 6.9 billion hours.[1] At the current estimated national value of a volunteer hour at $27.20, the estimated worth of this service tops $187 billion.[2]

Aside from the monetary value of their work, volunteers tend to have other important qualities:[3]

- They are twice as likely to donate to charity as nonvolunteers.
- They are much more likely to be joiners—belonging to groups, organizations, and associations at five times the rate of nonvolunteers.
- They are most likely to volunteer by fundraising or selling items to raise money (35.97%).

Another study by Fidelity Charitable found that 79 percent of their donors volunteered in the last year, with 89 percent of volunteers citing an overlap between their financial and volunteer support.[4] What's our takeaway? Volunteers are more likely to be donors, and donors are more likely to be volunteers. In other words, we must examine these two relationships together. When we look at individual supporters, we must consider the value of their total contributions in volunteer hours and real dollars donated. When looking at these groups as a whole, we should consider how one can positively or negatively affect the other. A positive experience as a volunteer can influence charitable giving and vice versa. Similarly, negative experiences with one can negatively affect the other.

## Why Do People Volunteer?

Much like giving, volunteering is a values-based exchange. According to the U.S. Trust, the main factors that motivated volunteering were:[5]

1. Responding to an organizational need (65%)
2. Believing that the individual can make a difference (56%)
3. Aligning the organization with the individual's values or beliefs (52%)
4. Being concerned about those less fortunate or about serving a particular cause or group (43% each)

People volunteer for different reasons. They may be motivated by altruistic intentions to help others or support what they view as essential community causes. People may be internally motivated to use or acquire special knowledge, skills, or experiences in other situations. They may use volunteer opportunities to help them transition into new employment areas or from work to retirement. Finally, some volunteers are motivated by the social aspects. They are looking for camaraderie and a sense of belonging.[6]

## Managing a Volunteer Program

Whether you have paid staff or not, your organization will likely benefit from a more proactive, formal approach to managing your volunteer program. By establishing clear expectations on both sides, you help ensure the experience is meaningful and fulfilling for the volunteer and productive for the organization. If you don't currently have a volunteer program or feel like yours could stand to be revamped, the suggestions below can help you get organized and move forward.

### Identify How Volunteers Can Help

Remember that volunteers are looking for meaningful, useful engagement with the organization's work. Make a list of tasks that volunteers can complete. Keep in mind that many people derive satisfaction from projects they can see through to the end. If the volunteer supports staff as part of a greater effort, clearly identify the volunteer's role. Be sure also to identify any skills or experience needed (or preferred) for each job. It may also be helpful to provide a time commitment estimate. Don't forget to consider whether your organization has any virtual volunteer opportunities that could be attractive for someone who prefers to work from home.

## Create Job Descriptions

As you consider specific assignments, time commitments, skills, and knowledge needed for each position, create a job description just as you would for a paid staff position. You may also want to note specific requirements or expectations. For example, legal and ethical considerations and best practices should be addressed when dealing with fundraising, such as privacy and confidentiality. It might be a good idea to mention these and other expectations in the description specifically.

## Identify and Recruit Volunteers

Some organizations don't spend much time or effort actively recruiting volunteers. They just wait for people to come to them. This may work if you're not looking to fill specific needs. However, you may have to engage in targeted recruitment if you're looking for people with special qualifications. Consider where you can promote your volunteer opportunities to attract the recruits you want. Provide an application so you can collect pertinent information and better understand potential volunteers' interests, motivation, and availability. This can help you make the most of the volunteer's skills and talents to personalize their experience.

The other side of this coin is to give your new members and supporters a little bit of breathing room when they first join. It can be tempting to meet a promising potential volunteer and inadvertently apply a little too much pressure to get them in a service role. Let them get to know the organization, provide information about opportunities, and keep in touch with them so you can pick up signals when (and if) they're ready to get more involved.

### VOLUNTEER RECRUITMENT

What volunteer roles are you looking to fill? Where do you find people with the skills to be successful in those roles? Use your list of volunteer jobs to help you decide where to recruit. Here are a few ideas:

- Word of mouth (networking)
- Your website and social media
- Volunteer websites and apps (like Volunteer Match)
- Tables at community celebrations, festivals, and fairs
- Community volunteer recruitment events (like job fairs, only for volunteers)
- Your newsletter
- Stories with local media
- Partnerships with other civic groups and businesses
- Targeted communication like direct mail or one-on-one conversations with volunteers who have the skills you need

## Provide Volunteer Orientation and Training

Volunteers need to know what's expected of them. They need to receive instruction to be successful. They also need to understand the organization's mission and how different departments and teams operate together. If volunteers assist with fundraising, they could benefit from an overview of the basics (such as the fundraising cycle). Moreover, they should also understand the organization's programmatic needs and how they influence cases for support. Create training activities to support volunteers' job tasks and remember the overarching goal. You want new volunteers to have an excellent initial experience while providing ongoing support to veteran volunteers.

## Use Their Time Well

Volunteer satisfaction is essential. You want them to feel that the organization's success is directly tied to their contributions and accomplishments. You also want to respect their time and energy limitations. Avoid introducing menial tasks not included in the original job description, and be aware of workflow on any given day. If their project is on pause because a supervisor is absent or a vendor has been delayed, let the volunteer know ahead of time if they aren't needed or give them to option to work on something else. And make sure you don't ask your volunteers to do anything you wouldn't be willing to do. Saving the grunt work for volunteers is a good way to kill a volunteer program.

## Conduct Volunteer Evaluations

Evaluations demonstrate how valuable volunteers are to the organization. They offer an opportunity to provide feedback to volunteers and to open dialogue about their service. Like employees, most volunteers want confirmation that their work is being done correctly to meet the organization's goals.

Volunteer managers should perform evaluations according to the job description, considering the information provided during orientation and training. They should include both positive assessments and constructive feedback with recommendations for improvement. Ideally, the organization would also offer support and training in those areas. While most volunteer supervisors hope to offer mostly positive reinforcement, there are instances where the evaluation process may lead to changes in current assignments, or even termination, if the volunteer consistently fails to meet expectations.

## Recognize Volunteer Service

Celebrate your volunteers. Provide recognition and appreciation to them whenever you get a chance. Some instances may be private and informal. If possible, organizations should try to recognize volunteers in more formal, public ways as well. This can be accomplished through special events, such as a volunteer awards dinner, and opportunities offered exclusively to volunteers such as guest speakers, (fun) team-building activities, or tokens of appreciation such as clothing items with the organization's logo. Showing appreciation to volunteers can contribute to their continued motivation to serve.

## Focus on Retention

As with donors and employees, it's far more effective to keep the volunteers you have than to recruit and train their replacements continuously. We must nurture volunteer relationships like donor relationships through cultivation and stewardship. This is especially important because donors and volunteers are frequently one and the same.

The average national volunteer retention rate is 65 percent, and the average donor retention rate is 46 percent.[7] It's not difficult to imagine that one can negatively or positively affect the other. A donor who has a positive experience with the organization might be more motivated to volunteer. Conversely, a volunteer who has a negative volunteer experience is probably less likely to donate. Although it's sometimes challenging to connect volunteer and donor data in our databases effectively, we have to assume that one affects the other. We should then look for instances to influence the outcomes in our favor.

## Volunteers as Fundraisers

When we think about volunteers helping with fundraising, we might picture them canvassing businesses to sell ad space or round up silent auction items. Certainly, this type of service has its place. However, we may be underestimating the contributions volunteers can make to help us professionalize our fundraising approach. Aside from their assistance with special projects such as those listed above, volunteers can serve as ambassadors for your organization, help you understand your community's needs, provide valuable feedback about appeals, and play a critical role in your stewardship efforts (and a few might even be up to helping you make direct asks).

Your most engaged volunteers probably have an unmatched passion for your organization's work. Their energy can be contagious. In addition to bringing their skills and their "material resources," such as personal and professional connections, these volunteers can testify to your organization's good work. They are invested enough in your cause—in the needs you meet, the programs you offer, and the outcomes you produce—to give their resource of time without financial compensation. These volunteers can be "bellwethers" for your community, helping you gauge both external needs and internal responses.[8] Let your volunteers help you better understand your audiences.

You want to engage volunteers in work that is meaningful to them. For some volunteers, this could mean they are well-suited for fundraising tasks. You may find that they are willing and able (or at least willing to be trained). Even if your volunteers aren't immediately interested in what they might view as typical fundraising tasks (such as making asks of others), you can still start them off slowly in an advisory role to provide feedback. Consider where their input might be most helpful.

Chances are, if you're creating case statements, communication plans, or other written reports or appeals, you are going to need a few people to review these documents anyway. Some volunteers might be able to provide useful input on these, as well as appeal methods and prospect evaluations. In some cases, these reviews might happen individually. In others, you might recruit several volunteers to participate in focus group discussions. These situations not only open an avenue for feedback but also provide an opportunity for volunteers to identify potential prospects and connections within their personal and professional networks.

You also can't underestimate the valuable contributions your volunteers can make to your stewardship efforts. They can help you add more personalization to your thank-yous with handwritten notes and phone calls. They may also be able to assist with sending membership renewal reminders or planning donor and member appreciation events. The key is to find where the organization's needs intersect with the volunteer's interests, expectations, and comfort level.

If you plan to engage your volunteers in more active fundraising, there are ways to make that experience easier for both you and the volunteer.[9]

1. Provide fundraising training. Just as you've sought additional information about the fundraising process and tips to make it go more smoothly, your volunteers will benefit from training that will help them feel more knowledgeable and confident about fundraising. Explain how fundraising fits into your organizational operations, who is responsible for its various aspects, and your expectations for volunteers in a fundraising role.

2. Encourage giving to the organization. It's much easier for volunteers to solicit donations when they've already made a financial commitment to the cause. By investing in the organization's success, they signal their commitment to the project and serve as an example for others.

3. Engage them in prospect identification and qualification. Let your volunteers help you create and cull your prospect lists. They may be able to recommend potential donors and provide valuable information about their capacity and motivations. In cases where a prospect is in their personal or professional network, they can help make introductions and set up meetings.

4. Ask them to host small groups of prospects. Volunteers can serve as hosts to prospective donors, helping them feel welcome and providing an opportunity for someone from the organization to speak about its mission and programs. Guests can be invited by the organization or by the volunteer. Depending on the situation, the gathering can be held onsite or in the volunteer's home.

5. Train them to be ambassadors. Volunteers can serve as ambassadors and advocates in the community, conveying important messages about the good work the organization is doing and encouraging others to visit or take advantage of programming. Provide them with the information and training needed, and they can become your best engagement officers.

Look for the intersections between the organization's needs and the volunteer's interests. Not every volunteer will help directly with fundraising. Still, even volunteers working in other areas of the organization can be trained and encouraged to build relationships on behalf of the organization. Provide them with the information they need to encourage visitation and answer basic questions, including how people can donate to the organization. Be sure that all advocates—paid staff and volunteers—understand the organization's value proposition (why the organization's work is important and worthy of support) and can communicate it in their own words. In this way, everyone can help with fundraising, even if they're not directly asking for money.

# Notes

1. "Research - Volunteering in America," AmeriCorps, accessed January 8, 2021, https://www.nationalservice.gov/serve/via/research.

2. "Value of Volunteer Time," Independent Sector, accessed January 8, 2021, https://independentsector.org/value-of-volunteer-time-2020/.

3. "Research—Volunteering in America."

4. "Time and Money: The Role of Volunteering in Philanthropy," Fidelity Charitable, 2014, accessed January 8, 2021, https://www.fidelitycharitable.org/content/dam/fc-public/docs/insights/volunteering-and-philanthropy.pdf.

5. *The 2018 U.S. Trust Study on High Net Worth Philanthropy*," Bank of America Private Bank in Partnership with the Indiana University Lilly Family School of Philanthropy, 2018, accessed January 27, 2021, https://scholarworks.iupui.edu/bitstream/handle/1805/17666/high-net-worth2018-summary.pdf.

6. Tyrone Freeman, "Volunteer Management," *Achieving Excellence in Fundraising*, ed. Eugene Tempel, Timothy Seiler, and Eva Aldrich (San Francisco: Jossey-Bass, 2011).

7. Eric Burger, "Converting Volunteers to Donors: Missed Opportunity for Most Nonprofits," *GuideStar* (blog), November 8, 2018, https://trust.guidestar.org/converting-volunteers-to-donors-missed-opportunity-for-most-nonprofits.

8. Tyrone Freeman, "Volunteer Management," 287.

9. Adapted from William J. Moran, "7 Ways to Engage Volunteers in Fundraising," The Moran Company, 2012, accessed January 27, 2021, https://morancompany.com/the-role-of-volunteers-in-fundraising-3/.

# Evaluation

Believe it or not, I have looked up the definition of the word "evaluation." It means "to judge or determine the value, significance or worth of" something.[1] The synonyms for "evaluate" are even more helpful. Words like "check," "look over," "measure," and "take account" make the process seem pretty agreeable. In this chapter, we're going to review the evaluation process. We'll bust some myths associated with program evaluation and hopefully provide some structure that will help you measure the effectiveness of your efforts.

## Evaluation in Fundraising

If you're making promises to your supporters, you're going to need a way to show results. Donors and funders want to know that their generosity is making a difference. One way to do this is with data because it measures change. It can help you identify and justify your needs, or it can help you demonstrate success, such as in a grant report. But much like fundraising, evaluation doesn't just happen. We have to make a point to set up our process and see it through. Unfortunately, it's easy to get derailed by some common evaluation myths. Let's walk through a few of these and be on our way to better evaluation.

## Evaluation Myths

### Myth #1: Only Big Organizations Need to Evaluate

The truth is that organizations of all sizes and missions need to take account of what they're doing. To do this, we will look at evaluation as a series of measurements.

What do we measure?

When we evaluate, we measure change. We look at what has changed, how it has changed, and what else happened due to that change. Program evaluation is intentionally and thoughtfully gathering data to document and measure

- what we did;
- what difference it made; and
- objectives met (Did we accomplish what we set out to do?).

So we can

- learn and improve; and
- inform our stakeholders.

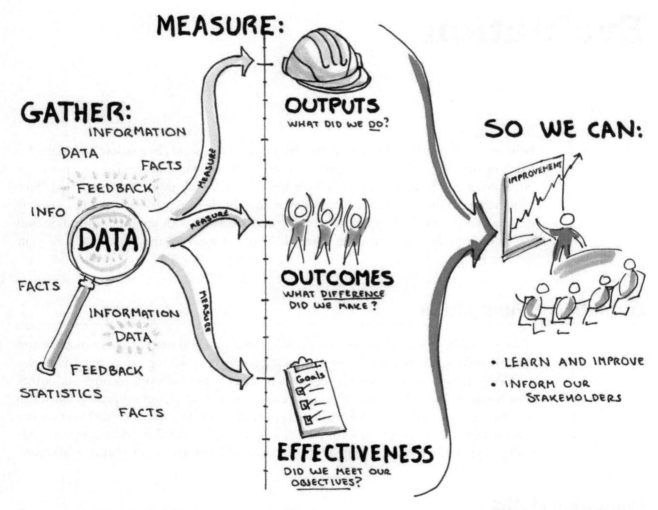

**Figure 19.1.** What Do We Measure?  Jeannette Rooney, original artwork in ink, Evaluating Your Outcomes Webinar, Indiana Historical Society Local History Services, December 14, 2017. Used with permission.

In evaluation-speak, we call these our outputs, outcomes, and effectiveness. And we need to address them for two main reasons. The first is to learn and improve within our organizations. The second is to make sure we can inform our stakeholders, such as our board, staff, volunteers, donors, funders, and others. Figure 19.1 shows the evaluation process in action.[2]

## Why do we measure?

We evaluate because we want continuous improvement. We also want to keep our stakeholders and supporters informed. But what does this actually look like? What are we trying to achieve with evaluation? In truth, evaluation serves different purposes at different times, or more likely, multiple purposes simultaneously. Let's take a look at why we measure:[3]

- To reinforce public trust in our mission: As nonprofit organizations, we must operate within the public's trust. Our organizations don't exist for their own sake. We exist to serve our community's greater good. The community gains confidence in our mission when we can explain why our work is important and then back it up with evidence.
- To demonstrate results to supporters: We rely on the generosity of donors and funders. We want to show them their investment is working by providing a positive ROI. Not only does this demonstrate that we are good stewards of their funds, but it inspires confidence for future investment. This also helps donors determine whether they are meeting their own impact goals.
- To ensure we are meeting community needs and providing valuable benefits: Our organizations don't exist for the sake of existing. We serve the public, and there is an expectation of beneficial services. Whether this is through proper collection methods, educational exhibits, or local history expertise, evaluation ensures we provide benefits the community finds valuable.
- To better understand program delivery: We put a lot of time and energy into our programs. Sometimes evaluation is critical to helping us understand how a program works. We can look at our programs' inner workings to know how they function, what might need to be changed to improve them, and sometimes even what is scalable for use in other organizations.
- To inform planning: Anyone who has ever participated in a strategic planning session knows that you need data to inform your decisions. Whether you are planning the budget, the calendar, or the "next big thing," data helps you evaluate where you've been, where you are, and where you should strategically go next.
- To improve projects, programs, and processes: Not every organization is trying to get bigger, but it's reasonable to expect that we all want to get better. Evaluation keeps us from making decisions based solely on internal assumptions. With data at hand, we can avoid "echo chamber" planning meetings where we reinforce each other's thoughts, assumptions, and biases. When we know how well we're meeting the wants, needs, and expectations of those we serve based on evaluation, we know where to focus our efforts.

## Myth #2: Evaluation Is Complicated and Takes Too Much Time

I used to work at a university research institute, and I was surrounded every day by brilliant professionals doing serious academic evaluation. It was both impressive and intimidating! If you've ever read a book about evaluation or even done an online search, maybe you were thrown off by some of the jargon or complicated processes. People get advanced degrees in evaluation and dedicate their careers to it. But it's important to remember that academic evaluation has its own goals (like scientific rigor, complete accuracy, and replicable studies). When it comes to project or program evaluation, it's okay for we practitioners to have different goals for evaluation.

To best use the results of our evaluation efforts, we should focus on utility and tailor our evaluation plans to our needs and questions. We are not undertaking evaluation for the sake of research. We are looking for practical, relevant information that we can turn around and use to improve our work. In project evaluation, we are only going to collect data we need to use. In baking terms: if we're making jam, there's no reason to measure out cake flour.

### Outputs: What did we do?

We want to answer two overarching questions when it comes to designing—and funding—projects:

1. What are we going to do (outputs)?
2. What difference will it make (outcomes)?

There are a lot of variables to consider when evaluating your success. If you're looking for a jumping-off point, I encourage you to start with outputs and outcomes. We've covered these in a few other chapters (especially chapter 16 about grant writing), but let's do a quick review.

Outputs are results, products, or services that come from a program's activities. You can see in figure 19.2 some sample questions we might ask about project outputs. We often measure these in terms of frequencies, rates, proportions, durations, or expenditures.

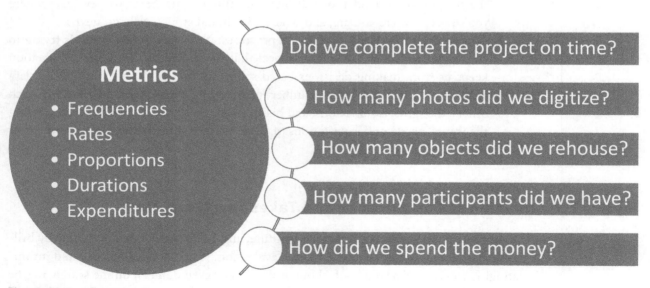

# Outputs – What did we do?

**Metrics**
- Frequencies
- Rates
- Proportions
- Durations
- Expenditures

Did we complete the project on time?

How many photos did we digitize?

How many objects did we rehouse?

How many participants did we have?

How did we spend the money?

**Figure 19.2.** Outputs

Outcomes are changes or benefits to a target population as a result of project activities. Answers to questions in the outcomes category are often expressed as reactions and feelings, learning, change in behavior, or change in values, attitude, or status.

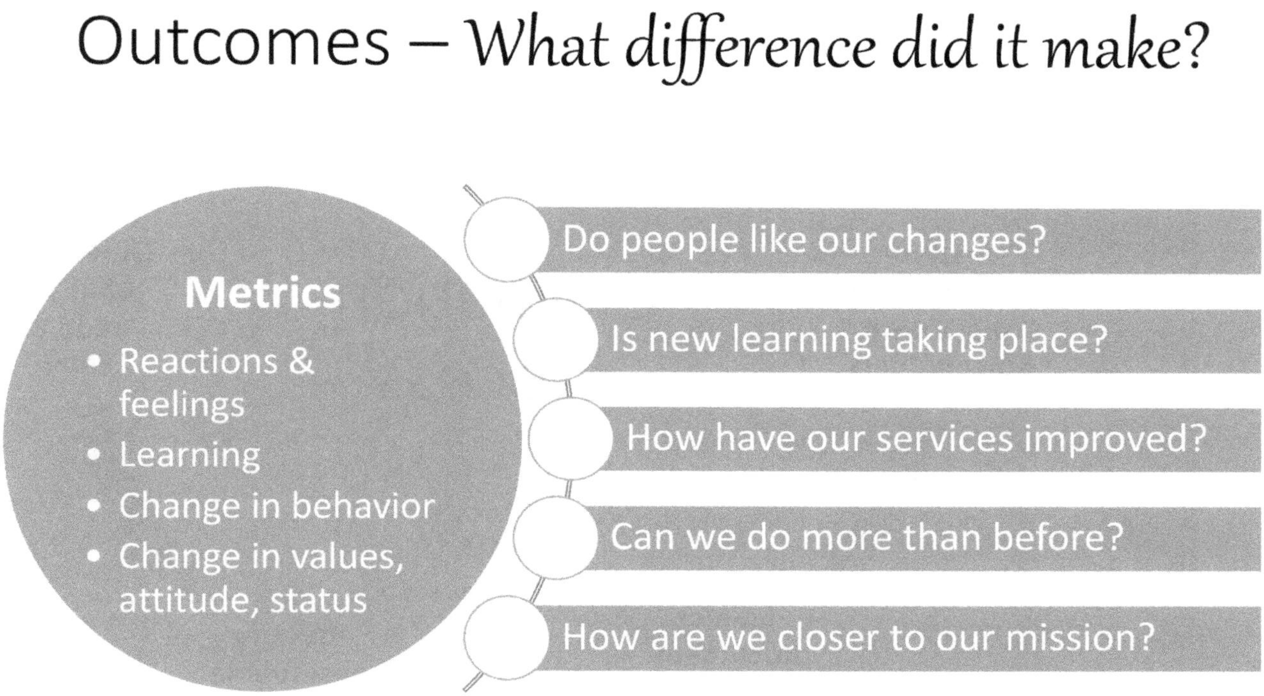

# Outcomes – *What difference did it make?*

**Metrics**

- Reactions & feelings
- Learning
- Change in behavior
- Change in values, attitude, status

- Do people like our changes?
- Is new learning taking place?
- How have our services improved?
- Can we do more than before?
- How are we closer to our mission?

**Figure 19.3.** Outcomes

## Myth #3: There's Only One "Right" Way to Evaluate

Sometimes we are our own worst enemies when it comes to evaluation. We delay starting because we're afraid we won't do it "right." To address this, we are going to walk through the evaluation process. Figure 19.4 shows an overview of the steps in this process. We will discuss each in detail, but keep in mind, this is a model, a framework. Feel free to change it and make it yours. Adapt it so that it's useful for your purposes.

1. ID primary users
You want your evaluation results to be useful to the people who will use them. Think about your stakeholders and the type of information they need to make good decisions. Then design your approach with them in mind. An excellent first step is to make a list of users, such as:

- Board members
- Management
- Program coordinators
- Marketing and outreach
- Fundraisers
- Funders
- Volunteers
- Community partners

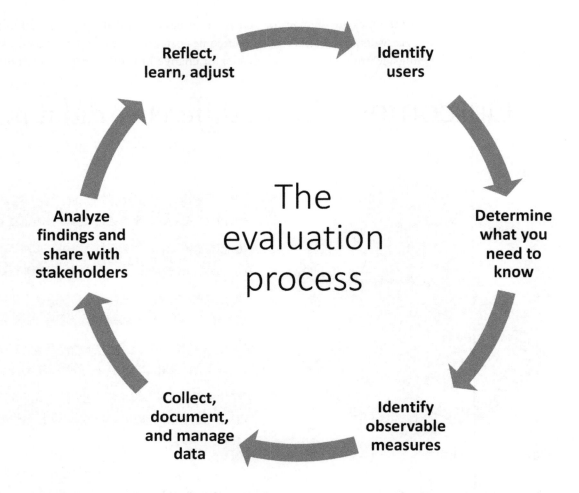

**Figure 19.4.** Evaluation Process

2. Determine what you need to know

Begin with the end in mind. What does success look like? Your success metrics, and therefore the questions you need to ask, depend on several factors. With your primary users and critical audience in mind, you can start thinking about what you're trying to accomplish.

We're all trying to balance different needs when it comes to programming. What you decide to measure will change depending on the situation. For instance, if your evaluation is part of a funding request, you may focus on measuring the project's impacts (which is basically a long-range "What difference did it make?" question). If you're trying to decide if the program should be a budget priority, you may need to determine the organization's return on investment before you continue allocating resources to it. The information you need will shape the questions you pose. (Tip: a logic model template can be a great reference tool when trying to determine what you should be tracking and measuring in your project.)

Involve other internal stakeholders in this part of the process. By inviting staff and volunteers to participate in the process (especially those who work closely with the areas you're evaluating), you can create buy-in for collecting data. The project will benefit from different perspectives, and including others may help you identify unique situations and explore new questions.

### 3. Identify useful indicators

Indicators are specific, observable, and measurable characteristics or changes that will represent an outcome's achievement. In other words, an indicator is a change that can equal success. Once you identify your indicators, you can determine what kind of data you want to collect. Remember that data is simply something known about a specific subject or situation. There are many different kinds of data (more on that in a bit). For now, try thinking of your indicators in terms of your senses:[4]

- How can you see change taking place? For example, in an attempt to be more interactive, our exhibit team created a blank wall and asked guests to use sticky-notes to tell us what they collected. We could clearly see from the number of notes accumulating on the wall each week that our guests were interacting through their participation.
- How can you hear change taking place? I once visited a museum that created a space for conversations around an art exhibit. They provided discussion questions and a comfortable place for small groups to sit. A gallery attendant lingered (in an unobtrusive way) making note of the discussions. It was not so much that she could hear what people were saying; she was measuring the fact that she could hear discussion where there had previously been none.
- How can you read change taking place? If you do surveys after programs, consider asking people what they learned or how they will think about something differently in the future. This provides a very insightful way to read about change taking place.

Sometimes it helps to think about your outcomes' characteristics in terms of "if/then" statements and then apply the "means that" rule.[5] For instance, if you want to provide better preservation of documents and also increase access to those documents through a digitization project, you might say

- "If we can digitize our most fragile courthouse records, then we will reduce the need for researchers to handle them."
- Similarly, "Making our most requested records available and searchable online means that researchers will be able to access this information from anywhere, 24/7."

Another way to take stock of your outcome indicators and the data you want to track is by using an evaluation matrix. Figure 19.5 shows sample headers you might use to set up your spreadsheet.

Under objectives, we look at what we're trying to achieve—our results. Remember that outputs are "what we did," and outcomes are "what difference it made." We often think about outcomes in the short- to mid-term range and impact in the longer term.

Under indicators, we're looking for changes we're hoping to see. Maybe that's learning taking place as the result of an educational program. Or perhaps it's rehousing and better storage of textiles to extend the life of the collection. If you're hosting a series of genealogy workshops, for example, one of your objectives might be to host one workshop in every library in your county. That would be an output. Another objective might be to teach attendees about free genealogy resources they can access from home or at their libraries. If a postworkshop survey question asked attendees if they learned about any new resources, that would be an outcome. Both would be indicators.

# Sample evaluation matrix

| Objective | Indicators | Data Collection Method | Person Responsible for Data Collection |
|---|---|---|---|
| **OUTPUTS** | | | |
| | | | |
| | | | |
| **OUTCOMES** | | | |
| | | | |
| | | | |
| **IMPACT** | | | |
| | | | |
| | | | |

**Figure 19.5.**   Sample Evaluation Matrix

4. Collect, document, and manage

Deciding how to administer your data collection process involves a series of "how and who" questions to work out the logistics of your data collection plan. We're going to look at this process in more detail to find answers to some of these questions.

*Baseline data:* You can't have a conversation about collecting and analyzing data without mentioning this critical step. This is the data you collect before you begin your project or program. It helps you answer those change questions we talked about at the beginning of the chapter:

- What has changed?
- How it has changed
- What else happened as a result?

We can better answer these questions when comparing "before" data to "after" data. Some examples of baseline data might include

- an organizational preself-assessment (such as a board assessment, for example);
- the number of objects cataloged before the start of a collection backlog project;
- the extent of mold present before a remediation treatment;
- "before" photos for a construction project.

*Data collection:* When you're formulating your evaluation plan, keep in mind how frequently and at what points you will collect and analyze data. Generally, we think of this in terms of formative or summative data collection. If you have a background in education, these terms are probably familiar to you because they are used for learning assessment. But I think they apply to project evaluation as well:

- Formative evaluation is ongoing and allows for feedback to be considered and implemented during the program or project. This can help you catch problems and work to solve them before they threaten project success.
- Summative evaluation occurs at the end of an operating cycle, and findings typically are used to help decide whether a program should be adopted, continued, or modified for improvement.

*Common data collection methods:* Let's take a look at some common data collection methods. As you design your evaluation plan, you may want to use several of these methods, depending on the type of information you're hoping to capture:[6]

- Observation: When we use observation, we are noting behavior, events, or physical characteristics. This may require us to set up a standard process for documenting and explaining what we see. For instance, a staff member or volunteer might conduct a gallery observation, noting which exhibits visitors gravitate to and how much time they spend at each. It's also worth mentioning that observations can be direct or indirect. Direct observations involve looking directly at the behavior or occurrence, whereas indirect means observing the results of those occurrences. An example here would be noting that kids at a coloring station prefer red crayons because that's the color the education manager most often replaces.
- Record review: A record or document review encourages us to use internal and external records to collect data. These can be paper or digital records and might include financial documents, after-action reports, visitor or activity logs, even actual versus budgeted expenses. For example, many museums and heritage sites track visitors by zip code. They then use this data to understand where their visitors live and what geographical areas are not well represented. While this is usually a cost-effective data collection method, it's important to remember that your data will only be as good as the records you keep.
- Surveys: Surveys are standardized written instruments administered by mail, email, online, or in person. The nice thing about surveys is that you can adjust them to meet your needs, and they are usually cost-effective. For example, you could create an exit survey for your visitors and make it available via an electronic tablet, QR code for an online version, or on paper administered by volunteers at the door. There are free and low-cost online survey platforms you can access to help you track and analyze your results (SurveyMonkey is probably the most well-known). Surveys are often criticized for low response rates, so be sure to consider this.
- Interviews: Interviews are another great way to get feedback from your constituents, whether formally or informally. They can be one-on-one or include multiple people, such as focus groups or town hall-style meetings. They provide an opportunity for participants to clarify questions and expand on topics through additional probing. You may want to use an outside facilitator to lead the discussion to make sure it isn't one-sided or biased. Because interviews generally reach a smaller audience, you will get a lot of feedback from fewer people, so use this method strategically.

As you're considering these, and possibly other data collection methods, remember to ask yourself

- What data can we capture?
- What is usable?
- What do we have the resources to do?
- What is most important (with an emphasis on quality over quantity)?
- Who will collect the data? Where will it be stored?
- Who will compile and analyze the data? How will they do this?

To gain even more perspective on those questions, here are some additional questions to consider:

- Can we collect this data when and where we need it?
- Do we have the systems in place to properly manage this data? If not, what would we have to do to make that happen?
- Is it cost-efficient?
- Can we get feedback from enough people?
- How susceptible is this method to bias? (This is especially true if you are conducting your evaluation internally without assistance from an external evaluator.)
- Will we get all the information we need from this method?
- Do we need to know "why" a specific change occurred? If so, which method could answer that question for us?

5. Analyze the Data

Generally, we speak in terms of two different types of data: quantitative and qualitative.[7] The way I remember the difference between the two is to think of quantitative in terms of quantities or numbers—things that can be counted. Qualitative data represents those qualities that can't be counted.

*Quantitative data:* When we're analyzing and reporting on quantitative data, we're often talking in terms of headcounts, testing results, data analysis, and comparisons. You can see some of the examples in figure 19.6. The main takeaway for quantitative data is that you're dealing with numbers, so think in terms of totals, averages, ranges, rates, and percentages.

| Counts | Testing | Data Analysis | Comparisons |
|---|---|---|---|
| • Records scanned<br>• Web hits or downloads<br>• Program participants | • Educational programming pre- and post-tests | • Percentage of participants who agree or strongly agree | • Temperature and relative humidity readings before and after HVAC installation<br>• UV light readings before and after window treatments |

**Figure 19.6.** Sample Quantitative Measurements

*Qualitative data:* We can break the process of analyzing qualitative data into simple steps, but it does take keen observation, critical thinking, and some practice to get your best results. To get started, try applying this process to your nonnumerical information:

1. Read and consider the comments or text in question. (I often use a highlighter to track key themes and ideas, and I make a lot of notes in the margins).
2. Organize the information into similar categories or themes as best as possible.
3. Label your themes (e.g., "lessons learned" or "suggestions").
4. Attempt to identify any patterns or relationships.

6. Share Your Findings

How you share your findings depends on the audience. Board members and funders may appreciate receiving information in formal summaries, such as quarterly or annual reports. Your newsletter may be the right place to share your results with your members and supporters. Visitors and the general public might get strategic bits of information on your website or through social media. And don't forget to share the results with other staff members and volunteers.

7. Reflect, Learn, and Adjust

The final step in the evaluation process is to pause long enough to reflect on your findings, learn from the process, and make adjustments going forward. Sometimes, this is the most challenging part of the whole process, but if we don't apply what we've learned from our evaluation, what was the point of doing it in the first place? Here are a few questions for your team to consider:

- Did the measurements you chose capture the data you needed?
- Was the information from your data analysis useful?
- Was the data collection plan functional?
- Who received the results? Should anyone else be included?

## Myth #4: Success = Implementing the Project Perfectly

We often convince ourselves that if programs don't run perfectly—if we don't adhere exactly to project timelines or if our outcomes don't happen as perfectly as we told our funders they would—our work was not successful. When we've invested time, money, energy, and emotion into a project, it's deflating when things don't go as planned. In these cases, we need to remind ourselves of the value that comes from lessons learned.

If you've ever completed a final grant report, you've probably been asked about lessons learned. Funders don't expect your projects to go perfectly. However, they do want you to take deliberate note of what you learned when things didn't go as planned and how that might influence future decision-making. Even if you're not reporting to a funder, it will be worthwhile to consider and make a note of the following questions:

- What did we learn?
- What new ideas did we get?
- What worked well?
- What can we do better next time?

Once you have the answers to these questions, implement them in your programs and your future funding requests.

## Myth #5: We Always Know What Our Visitors (Volunteers, Staff, Community) Need

Our final myth leads us into how we can use data collection and evaluation in our everyday work. Formal evaluation plans for programs are important, but we want to be careful not to box them up and keep the idea of measuring outcomes separate from the work we do daily. Often, we're already collecting data (or could be) that we could put to good use.

We have a lot going on in our organizations. There's potential for data collection in almost every area, depending on what we're trying to accomplish. Ask yourself and your team members about the data you are already collecting and how you are using it. You may find that you have untapped data available waiting for someone like you to organize and analyze it. Areas to consider include:

- Visitors (Are you already tracking numbers? Is it broken down by days of the week? If so, you can look for patterns);
- Collections (Are you already tracking temperature and humidity readings? If so, you will have the data to back up any fluctuations caused by failing equipment);
- Exhibits (Do you notice that visitors spend more time with a certain exhibit? Try setting up gallery counts or asking guests a few short questions to understand what they like about it);
- Research (Do you track your most requested materials from your archives? If so, this might help you prioritize which documents should be digitized);
- Fundraising (Do you know your donors' average gift? With this information, you can put that amount in the middle of an ask string. For example, if the average is $50, you can give them a gift range of $10, $25, $50, $75, or $100); and
- Programs (Do you already track attendance to your programs and events? Can you use this information to identify factors that could be carried over to other programs?).

## Evaluation Resources

There's a lot of information out there about evaluation. If you're looking for resources specifically for museums or local history organizations, I encourage you to visit websites for the American Association for State and Local History (AASLH) and the American Alliance of Museums (AAM). If you think you might be interested in getting help from an outside evaluator, consult with the Committee on Audience Research and Evaluation through AAM, the American Evaluation Association, or even a local university or community foundation for recommendations.[8]

You don't have to be part of a large, resource-rich organization to conduct a good evaluation. You can start small, adding to and refining your process as you go. Just remember to begin with the end in mind. Track the information you will use, and don't measure too much. It's fine to prioritize the data you need most. Finally, make sure your evaluation collection, management, and reporting methods fit the project. With good measurements in hand, you will be able to talk to donors and funders about data-informed needs and track how well your outcomes are serving your community.

# Notes

1. "Evaluate," dictionary.com, accessed January 27, 2021, https://www.dictionary.com/browse/evaluate.

2. Jeannette Rooney, "What Do We Measure?" original artwork in ink, Evaluating Your Outcomes Webinar, Indiana Historical Society Local History Services, December 14, 2017. Used with permission.

3. Adapted from "Why Evaluation Is Important for Your Nonprofit," TSNE MissionWorks, January 1, 2019, https://www.tsne.org/blog/why-evaluation-important-your-nonprofit.

4. "Measuring Outcomes, Strengthening Nonprofits: A Capacity Builder's Resource Library," Compassion Capital Fund National Resource Center, accessed December 12, 2017, http://www.strengtheningnonprofits.org/resources/guidebooks/Measuring Outcomes.pdf (can now be accessed at https://nonprofit.uwazi.io/en/document/pikuqnx 030hc9d3q11431sjor and other open-source document websites), 19.

5. "Measuring Outcomes," 20.

6. "Measuring Outcomes," 22–23.

7. "Did It Work? 5 Tools for Evaluating the Success of Your Project," *Sumac* (blog), August 3, 2013, https://www.sumac.com/blog/nonprofit-management-and-hr/did-it-work-5-tools-for-evaluating-the-success-of-your-project/.

8. Additional resources consulted: "Evaluation Toolkit," The Pell Institute and Pathways to College Network, accessed January 27, 2021, http://toolkit.pellinstitute.org/evaluation-guide/; Paul W. Mattessich, *The Manager's Guide to Program Evaluation* (St. Paul, MN: Wilder Publishing Center, 2003); James Aaron Quick and Cheryl Carter New, *Grant Winner's Toolkit: Project Management and Evaluation* (Hoboken, NJ: John Wiley & Sons, 2000).

# Fundraising for Local History

While fundraising guidelines apply regardless of a nonprofit's mission, fundraising for museums has its own unique considerations. Because our missions usually revolve around education, interpretation, and collections care, we must consider how these efforts influence the work we do and, by extension, the asks we make when raising funds. This chapter provides a brief look at a few lessons learned in fundraising for museums and historic sites.

## Collections Care

For collections-holding institutions like museums, collections care is of paramount importance. The organization is charged with managing and protecting its objects in public trust. In other words, the museum is responsible for ensuring that the collection—which is held for the good of the public—is well taken care of and used properly.

As you very likely already know (perhaps too well), caring for collections takes money. First, there are the actual expenses such as archival-quality storage containers and extra costs associated with maintaining proper temperature and humidity, blocking harmful UV rays, and preventing pest infestations. There are also intangible costs such as valuable space used for collection storage and staff and volunteers' time and expertise caring for the objects.

If you don't currently have a line item in your budget for collections care, it's worth serious consideration. Adding collections care to your annual accounting signals your commitment to it and helps you estimate your needs and how much money you should bring in to cover those needs. If you're going to fundraise for collections care, you need to understand your goal. This fundraising can be accomplished through a combination of individual donations and grant funding. Still, you have to be able to talk about the collection with honesty and optimism, even if you're staring at a ceiling-high backlog. Here are a few tips to help with collections care fundraising:

If the sight of your collections care processing or storage areas raises your blood pressure, take comfort in the fact that you're not alone. Many museums (of all sizes) struggle to keep up with processing their collections; it's very easy to get behind when things start to pile up. If you're facing a collections backlog, or if you've outgrown your current storage space, your best first step is to come up with a plan to address it and then start sharing that plan with donors and funders. Don't feel like you need to hide the situation, especially if it's a problem they can help you solve. If you invite them into your messy space (in person or through "before" photos), share your plan and help them visualize how their support can make a difference.

- Be prepared to talk about your collection. You never know when a conversation with a donor or community member may uncover an interest in the objects in your collection and your efforts to preserve them. In addition to generally speaking about the collection's scope and how you use it for interpretation, understand where your needs lie. What are your collections care priorities? Are there special projects waiting for funding?
- Be prepared to talk about your collections *process*. This is how you will explain what you do and why it costs money to people who aren't familiar with museum work and the jargon that goes with it. From accession and processing to storage and exhibition (and possibly even to deaccession), potential donors and funders need to be able to understand how you do your work. You may find opportunities to help them understand the costs associated with ensuring objects are appropriately stored and exhibited. You could even go so far as to draw up price points for different types of items. Don't be afraid to share this information, as it's highly likely that many donors have never considered the expenses associated with museum collections. And don't be shy about sharing your process and the cost with object donors. They need to understand what goes into caring for grandma's quilt if you agree to make it part of your collection.
- Know the details. Suppose you want to speak to a prospective donor or write a grant application for a specific collections-related initiative. In that case, you will likely need to provide details such as the number of objects, percent currently cataloged and stored, and the status of any special collections. Estimates will even help you and your supporters understand the scope of work for any given collections-related project.
- Have your collections management policy handy. Although donors may not ask if you have this critical document, funders specializing in collection care initiatives may inquire whether you have one (and may even request that you include it with your proposal). If you don't have a written collections management policy, there's no time like the present to draft this critical document.[1]
- If you have a backlog, address it. There's no use tiptoeing around a collections backlog. You might even be surprised to find out that funders interested in collections care already know about backlogs, so admitting to one probably won't surprise

them. Furthermore, avoiding a backlog won't make it go away, so handle it head-on with a plan to remedy the situation. Donors and funders may expect information about how you're addressing the backlog but still understand that clearing it can be a years-long process. It will be helpful to potential funders if you can also explain how the backlog occurred. Whether it was lack of staff resources, tight storage space, or loose accession guidelines ("If it's old, we take it"), if you can identify what caused the backlog, you can build confidence in your plan by addressing the situation directly.

- Don't overlook personnel training. Professional development is an integral part of museum work, and this is undoubtedly true for collections management. Even if you're working with volunteer staff, you might still consider building training opportunities into your project plans and proposals. This helps increase institutional knowledge and build capacity. It also helps organizations adhere to industry standards and best practices while addressing sustainability and improving the donor's ROI.

## Education and Interpretation

Education and interpretation are at the heart of museum work. Using our collections and our people's expertise, we create opportunities for our community to learn, think, and discuss. While we may be using objects from our collection or those borrowed from another museum, there are still costs associated with designing, building, and installing impactful exhibits. Likewise, there are upfront expenses for educational programming, even if we are charging registration fees to offset some of those costs. Here are a few things to consider when trying to fund education and interpretation.

- Understand the interpretive "big idea." What are your visitors' takeaways from the exhibit or program? What are you trying to convey? While it can be tempting to design an exhibition based on a list of stuff that hasn't been out of storage in a while, the interpretation still needs a theme to make it relevant to visitors and intriguing to funders.
- Submit visuals. Help donors, sponsors, and funders visualize how the exhibit or program will look. Create a floor plan and design mock-ups using photos and branding (colors, logos, fonts), so they can get a feel for what you're trying to accomplish. Provide a summary of the exhibit's different sections and a list of possible objects to display.
- Clearly identify learning objectives. What do you want visitors or participants to learn? How do you hope to influence their thinking or behavior? Take the time to identify the learning objectives first and then design your exhibit and programming around those objectives. When appropriate, demonstrate that you sought feedback from educators and representative audiences when creating your educational content.
- Exhibits and educational programming are "sexier" than some of the behind-the-scenes work. Use this to your advantage. Seek sponsorships for new exhibitions. Plan events around exhibit openings and give your members and donors a special exclusive preview. Use crowdfunding to raise money for educational materials or conservation of a particular object before exhibition.

- Plan for visitor evaluation. You'll be hard-pressed to find a grant application that doesn't ask for details about how you'll evaluate your project. Build metrics measurement into your plans from the beginning and decide how you will use the feedback you receive. Whether you're piloting a program with a focus group or collecting data from exit surveys, address how you will integrate evaluation information into improving your program.

## Human Resources

If you're looking for donor support or foundation funding for personnel, it may take a little more searching and relationship building. When you find a prospective funding source, you will want to have a well-developed plan for the position. You may have more luck finding funding for short-term, temporary, project-based workers than for permanent positions. Grant funders are often hesitant to fund someone's salary without a concrete plan for continuing to pay that person after the grant cycle. As you develop your case for support, consider the following:

- Endowment funding might be a consideration when trying to secure consistent income to pay for personnel. You may be able to secure major gifts toward creating an endowment to fund a permanent staff position in perpetuity. This is where knowing your donors and their interests, as well as making a good case, will be essential.
- Identify the desired qualifications you're seeking. Write up the job description ahead of time and if you already have a candidate in mind, have a copy of that

person's résumé. What kind of work will this person be doing? Develop a scope of work with details about the assignment or include any you have received from potential consultants.

- Classify the position correctly for tax purposes. Businesses, including nonprofits, do not get to decide for themselves whether someone is a temporary employee or a contractor (and subsequently, who handles payroll taxes for the employee). Instead, this is determined at the federal level using specific threshold tests. Therefore, you should consult your accountant or employment attorney and refer to IRS and Department of Labor guidelines to ensure you've handled the classification correctly.[2] If you've determined that your new hire will be an employee (rather than a contractor), be sure to factor payroll taxes, benefits, and organizational insurance costs into your budget and proposal. You don't want those to sneak up on you.

## Digitization Projects

While many of us are familiar with the concept of digitization, there's more to it than just hitting the scan button. In addition to capturing and editing the image, you must decide how it will be stored, accessed, and used. If you're looking to embark on a digitization project, you will want to address a few things up front:[3]

- Consider the need: Why are you digitizing part of your collection? Is it for access, preservation, or both? If you plan to make part of your archives available online, you will need to decide your best course of action to provide access to the images. On the other hand, suppose you're hoping to preserve a deteriorating document by digitizing it to reduce handling. In that case, you will need to establish a long-term file management system and consider making high-quality copies of the image in the future.
- Address which collection(s) you've selected and why. A potential funder may want to know why you've chosen to digitize one part of your collection over another, and you should be able to provide a sound rationale for your decision. For example, perhaps you've chosen your most requested and handled documents, or you're digitizing a selection for an upcoming community anniversary or celebration. Maybe you've identified resources needed for a primary source partnership with a local school, or perhaps you're just starting in chronological order. Whatever your reasons, be able to speak to them.
- Provide a detailed work and storage plan. As stated above, digitization is more than just scanning. Once you have a good image, it will need to be edited, metadata will need to be assigned, and you will need a secure storage system (preferably with duplicate copies and automatic backups). You will also need to know how the digital files will be accessed and used. If you plan to make the images available online, they will need to be stored on a server, so you may need to involve your IT providers to understand your needs better.
- Set goals and milestones. Determine how long it takes you to process one image and apply that to the entire collection you will be digitizing. How long will the whole project take you? Determine your goals, such as how many hours you'll work on the project each week and how many digital images will be created. Identify milestones where you'll pause to evaluate your progress and adjust your goals.

# Building Projects

It's no surprise that many heritage organizations have capital needs. Between aging historic buildings and ever-growing collections, we often find ourselves looking for money to address building issues. Whether you are soliciting donations or applying for grants, there are a few things to keep in mind when seeking funding for building projects:

- Address your building ownership or lease. Do you own your building? If not, who holds the title, and what are the terms of your lease? Donors and grant funders may be hesitant to pay for improvements to buildings you don't own, especially if you have a short-term lease. If you don't own the building you occupy, do you have the owner's permission to make capital changes? These are things you may need to address in your case for support or grant application. It may also be good to check with an attorney about any laws addressing property improvements or other kinds of building legal issues that aren't common knowledge.
- Be mindful of easements, covenants, and other restrictions. Historic preservation easements on buildings are usually voluntary legal agreements with a nonprofit or government entity that protect the historic character of the building and sometimes the landscape by preventing certain changes to the structure. These can be exterior only but also sometimes include interior changes. (Easements may allow for federal and state tax deductions and can sometimes lower property tax assessments.)[4] Covenants may require building owners to adhere to certain expectations for maintenance or submit restoration plans for approval.[5] These easements and covenants may affect what you're legally able to do to a historic property.

- Consider the Secretary of the Interior's Standards for the Treatment of Historic Properties. These standards offer guidelines for four areas of historic property "treatments," including preservation, rehabilitation, restoration, and reconstruction.[6] Although the standards are only required for projects receiving federal grant-in-aid assistance and are not regulatory for other projects, funders may look favorably on a consultation of the standards.[7]
- Provide historic structure reports and other types of building assessments and studies, if available. Historic structure reports are prepared by experts who examine the building's history and current condition to provide an evaluation that considers the most appropriate treatments for a historic property and a scope of recommended work. The report should also consider the owner or user's goals for the property. A historic structure report can be a valuable piece of information for planning a project and justifying evidence-based needs. If you think your organization could benefit from a report, you may be able to find a grant or private funding to cover the cost.[8]
- Use contractors with historic property experience. Not every local contractor has the knowledge or expertise to deal with historic structures. When possible, treatments, materials, site use, and compliance updates (such as those associated with the Americans with Disabilities Act) should be addressed by someone familiar with the "quirks" that often accompany historic buildings and landscapes.
- Add contingency funds to the budget. Perhaps more than any other type of project, building treatments are subject to unforeseen circumstances. The weather can delay progress. A contractor might find unexpected electrical or plumbing issues behind a wall. Materials may not be delivered on time. Consider adding contingency funds to your building projects to help mitigate surprises that might otherwise cause you to run over budget.

## Final Thoughts and a To-Do List

This is not an exhaustive list of lessons learned, and you probably have a few additional tips of your own. I don't think there's been a day since I started working with museums when I didn't learn something new (and I'm confident I could say the same about fundraising). One of the greatest joys of my career has been meeting and working with leaders and volunteers at heritage organizations from across the country. I have tried to soak up each new lesson—every tidbit of information—to use in my own practice, but more importantly, to share with others who are doing this good, important work.

Several years ago, a museum colleague and friend posed a question: "What advice would you give to a brand-new small museum director who is trying to get a handle on fundraising?" With pangs of empathy, I set to work on a list of ten "to-do's" I would recommend to her if we strategized over coffee. That list morphed into a blog post for American Association for State and Local History (AASLH) and provided a baseline for a lot of the recommendations you've read in this book. So it seems fitting to go full circle and take one last look at these key takeaways.

Many of us wear multiple hats—not the least of which is "museum person" and "fundraiser." As we continue to build our skills in this area as local history fundraisers, the most important thing we can remember is that above all, we are in the people business. If you ever feel overwhelmed by the fundraising tasks ahead of you, don't lose sight of the

## TEN FUNDRAISING TO-DO'S

Below are ten fundraising to-do's for local history organizations:[1]

1. Consider how you're tracking your friends (aka your constituents). Capture and update *at least* basic information (name, address, email, phone, membership/gift history) for all donors (object and monetary) and members. This can be done through commercial software, the PastPerfect contacts module, or even a simple database.

2. Take a look at membership and donation history. Know how much money comes in through memberships, annual donations (usually going into the general fund), major gifts (usually toward special projects), grants, and events. Get a handle on when and how you currently ask people for money (whether through direct asks like mailings or "soft" asks like a donate button on your website). If not already in place, develop a formal process to request membership renewals.

3. Examine how memberships and gifts are processed. Identify how money is received (cash, check, credit card, online payments), who is responsible for processing donations, who is responsible for updating donor records, and who will generate and send the thank-you (ideally within forty-eight hours).

4. Identify, meet with, and get to know long-time supporters and donors who've given significant gifts. Identify ways to build better relationships and show them their support matters. Invite them to become more involved with the organization. Ask for advice and input.

5. Help your board understand why they are critical to successful fundraising. Define their responsibilities (in writing) and help them decide how they can participate within their comfort zone. Establish a board development committee and get fundraising training for the entire board to understand their role in the process. If you've identified specific gaps or "hot button" issues, ask your fundraising trainer to focus on those areas.

6. Define immediate and long-term priorities and make sure they are included in your annual budget. Then, establish fundraising goals for each priority so you and your board understand how the individual components contribute to the bigger fundraising picture.

7. Compile basic organization information and fundraising priorities and put them in one document or file for quick reference. The basics include mission, goals, programs and services, finances, governance, staff and volunteers, planning and evaluation methods, and organization history.

8. Create boilerplate language. This ensures consistent messaging and saves time. Use it for brochures, websites, appeal letters, grant applications, etc.

9. Develop your organization's "elevator pitch" and train your spokespeople to make it their own when serving as organization ambassadors. Make sure they understand the agreed-on priorities and encourage them to have conversations that can help them match interested donors to the organization's priorities.

10. Lay out a one- to two-year development calendar. Identify membership drives, annual giving appeals, special events, newsletter mailing dates, and any other significant events or scheduled communication. Share among the board, staff, and volunteers.

---

1. Jamie Simek, "Ten Fundraising To-Do's for Small Museums and Nonprofits," *AASLH* (blog), August 29, 2016, https://aaslh.org/ten-fundraising-to-dos-for-small-museums-nonprofits/. Adapted with permission from AASLH.

fact that fundraising is more about people than money. Focus on building personalized relationships and creating opportunities to help donors make a difference in the community *through* your organization.

Most of us do this work because we love local history, and we want to protect and share it with others. The efforts we make today will ensure that history is still available for future generations. The work we do is important and worthy of support. I sincerely hope you can apply some of what you've learned from this book to that work and your fundraising efforts. Keep sharing your stories and building genuine relationships. Have confidence in your ability to make good cases for support. And most of all, get out of the kitchen and into your community. You're ready to go beyond the bake sale.

## Notes

1. For more information, see "Developing a Collections Management Policy, Alliance Reference Guide," The American Alliance of Museums, 2018, accessed January 29, 2021, https://www.aam-us.org/wp-content/uploads/2018/01/developing-a-cmp-final .pdf and "Essential Elements of a Collections Management Policy," Connecting to Collections Care, October 2, 2013, https://www.connectingtocollections.org/coming-up -essential-elements-of-a-collections-management-policy/.

2. For more information, see "Understanding Employee vs. Contractor Designation," The Internal Revenue Service, July 20, 2017, https://www.irs.gov/newsroom/ understanding-employee-vs-contractor-designation.

3. For more information, see "Preservation: Digitization," The American Library Association, May 15, 2018, https://libguides.ala.org/libpreservation/digitization; "Preservation Guidelines for Digitizing Library Materials," Library of Congress, accessed January 29, 2021, https://www.loc.gov/preservation/care/scan; and Janet Gertz, "Preservation and Selection for Digitization," Northeast Document Conservation Center, accessed January 29, 2021, https://www.nedcc.org/free-resources/preservation-leaflets/ 6.-reformatting/6.6-preservation-and-selection-for-digitization.

4. Charles Fisher, "Easements to Protect Historic Properties: A Useful Historic Preservation Tool with Potential Tax Benefits," National Park Service Technical Preservation Services, accessed January 29, 2021, https://www.nps.gov/tps/tax-incentives/ taxdocs/easements-historic-properties.pdf. James C. Massey and Shirley Maxwell, "Easements Explained," Old House Online, April 30, 2020, https://www.oldhouseonline.com/ repairs-and-how-to/easements-explained.

5. Anne Nelson, Raina Regan, and Greg Sekula, "Easements and Covenants as Preservation Tools" (presentation slides), Indiana Landmarks, accessed January 29, 2021, https://www.indianalandmarks.org/wp-content/uploads/2018/07/PHP-2018 -Easements-and-Covenants-as-Preservation-Tools.pdf.

6. "The Secretary of the Interior's Standards for the Treatment of Historic Properties," Technical Preservation Services, National Park Service, U.S. Department of the Interior, accessed January 29, 2021, https://www.nps.gov/tps/standards.htm.

7. Kay D. Weeks and Anne E. Grimmer, "The Secretary of the Interior's Standards for the Treatment of Historic Properties with Guidelines for Preserving, Rehabilitating, Restoring and Reconstructing Historic Buildings," Heritage Preservation Services, National Park Service, U.S. Department of the Interior, 1995, https://www.thempc.org/ docs/lit/hist/interiorstandards.pdf.

8. Deborah Slaton, "The Preparation and the Use of Historic Structure Reports," Technical Preservation Services, National Park Service, U.S. Department of the Interior, April 2005, https://www.nps.gov/tps/how-to-preserve/briefs/43-historic-structure-reports.htm.

# Index

general operating funds:
    annual giving, 62–63, 119, 151–52;
    grants, 173–74;
    unrestricted gifts, 27
gift processing, 109, *111*, 232
giving methods, 61
giving societies, 113, 156
Giving USA, 6
grants:
    budgets, 180–83;
    checklist worksheet, *185*;
    funders, 173–76, 184;
    proposals, 176–84, *185*;
    reporting, 184

identity-based philanthropy, 59–60
implementation plan, *181*
income. *See* financial statements; revenue
indirect costs, 182
individual giving, 5–6, 61.
    *See also* annual giving
in-kind donations, 50, 62, 182, 190
Internal Revenue Service (IRS), 12, 29, 110, 183
investment income, 5, 50, 119
IRS. *See* Internal Revenue Service

letter of inquiry (LOI), 177
linkage, interest, and ability (LIA), 164
logic model, 178–80, 216

major gift, 62, 161–71.
    *See also* capital campaigns
managing volunteers, 204–7.
    *See also* volunteers
matching gifts, 80, 170, 200
membership, 61, 113, 119, 122, 152–56
mind mapping, 40–42
mission:
    and affinity members, 155–56;
    board support of, 26, 139–41;
    and core standards for museums, 21;
    gift acceptance in support of, 28;
    and grant eligibility, 176;
    mission creep, 173;
    and operational needs, 132;
    questions to ask donors, 166;
    reinvestment of profits into, 11;
    and special events, 188–89;

    and statement of functional expense, 16;
    and strategic planning, 36, 40–43;
    and the big "So What?", 146–47.
    *See also* Donor Bill of Rights; donor motivation; revenue
monthly giving, 60–61, 65, 78, 95, 100, 119, 155–57
museums:
    accounting standards for, 19;
    accreditation, 21, 37;
    best practices for, 5, 21, 86, 145, 169;
    conflict of interest disclosure for, 140;
    core standards, 21;
    grants for, 174;
    small museums, 176.
    *See also* collections care

The National Council of Nonprofits, 18, 25, 119
Nonprofit Finance Fund, 46, 51
nonprofits, 11–12

online giving. *See* solicitation
operating reserve funds, 13, 42, 51, 119
outcomes:
    donor expectations for, 166;
    evaluation, 215, 217, 221–22;
    in grant proposals, 176–77;
    if/then means that, 217;
    in special projects, 169–70;
    and writing appeal letters, 96.
    *See also* persuasive requests
outputs, 178–80, 212, 214, 217

peer-to-peer fundraising, 93, 98, 149, 191
personnel, fundraising for, 228–29
persuasive requests, 133–35
planned giving, 6, 61, 157
pledges, 60–61, 95, 103
policies, 25–29, 108;
    fundraising policies worksheet, *30–31*.
    *See also* procedures
procedures, 13, 21, 29, 63, 108, 109;
    gift processing worksheet, *111*.
    *See also* policies
profit and loss statement. *See* financial statements

qualifying donors, 79
quid pro quo, 62, 110, 152, 154

# About the Author

**Jamie Simek** is a resource development professional, writer, and champion for small organizations that make a big difference. She believes anyone with a passion for their cause and a willingness to build relationships can be a fundraiser. With twenty years of nonprofit experience, working with college students to veterans to local history leaders, Jamie is committed to a listen-learn-teach-repeat approach to practicing, training, and writing about fundraising.

An unabashed history geek and museum person, Jamie has presented sessions, workshops, and webinars for the American Association for State and Local History, chaired the STEPS Enhancement Fundraising Committee, authored a *History News* technical leaflet on fundraising basics for local history organizations, and facilitated fundraising training to the Field Services Alliance on behalf of the American Alliance of Museums. She has also provided training to individual museums and organizations, including the Indiana Historical Society and the New Jersey Historical Commission and New Jersey Historic Trust. In 2019, she was recognized as a national government sector winner of the Winning Grant Proposal Competition sponsored by the Grant Professionals Association and GrantStation.

CPSIA information can be obtained
at www.ICGtesting.com
Printed in the USA
BVHW051007290122
627167BV00003B/14

9 781538 148778